D0655359

Art
Treasures northern
Italy

AUSTRIA

Friuli-Venezia
Giulia

Gemona
Cividale del Friuli
Udine
Passeriano

Grado
Trieste

Treviso
Torcello
Murano
VENICE

Pomposa

YUGOSLAVIA

Rimini

Pesaro

Urbino
Fano

Ancona

Iesi
Gubbio
Marches
Loreto

ADRIATIC SEA

Assisi
Spello
Fermo

rugia
Montefalco
Ascoli Piceno

Umbria
Todi
Spoleto

San Clemente Casauria

Aquila

Civita Castellana

Abruzzi and Molise

Latium

Art Treasures in Italy

Art Treasures in Italy

Monuments, Masterpieces, Commissions and Collections

Introduced by Giulio Carlo Argan
Professor of the History of Modern Art, University of Rome

Paul Hamlyn
London   Sydney

General Editors
Trewin Copplestone
London
Bernard S. Myers
New York

half title illustration
Jewel in the form of a cock,
seventeenth century;
Museo degli Argenti, Florence
frontispiece
Detail from *The Journey of the Magi*;
Benozzo Gozzoli;
Palazzo Medici-Riccardi, Florence
opposite
David, 1623; Gianlorenzo Bernini;
Galleria Borghese, Rome

Published jointly by
The Hamlyn Publishing Group Limited, London and Sydney
Hamlyn House, The Centre, Feltham, Middlesex
and McGraw-Hill Book Company, New York and Toronto
© The Hamlyn Publishing Group Limited, 1969. All rights reserved
Printed in Italy by Officine Grafiche Arnoldo Mondadori, Verona
Phototypeset by Filmtype Services, Scarborough

Contents

Introduction

Italy did not achieve political unity until the nineteenth century; even the idea of the nation as a geographical and historical entity took shape later in Italy than elsewhere in Europe. Yet despite its division and subjection to foreign rule, for many centuries Italy played the rôle of example and guide within the European artistic tradition. The explanation for this is not to be found in any consistency of style and subject matter, for there are profound differences between the creations of various periods and regions, but in the universality of its art.

THE CAMPO VACCINO, ROME
after Piranesi

The Forum, which had been the centre of civic and religious life in ancient Rome, shared in the general decay of the city after the decline of the empire. The temples were neglected by the Christians, barbarian invasions and earthquakes brought destruction and the ruined buildings were used as foundations for medieval fortresses. Even the awakening of interest in classical Rome during the Renaissance did not save the Forum from further destruction, though it inspired many buildings. During the late eighteenth century, however, systematic excavation began. Though our knowledge has immeasurably increased as a result, the

picturesque chaos of the eighteenth-century Campo Vaccino seen in this engraving has disappeared. Visible in the right foreground of this picture is the top of the three Corinthian columns of the Temple of Vespasian (see also plate **45**); the Arch of Septimus Severus appears on the left; the solitary Column of Phocas is in the centre; the three columns of the Temple of Castor and Pollux stand further away on the right, while the Colosseum (plate **55**) dominates the background.

The one relatively autonomous culture in Italy was the Etruscan and this came to an end with the Roman conquest. The empire made Rome the centre of the known world and everything outside the capital was considered as one vast province. Florence, Padua or Bologna did not stand for anything substantially different from Trier, Cologne or Marseilles. From the idea of the universality of the state grew the idea of the universality of the church; throughout the Middle Ages Italy was the link between the Byzantine east and the European west.

Then, around 1400, Italy's artistic tradition freed itself from Byzantine influence and claimed its legacy from Rome. The aim of Nicola and Giovanni Pisano, Arnolfo di Cambio and Giotto was not to set Italian art in opposition to the spread of Gothic from France and Germany but to give the Gothic a Latin rather than a Greek (or Byzantine) basis. This was Italy's contribution to Gothic, the first great *European* artistic phenomenon.

Nevertheless, with the spread of humanistic culture, Gothic was to be contrasted unfavourably with the fundamental experience of classical art. The various Italian schools were formed during the Renaissance when a typically urban civilisation evolved. Every city was proud of its own history and sought to equip itself with its own culture. The rulers invited artists to express the character and importance of their city in the planning of the streets, churches and palaces, and in statues, reliefs, frescoes and paintings. Thus the artistic schools of many cities such as Florence, Siena, Ferrara, Venice and Urbino were alike in aim but diverse in effect. But in the very diversity of these schools the universality of art is emphasised, this universality found expression in the historical classicism of Raphael, in the ideological classicism of Michelangelo and the naturalistic classicism of the Venetians. Even Leonardo, who spurned the teaching of classicism, was still intent on universal experience when he studied directly from nature. In the Mannerist period art became a search for pure forms and Italy then assumed the leadership of an international culture which stretched from Spain to France and the Low Countries. In fact, the only national characteristic of Italian art is that it has none.

By Giotto's time artists were already persons of importance, commissioned by religious authorities to illustrate and reinterpret major historical and religious subjects. The princes of the Quattrocento were also great patrons who rivalled each other for the services of the most celebrated artists. In the sixteenth century the most enthusiastic patrons were the popes, who commissioned large projects for political reasons, and the principal sovereigns of Europe, who considered the possession of Italian art treasures to be essential to their rank.

In the seventeenth century the artist achieved professional independence when the rôle of the patron who commissioned the work and was able to influence its progress became subordinate to that of the collector who acquired works of art made expressly for a market and conditioned therefore by the tastes of an educated public. This happened particularly in Rome which became the outstanding centre in Europe in the eighteenth and early nineteenth centuries. Foreign countries maintained academies there and French, German, English and Dutch artists settled there to study the masterpieces which this book describes. The idea of a universal art which had been established with the classicism of the Renaissance was transformed into the idea of an international art which is an essential part of world culture today.

Giulio Carlo Argan

In the thousands of years of Italian history two periods, the Roman and the Renaissance, have been abundantly creative. Both are at the heart of western culture and their influence is abiding. Magnificent works of art, however, survive from all ages: the medieval, the Baroque, the nineteenth century and even the prehistoric. The inhabitants of prehistoric Italy were nomadic hunters and later primitive farmers, but they drew, painted, built houses and made pottery. The works that survive are not merely interesting historically, but are also beautiful.

Small female statuettes carved in stone and known as venuses are one of the most frequently found art forms from prehistoric Italy, and, although much uncertainty surrounds the culture from which they come, they are probably the earliest art form so far known. In the series of fifteen venuses found at Grimaldi and in the Savignano and Chiozza venuses the features which are most emphasised, the breasts, stomach and thighs, all seem to have a sexual connotation, while other parts of the body are left undefined. Some kind of fertility symbolism seems to lie behind these figures.

The early hunters

The earliest cave paintings were found in the Paglicci cave on Monte Gargano. In a short side passage, where man had been in permanent occupation and had left art objects, are four red painted hands and some horses. The hand designs were made by placing the hand flat on the wall and blowing the liquid pigment around it, leaving the wall blank where the palm had been.

These designs are significant for our understanding of the society of early man. Among Australian aborigines, for example, such silhouettes were made during ritual ceremonies under the control of a shaman (witch doctor) or other recognised authority on religion and ritual. Strict observance of the ceremony would be his responsibility and thus, in a sense, this art would be carried out under his patronage. Harder to interpret in this context is a pebble, also found in the Paglicci cave, engraved with what appears to be a man pierced with at least three arrows or spears. One would more naturally look for speared animals (indicating the sympathetic magic of the hunter who wished to gain a magical advantage over his prey). Perhaps the speared man has the same significance as a voodoo doll and betrays some kind of enmity in the society.

The best Italian example of sympathetic hunting magic and ritual spearing comes from the slightly later Romanellian period, which takes its name from the Romanelli cave in Apulia. It is a carnivore engraved on a pebble which was found in the Polesini cave at Tivoli. Small marks probably indicate that it had been speared or pricked with a pointed object.

An almost unique glimpse into one of the most revealing of all primitive ceremonies is provided by a remarkable panel found in the Addaura group of caves. On it are some fifteen human figures and a large fallow deer in the lower part. Many of the figures seem to be watching two people in the centre of the panel who are lying on their stomachs. The most likely suggestion is that the scene shows an initiation ceremony and that in the centre are two young men undergoing the initiation rites, surrounded by elders who are performing the appropriate ritual dance.

Pride of place as the finest of the Romanellian art sites should probably go not to Addaura, but to the remote Levanzo cave on the Egadi islands west of Sicily. Engravings were discovered there in 1950, and the outline of a young deer turning its head has become the most famous. Elsewhere in the cave are more deer, bulls and a small horse. Throughout Romanellian art, distinctive bulls' profiles occur, their horns bent forward, often curling up again at the ends. Levanzo also has human figures dressed up and wearing

1
THE AREZZO CHIMERA
detail of plate 10
c. 480 BC
bronze
Museo Archeologico, Florence

Fifteenth-century Florentines believed that ancient Tuscany had a very different civilisation from Rome, and they were fascinated by Etruscan works. This bronze was found in 1554 and acquired by Cosimo I, grand duke of Tuscany.

on their heads what can only be described as chefs' hats. They are probably masked and engaged in a ritual like that of Addaura.

Art of the early farmers

As the climate approached that of the present day, the way of life of the hunters of Italy had to be modified, and the emphasis moved from herd game to smaller prey. But this was as nothing compared to the revolution caused by the arrival of the first farmers. These colonists from further east brought with them the essential equipment for the cultivation of plants and some domestic animals. Influences from the Aegean are evident in their art. A good example of this are female idols or statuettes in the Cycladic style, which have been discovered at Senorbi on Sardinia. From these we may infer that the mother-goddess cult of the early Greek world had penetrated this far. Decoration on the pottery of these peoples, which also has stylistic affinities with pottery from the Aegean, includes scratched rectilinear patterns and painting in red and black. The Serro d'Alto pottery, for example, has stumpy spirals and meanders painted on it.

A later and more important kind of art expression is found in the third and second millennia in association with a style of monumental architecture made of large stones known as megaliths. The constructions consist usually of one or more capstones resting on upright stones so as to enclose one or more chambers, which were used for collective burial. In some cases, especially in Italy and the surrounding islands, very similar tombs were made by tunnelling into soft rock.

On Sardinia both rock-cut and surface megalithic tombs are found. The so-called giants' graves are probably of the second millennium and represent some of the latest surviving megalithic architecture in the area. Carving on megaliths is perhaps best represented at Castelluccio, where opposed spirals recall 'oculi' designs, which have some kind of parallel both in the megalithic art of the west and in the Mycenean world. Numerous bone plaques carved with circular and spiral designs from Castelluccio add to the artistic heritage of the period.

Little is known of the social circumstances surrounding the megalithic cult, but the communities which supported it were presumably efficient agriculturalists, living sometimes in villages of stone huts. The houses known on Sardinia are associated with nuraghi, circular stone towers of which there are some 6,500 on the island. Perhaps piracy had already made it necessary for such peoples to have defensive strongholds where they could retreat in time of attack. This in turn would indicate that there was already enough wealth to make piracy for such commodities as precious metals, cattle or slaves worthwhile. Connected with the latest stage of the nuraghic civilisation are curious miniature votive figurines, often of warriors with weapons, deities and priests, which show Etruscan influence.

Considerable uncertainty surrounds the age of the extensive rock carvings of the Alpine periphery in the north. Those from Val Camonica near Lake Garda are the most famous. Pecked into the rock are figures of armed warriors and herds of oxen, which probably indicated wealth as understood by prehistoric farmers. In addition to numerous weapons such as daggers and halberds, there are some symbols which probably represent the sun and are related to other sun cults known towards the end of the Bronze Age. There are also tall houses, with pitched roofs, reflecting domestic architecture. Spanning the later Bronze Age, some of these engravings may be as late as Etruscan times. Whether Etruscan art developed from these Bronze Age works or whether the Etruscans themselves came in from outside bringing their art with them remains an unsolved problem.

Desmond Collins

A SARDINIAN NURAGHE
1000 BC, rough blocks without mortar
h. about 40 ft (12·805 m)

The nuraghi are stone-built towers of cylindrical shape, tapering a little towards the top. Usually the only entrance was a low tunnel leading to the interior. A staircase within the thickness of the wall gave access to the higher parts. Spaced as they are at regular intervals in the cultivable areas, they seem to imply a clan society in which defence against marauders was the overriding consideration.

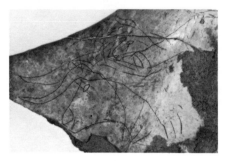

3
HEAD OF AN AUROCHS
c. 20,000 BC
fine line engraving, width 6·5 in (17 cm)
Museo Civico di Storia Naturale, Verona

The head of an aurochs, an extinct species of wild cattle, is clearly visible and at least one other animal is present. The piece was found in the Paglicci cave, Gargano.

4
CARVED SLAB
c. 1800 BC
limestone
h. 39·5 in (100 cm)
Museo Archeologico Nazionale, Syracuse

The double opposed spirals, which form the most conspicuous part of the design, are to be found widely elsewhere on tombs of this age. The slab closed the entrance to a tomb at Castelluccio.

5

THE VENUS OF SAVIGNANO

early to middle Leptolithic, c. 25,000 BC
green serpentine
8 in (22 cm)
Museo Preistorico Pigorini, Rome

This statuette was found by workmen
near Savignano in Emilia. After much
controversy it has generally been
attributed to the Leptolithic series of
venuses. The possibility remains that it
may belong rather to the east
Mediterranean series associated with early
farming colonists. The failure to show the
face or the feet in any detail is typical of
the Leptolithic period, as are the large
breasts, stomach and buttocks. It is one of
the finest venuses known.

6

SARDINIAN WARRIOR

early first millennium BC, bronze
h. 3·5 in (10 cm)
Museo Preistorico Pigorini, Rome

Hundreds of these small bronze figures
have been found in Sardinia, mainly in
temples or religious centres associated with
the nuraghi, but generally a little later in
date. They are thought to be votive, and
include, besides warriors and chieftains,
priestesses and other figures of apparently
religious significance. This warrior wears a
horned helmet, breeches and a tunic
coming down to his thighs. The face is
particularly realistic. They are among the
earliest costumed figures in Europe.

7

THE VALLELUNGA VASE

c. 1700–1400 BC
Museo Archeologico Nazionale, Syracuse

This 'fruit stand' was found at Vallelunga
near Caltanissetta, Sicily. It is of a shape
widely found in the area.

From the seventh century BC until the fifth, the Etruscans were the greatest sea power of the western Mediterranean. On land, the twelve cities of the Etruscan confederation dominated central and northern Italy from the Alps to Campania, and their alliance was courted by both the Greek cities of southern Italy and by the Carthaginians. Yet despite the wealth and power of their rulers, the Etruscans were a mysterious people even in antiquity, with a strange language and institutions unlike those of any of their neighbours. Most of the Greek and Roman writers, for example Herodotus, believed that they were immigrants from Lydia in Asia Minor, and that famine in the thirteenth century BC had forced them to leave. Others, who included the great geographer of the first century BC Dionysius of Halicarnassus, thought that the Etruscans were indigenous to Italy.

Many features of Etruscan culture, including their magic practices and religion, may have an oriental origin, but the art of the eighth century in central and northern Italy (called Villanovan after an important cemetery) is merely a variant of the geometric style of central Europe. From graves we can see that the social context of Villanovan art and of the exotic orientalising manner which succeeded it are the same. The difference between the two periods is that whereas the Villanovan bronze belt buckles, simple brooches and pottery cremation urns of the early period show no foreign influence, towards the end of the eighth century vessels of eastern appearance and rich jewellery are found with the dead. The Etruscans obviously believed that the dead chieftain required ornaments and weapons for the afterlife, and as foreign trade in metals and other raw materials expanded so did their taste.

Etruscan lovers of magnificence

The age of splendour which followed was one in which burial chambers of stone actually simulating houses replaced hut-shaped urns. The wealth of the period is seen in the great tombs of the seventh century, particularly the Regolini-Galassi tomb at Cerveteri (Caere) and the tombs of Praeneste, in which the dead were buried with sumptuous silver and silver-gilt vessels. In the realm of the minor arts the charm and spontaneity of the Etruscans really showed itself. Thousands of mirrors and coffers reveal their skill in engraving on metal, and from the first they established themselves as masters of the craft of jewellery. Gold and silversmiths, working in filigree and with granulation, produced numerous necklaces, rings, bracelets and earrings of extraordinary beauty with a technical skill which has never been matched. The reaction of the Etruscans on first meeting foreign art styles was undisciplined and over-indulgent. Riches were accumulated for their own sake and funerary pomp became increasingly pronounced. Among the most successful products of this time is the black, shiny pottery known as Bucchero. Often decorated with relief scenes, vast quantities were traded with neighbouring peoples.

Although, politically, in the sixth century Etruria usually supported the Phoenicians against Greek expansion in the western Mediterranean, the culture of the latter prevailed. The Etruscans probably continued to value power and display as much as ever, but their art now emphasised enjoyment rather than wealth. Fine black-figure pottery from Greece, painted with scenes of festivity and athletic prowess, reveals a view of the afterlife as a banquet. One particularly interesting group of painted water-pitchers (hydriae) found at Cerveteri is the work of eastern Greeks who were probably resident in Italy, for pitchers like them have been found nowhere else. Browns and ochres are used in addition to black, and the mythological scenes have a freshness and originality that make them pre-eminent among the pots of this period. A famous wine jar, the so-called François

8

FIBULA
c. 650 BC
gold
h. 12 in (31·5 cm)
Museo Etrusco Gregoriano, Vatican Museums, Rome

Etruscan goldsmiths were experts in the art of filigree and granulation. The lower part of this elaborate brooch from the Regolini-Galassi tomb at Cerveteri is ornamented with tiny griffins decorated in this way, in a style ultimately derived from oriental art. In contrast, the plate of sheet gold embossed with five lions seems rather crude. It too is influenced by the near east. The surround of palmettes, however, is closer in spirit to Greek art, although western motifs did not become common in Etruscan jewellery until the following century.

Vase, found at Chiusi and now in Florence, is a purely Greek vessel made by Ergotimos and painted by Klitias, but so elaborately decorated that it must have been produced for an Etruscan market, for a people who appreciated detail and fine workmanship above all things.

It is very easy to take the superficial resemblance of sixth-century Etruscan and Greek art at its face value, but their purpose was so different that inevitably there are subtle contrasts. The Greeks glorified man but feared the natural world and were pessimistic about death: Achilles tells Odysseus that it is better to be a poor shepherd 'than to be king over all the un-numbered dead'. The Etruscans, with independent traditions and trading contacts with Phoenicia, had a more positive conception of death. Soon not only cups but the very walls would proclaim an existence of idyllic happiness beyond the grave – feasting, hunting, fishing and athletic **18,** competition. This sense of joy and liberation, characteristic of the sixth and early fifth centuries, was achieved by a confident denial of death itself.

Although there is some evidence for town planning in Etruscan cities, as at Marzabotto near Bologna for example, the towns are not well known. A few temples have been excavated, however, and the Roman writer Vitruvius also discusses Etruscan shrines. The upper parts were usually of wood, decorated with terra-cotta ornaments which are sometimes of high quality: the statue of Apollo from Veii by the great early fifth-century **20** sculptor Vulca and the fourth-century winged horses in the Tarquinia Museum both show Etruscan mastery of the medium. The foundations, which are all that survive of the temples themselves, are rectangular rooms fronted by porches. Recently, discoveries at Pyrgi near Rome have brought to light two rather different temples. The earlier of them was built around 500 BC in the Greek style with a colonnade running all the way round instead of merely a porch in front as in Etruscan examples. It is very likely that the architects were Greeks from south Italy, like those of the Temple of Apollo at Pompeii.

Tarquinian frescos

The early frescos at Tarquinia, like those at Chiusi and Orvieto, reveal the lyricism of the Etruscans and are all the more valuable in view of the scarcity of ancient paintings still in existence. The simplicity of their draughtsmanship and the limited but bright range of colours convey their immense joie de vivre. Some, like the Tomb of the Bulls, show events in Greek mythology, others show wrestling, horsemanship or athletics. The Tomb of the Augurs has a representation of a dog attacking a man with a sack over his head, which demonstrates the cruelty that was a feature of Etruscan character. The Tomb of Hunting and Fishing in contrast has a landscape com- **18** position that prefigures the naturalism of Roman painting. However, the feast predominates over all other subjects. According to Diodorus Siculus, a **19** Greek writer of the first century BC, sumptuous tables were set out twice a day in the houses of nobles. Around them, as can be seen in the paintings, men and women recline on couches, together or singly. They are simply and informally dressed and their servants – waiting men, dancers and flautists – are either naked or wear very sparse clothing. The forwardness of the women, the naked servants and the excellence of the flute-playing all occasioned comment amongst the Greeks, for whom these feasts must have seemed a far cry from their own where no women would have been present.

The later frescos at Tarquinia show a new wave of formalism. In the truly Greek frescos of the Tomb of the Baron, the Tomb of the Leopards, **19** and the Tomb of the Triclinium instead of frenzied activity there is a graceful restraint. Against neutral, non-naturalistic backgrounds banqueters, dancers and musicians make delicate gestures and seem to glide along. The

9
DISH
seventh century BC
silver gilt
diameter 7·5 in (19 cm)
Museo Nazionale di Villa Giulia, Rome

The catholicity of Etruscan taste in the seventh and sixth centuries gave foreign craftsmen a rare opportunity to follow their own inclinations rather than their native traditions. This vessel, perhaps made in Cyprus specifically for export to Etruria, demonstrates the entry of foreign motifs into Italy. The centre shows an Egyptian pharaoh overcoming his enemies, the frieze of horses and birds in the middle register is in the archaic Greek style, while around this is an Assyrian hunting scene. The surrounding snake is also an Egyptian device.

famous horses in the Tomb of the Baron and the Tomb of the Funeral Couch are almost monumental and convey an impression of ordered pomp. The same solemnity is found in terra-cottas like the winged horses at Tarquinia and in naturalistic bronzes, for instance the Arezzo Chimera or the 10 statue of Mars from Todi in the Vatican and a number of portrait heads.

Decline

This seriousness is appropriate to a society in competition with others, and to one where constitutional change was possible. Indeed revolution by certain classes in fringe cities to the south – notably at Rome – and incursions by Celtic tribes from the north soon developed a strong sense of

10
THE AREZZO CHIMERA
c. 480 BC
bronze
31·5 in (80 cm)
Museo Archeologico, Florence

The Etruscans adopted many of the monsters of Greek mythology. The chimera was a fire-breathing dragon with the head of a lion, a serpent as a tail and a goat's head in the centre of its back. This fine bronze exhibits strong Greek influence in the sensitive modelling of the body, but is also an eloquent tribute to the high standards of Etruscan bronzesmiths. It was found as early as 1554 and skilfully restored by Benvenuto Cellini.

II
GRAVE STELE
c. 400 BC
sandstone, h. 71 in (180 cm)
Museo Civico, Bologna

The sandstone grave stones of northern Italy illustrate the growing uncertainty of life in the face of the Celtic advance during the late fifth and fourth centuries BC. Their sombre power contrasts with the gaiety of early Etruscan painting. The most interesting scene is the bottom one. In it an Etruscan knight mounted on a rearing warhorse is battling with a Celtic foot soldier. The Etruscan is wearing fine armour, but the barbarian is naked. By 350 BC the area from which this stele comes had been conquered by the Celts.

foreboding among the Etruscans. Battles against the Celts feature on several 11 tombstones from Bologna. The Etruscans are shown better armed and disciplined, but nevertheless they were inferior in numbers to the numerous barbarian hordes from the north and were ultimately to be overwhelmed. Further south allusions are more veiled – sometimes the dead person is shown being drawn to hell by a winged demon. On fine, sculptured coffins, guarded by demons or showing scenes of pain and violence, the dead recline on couches. Their features are depicted with an attention to detail that makes them very interesting, yet many people have rightly seen in them the very opposite of the joy associated with art of the early period. The sense of pain and loss is as ever most graphically represented in the funerary painting of Tarquinia.

In the Tomb of Orcus we see the demon Charu with his great vulture-like wings, hideous visage and snake-entwined hair and another winged demon leading a soul, the three-headed monster Geryon and the shades of Agamemnon and Ajax, now confined to the lower regions. There are more monsters in the Tomb of the Typhon and the François Tomb (the paintings are now in the Museo Torlonia, Rome), and we feel increasingly that the observance of ritual, the mere depiction of a banquet in a tomb and the performance of the right sacrifice was more important than entering into a spirit of rejoicing. This is borne out by the extraordinary Tomb of the 14 Painted Reliefs at Cerveteri, in which a large number of ritual objects are shown in painted stucco.

The aristocracy of Etruria ceased to be the ruling class of a great empire, and the paintings of men and women in the later tombs, for example the Tomb of the Shields, are very provincial. It is clear that the great nobles of Etruria had sunk to the level of a local squirarchy. Etruria, conservative and aristocratic, was outpaced by Rome with her broader-based society. Yet Etruscan influence on Roman temple design, portraiture and wall painting was immense, indeed it is likely that much of the legacy of Greece came to Rome indirectly through Etruria.

Martin Henig

12
THE CERTOSA SITULA
detail, early fifth century BC
bronze, h. 12·5 in (32 cm)
Museo Civico, Bologna

Skill in metalworking techniques extended beyond Etruria proper into the territory of the Veneti at the head of the Adriatic. Here fine ceremonial buckets embossed with scenes of daily life were produced. The Certosa Situla is one of the best. Originally owned by Etruscans, it is a remarkable testimony of their appreciation of the art of a neighbouring people. One of the scenes shows two Venetic musicians wearing distinctive hats and playing musical instruments. Above them hangs a situla.

13
BELT PLATE
eighth century BC
cast bronze, length 18·75 in (47·7 cm)
Museo Civico, Bologna

This belt plate is a typical product of a society whose ideals were still centred on martial display. Yet even in this early stage of Italian culture, the Villanovan bronzesmith shows remarkable skill in marrying the various elements of his design, which is an abstract pattern based on a representation of swans pulling the sun disc across the sky.

14
THE TOMB OF THE BAS-RELIEFS
third century BC, stucco
Cerveteri

Many ancient peoples including the Etruscans have provided grave goods for the use of the dead in another world. Here an amazing variety of kitchen utensils, toilet articles, arms and armour, musical instruments as well as domestic animals have actually been carved in stucco around the walls and naturalistically painted. The entrance to the tomb is flanked on either side by a dish with handles and a ceremonial trumpet, while other vessels and implements are placed above the burial niches.

15

BUCCHERO VASE

end of seventh century BC, h. 11·25 in (28·5 cm)
Museo Gregoriano Etrusco, Vatican Museums, Rome

Native ceramics reflect the mixed origins of Etruscan art long after the more sophisticated works in precious metal have become imbued with Greek and Syrian motifs. This decanter in the form of a charioteer and horses was found in the rich Regolini-Galassi tomb at Cerveteri, but is clearly the work of a village craftsman. The engraved decoration of the vessel remains close to the Villanovan geometric style, but the pedestal foot is beginning to show Greek characteristics.

16

GOLD CUP WITH SPHINXES

seventh century BC, gold, diameter 3·5 in (9 cm)
Museo Nazionale di Villa Giulia, Rome

Although ultimately derived from Greek prototypes, the precious material of which this cup is made and the four sphinxes sitting upon the handles proclaim the rich tastes of the Etruscan nobility and the skill of the native smiths in fashioning objects from sheet gold. The sphinxes give the vessel a luxurious, jewelled quality, but also perhaps protected the owner from harm in a world peopled by demons and supernatural forces.

17 *bottom*

BREASTPLATE *detail*

c. 650 BC, sheet gold, length 9·5 in (29·3 cm)
Museo Nazionale di Villa Giulia, Rome

The nobility of south Etruria went to the feast wearing jewellery of royal magnificence, and when they died it was buried with them. Ornaments of this nature express the flamboyance of successful merchants. The lions, griffins and sphinxes worked 'en repoussé' and covered in granulation were adopted from the repertory of near-eastern art as a result of trading contacts with Phoenicia.

18

BOATING PARTY *detail*

c. 520–510 BC
Tomb of Hunting and Fishing, Tarquinia

The strong element of naturalism in late sixth-century painting reflects an increasing Greek influence in Etruria. Yet the spontaneous gaiety of the frescos in this tomb are typically Etruscan. This painting shows four men relaxing and fishing in a brightly coloured boat. The whole composition presents a charming picture of the leisure hours of the Etruscan aristocracy.

19

BANQUETING SCENE *detail*

early fifth century BC
Tomb of the Leopards, Tarquinia

Feasting was the favourite occupation of the luxury-loving
Etruscan aristocrat, and so it is not surprising that banqueting
scenes appear on the walls of their tombs, almost as a denial of
the power of death. Indeed the man on the right of the fresco is
holding up an egg in front of his wife as a symbol of hope and
new life. The painting illustrates two features of Etruscan life
which scandalised their Greek contemporaries: the freedom of
women in society and the employment of naked cupbearers.

20

THE VEII APOLLO *detail*

c. 510 BC, Vulca
terra-cotta, h. 69 in (175 cm)
Museo Nazionale di Villa Giulia, Rome

The excavation of a major Etruscan sanctuary, the Temple of
Apollo at Veii, resulted in the rediscovery of a group of terra-
cottas produced by the artist Vulca, who worked on the Capitol
at Rome and was a citizen of Veii. This fine terra-cotta shows
him to have been a great and original artist who used rippling
hair and flowing drapery to soften the hard outlines of Greek
archaic sculpture. The expression, however, is forceful and
maintains an aura of divinity.

21

SEATED MALE FIGURE

end of seventh century BC
terra-cotta
h. 10·5 in (27 cm)
Museo del Palazzo dei Conservatori, Rome

Portraiture was born of a desire to
preserve the features of the dead from
bodily decay. This statuette from a tomb
at Cerveteri is one of the earliest examples
from Etruria. Most of these figures have
an oriental appearance, which confirms
the political and cultural dominance of a
foreign element in the population.

Men left Greece in the eighth century BC for the same reasons as they have left Europe in more recent times. Many voluntarily sought adventure and wealth, but most were driven by fear of over-population at home with its accompaniments of land shortage and famine. Although a number of colonies were founded in Thrace, around the Black Sea and in north Africa, the America of the ancient world lay in the west, in Italy. The Spartans founded Taras, the Achaeans Metapontum and Sybaris, while Corinth played a major part in the establishment of Syracuse in Sicily.

All these cities shared a common language and literature, religion and art, both with each other and with their Greek parent cities. Yet the Greeks in Italy did not intend merely to play an imitative role, for their adventurous spirit revelled in the opulent and the grandiose. They made up for a lack of history by an intense and often violent city life. Their architects and artists were untrammelled by tradition and felt free to experiment in ways that would have been denied them elsewhere. Moderation, which most Greeks prized before everything, was a quality they rejected.

The highest surviving achievements of western Greek art lie in temples and coinage. Both were intended to indicate power. A coin was a seal of the state and attempted to express its personality. Temples were, of course, religious shrines where people could make offerings to the gods. It was also hoped that these deities would protect the city and, in human terms, that a spy from another city would equate the seven large temples of Selinus and similar complexes at Agrigento (Acragas), Syracuse and elsewhere with great wealth and strength.

In the early period most of the colonies were governed by an aristocracy drawn from the descendants of original settlers. The Temple of Apollo in Syracuse, Temple 'C' at Selinus and the first temple dedicated to Hera at Paestum (Posidonia) are typical of sixth-century Doric structures in their surrounding colonnade of squat columns which terminate in bun-shaped capitals and in the somewhat dark and ill-organised central shrine, where the cult image was kept.

The age of tyrants

Other ideas emerged with the rise of powerful rulers, known as tyrants, in several Sicilian cities, especially Agrigento and Syracuse, at the close of the century. Theron constructed a great temple to Zeus at Agrigento which was over 110 metres long and clearly intended to rival the similar temple at Selinus, which may also have been built by a tyrant. Instead of the usual peristyle, the outer wall is blank and the entablature above is supported by pilasters and enormous figures, which may represent the Carthaginians routed at Himera in 480 BC. This triumph was also celebrated in Syracuse by Gelon, the other victor in that war. He constructed the fine Temple of Athena, which still survives embedded in the fabric of the cathedral. Although no decorative work from these reigns remains, the 'Demareteia' coins, struck from the proceeds of gifts which the Carthaginians gave to Gelon's wife Demarete, show the excellence of Sicilian craftsmanship in precious metals.

There were also wealthy cities on the mainland of Italy. One of the richest was Sybaris, which became a byword for elegance and luxury. Although Sybaris was destroyed by neighbouring Croton in 510 BC and no material trace survives above ground, three beautiful temples still stand at Paestum, its daughter town. The early Temple of Hera was, as we have seen, illogically planned and slightly rustic, but the late temple to the same goddess vies with the so-called Temple of Concord at Agrigento in being one of the best-preserved temples in existence. The main part is like a church, with aisles consisting of two rows of columns in two tiers, and

22
THE TAZZA FARNESE
181–174 BC
sardonyx
diameter 8 in (20 cm)
Museo Nazionale, Naples

Engraved gems were much appreciated in Rome; this magnificent specimen may have been brought to Italy after the fall of the Ptolemies and the Roman annexation of Egypt in 31 BC. Its fine state of preservation suggests that it continued to be a prized possession throughout later antiquity and the Middle Ages. During the fifteenth century it is known to have belonged to Pope Paul II and to have passed to Lorenzo de' Medici in 1471. It is a double-sided cameo in the form of a cup; the interior glorifies the Egyptian queen, Cleopatra I.

must have formed a magnificent setting for a great statue of the goddess. The bold colonnade has the fine strong columns and compact capitals typical of the fifth century. The effect of delicate, southern antiquity is enhanced by the warm honey-coloured limestone, which the Greeks plastered in imitation of marble. The Temple of Athena comes between the two temples to Hera in date, with the capitals of the first and a plan like the second.

The limestone reliefs at Paestum come from a shrine a few miles away also dedicated to Hera. There are some battered early sixth-century ones showing the deeds of the universal Greek hero and giant-killer Heracles,
24 but the portrayals of dancing girls are very fine, although their features are fixed in an enigmatic smile and their bodies are still solid and wooden.
25 The metopes from Selinus are more lifelike.

Unfortunately very few statues such as might have adorned temples and public places have survived the looting of Roman and later times. Because of the lack of suitable local stone or marble, terra-cotta was widely used for this sort of monumental art. As terra-cotta is so fragile a material, few examples exist today, although there are decorative slabs in the form of
27 gorgon's heads. There are even a few large terra-cotta statues which stood on temple pediments, although most statues of this type which survive are of high-quality marble imported from Naxos and other sites in Greece. The only terra-cotta statues discovered in large numbers are small votive figures. Particularly frequent are representations of the mother goddess. Among the marble statues which still exist are a number of figures of nude young men, known as kouroi. These might represent gods, heroes
29 or famous people, who, as in the case of the kouros from Megara Hyblaea thought to represent a physician, were not necessarily young at all.

At first most of the painted pottery used in south Italy was imported. However, in the second half of the fifth century BC, Athenian craftsmen
30 established workshops in southern Italy and began to make red-figure vases similar to those manufactured in Athens. The industry quickly adapted itself to the tastes of the south Italian clientele, which demanded highly ornamental vases in a monumental style and a variety of colours. Despite its mediocre content, fourth-century painted pottery illuminates many details of local custom, religion and dress that are otherwise obscure.

In the fourth century, violence and renewed tyranny alternated with periods of milder rule. Apart from Syracuse, Taranto in southern Italy seems to have retained a lively and independent civic life, developing luxurious jewellery and a local school of terra-cotta figures, mainly of
31, 32 dancing girls. In both cities an age of theatre followed the age of temples. Theatrical scenes are often depicted on vases. One shows the chorus of a play and may have been produced for a company as a souvenir. Others show rough country farces being performed.

It was inevitable that eventually either Carthage or Rome should rule the western Mediterranean, and the latter was to prove a worthy master. However, although the Roman aristocracy was sympathetic to Hellenism, the continued existence of powerful Greek states in southern Italy was out of the question. Taranto was captured in 272 BC, but Syracuse continued to be free for a time, and under Heiron II enjoyed both good government and prosperity. The theatre was rebuilt during his reign and so was a great altar to the east of it at which a thousand animals could be sacrificed at the same time. But co-existence was not possible for long and in 211, after a prolonged siege, Syracuse fell to a Roman army. Ultimately this meant that Greek ideas would be spread from Britain to the Euphrates, but in the short term, the history of 'Magna Graecia' – Great Greece – was ended.

Martin Henig

23
COIN FROM SYRACUSE
c.405 BC
silver
Cimon
diameter c.1·37 in (c.3·5 cm)
Museo Nazionale, Syracuse

24
A PROCESSIONAL DANCE
c.500 BC
sandstone
h.33·5 in (85 cm)
Paestum Museum

The cult of Hera was widespread in the neighbourhood of Paestum, and this metope from a temple at the mouth of the river Sele probably represents part of a processional dance in her honour. Although the faces still wear the fixed expressions of the archaic period, the handling of the drapery shows a new confidence. The soft modelling of the relief has the refinement of Ionian sculpture and emphasises the importance of an eastern Greek element in the artistic development of southern Italy.

This coin was minted by Dionysius I to commemorate his victory over the Carthaginians. The obverse shows a personification of victory crowning a female charioteer, with some of the spoils taken from the enemy depicted below. On the reverse is the profile of the nymph Arethusa, patroness of the city, surrounded by four dolphins. Despite its size this is one of the greatest masterpieces of Greek art and no finer monument to the pride and magnificence of ancient Syracuse exists.

25
ARTEMIS AND ACTEON
470–450 BC
limestone and Greek marble
h. 63·75 in (162 cm)
Museo Nazionale Archeologico, Palermo

The myth of Acteon, torn to pieces by his hounds because he saw the goddess Artemis naked, emphasises the unbridgeable gulf between man and the gods. The West Greek sculptor, who carved this metope for the Temple of Hera at Selinus, has produced a terrifying image of mortal suffering in the figure of Acteon. The most striking feature of his work, however, is the marble head of Artemis. Her expression is of gentle concentration; she is killing a man out of duty rather than from hatred.

In 616 BC an army from Etruria seized Rome. During the hundred years of its rule that followed, the Tarquin dynasty transformed the village that was Rome into an Etruscan city, with its inevitable class divisions based on wealth and political status. Works of art in terra-cotta and bronze bear witness to an emergent consciousness, which was emphasised all the more after the nobility rebelled in the early fifth century against the misdeeds of the violent and tyrannical king, Tarquin the Proud.

The origins of this nobility will never be known, but it may have contained a large Etruscan element. Certainly Roman religious practices, temple and tomb architecture and even the planning of cities were influenced by Etruscan example, and it was in the houses of the aristocracy that the custom of the ancestors was most revered. From the beginning, friction between the aristocracy and the common people was acute. It says much for the good sense and moderation in the Roman character that, although the ideological breach between the two sides was irreconcilable, it was not until the second century BC, when the problems of poverty and landlessness increased, that social revolution became a real danger. Powerful demagogues like Gaius and Tiberius Gracchus and great generals, Marius, Sulla, Pompey and Caesar, eventually brought the republic to an end, but something of its spirit continued to flourish under the early emperors.

Roman art reflects the history of Roman society. At first, when the city-state of the Greeks and Etruscans seemed to be the only possible form of government, Roman art was conservative and imitative. Later, as Roman merchants profited by trade and soldiers brought Italy and the eastern Mediterranean under their rule, art treasures came into the hands of private individuals or were dedicated in temples by triumphant generals. Marcellus who captured Syracuse in 211 BC claimed that he had taught the Romans 'who had previously understood nothing' to appreciate the wonders of Greek art. From the first century BC, Roman civilisation was shaping the artistic achievements of Etruria, Greece, Asia Minor and Egypt into its own mould. The mission of Rome was defined by Virgil as one of holding a balance between the nations: 'Spare the conquered and subdue the proud'. Roman art evolved in the same spirit.

Roman towns

The heart of Rome was the Forum which began as a market place, but was **45** gradually transformed into the religious and administrative centre of an empire. Compared with the orderly planned layout of other fora, at Ostia or Pompeii for example, the arrangement of buildings seems haphazard. Administrative necessity and traditional piety led to the crowding of official buildings and temples into a tiny space. The Tabularium (record office) dates from the first century BC, but the Senate House itself was erected in late imperial times. It reminds us of one reality of power under the republic – the great families who, with a sprinkling of new men, had been elected to magistracies by a vote in the popular assembly. From the Rostra the consuls, the chief magistrates of Rome, addressed the people, while behind it was the Temple of Saturn which, like many Greek temples, held a treasury.

Roman temples of various periods cluster thickly round the Forum, but the best-preserved early buildings must be sought elsewhere. There is a great variety of plan, but like the temples of Greece they mostly consist of a central shrine and a surround of columns with capitals, plain Doric at Cora, elegant curly Ionic in the Temple of Fortuna Virilis in Rome **47** and leafy Corinthian at Assisi and Tivoli. Although the great size of some **34** Roman ventures and the willingness to experiment show southern Greek influence, the majority follow the Etruscans in their conception of planning.

The temples are set square within their forecourts, stand on high bases and have elaborate façades to the front. The use of concrete was a major innovation encouraging the construction of round buildings such as the
34 Temple of Vesta at Tivoli. It also made possible the building of elaborate complexes of great size as at Terracina, where the platform of the Temple of Jupiter guards the town. Similarly at Praeneste, a series of terraces and ascending staircases are landscaped into a hill and culminate in a great hemicycle of columns with a circular shrine dedicated to Fortune behind it.

Colonies of Roman citizens were founded in various parts of Italy, and at Cosa, Alba Fucens and Ostia we find the regular street plan and rational arrangement of public buildings which are typical of Roman towns. Little building which has not been modified in later times survives anywhere prior to the imperial period. The great sewer (Cloaca Maxima) in Rome is early, so is the fine warehouse (Porticus Aemilia), but the best range of republican architecture is to be found at Pompeii. Here the basilica or town hall, several temples, baths with rooms of varied designs for the complicated procedures of bathing, a small theatre for intimate entertainment and an amphitheatre for blood sports indicate a developed city life.

From the time that Fabius Pictor decorated the Temple of Salus in 304 BC, painting by Roman and Greek artists had been much appreciated. None of the works mentioned by writers survive, but it is possible to gain some
52 idea of its quality from the mosaic showing a scene of the Battle of Issus where Alexander the Great defeated the Persian king and from the colourful fresco portraying strange religious ceremonies in the Villa of the Mysteries at Pompeii.

Great advances were made in sculpture, especially in portraiture. Like the Etruscans, the Romans conserved effigies of their ancestors to ensure their happiness in the next world and as assistance to their descendants in this one. These images were kept in little shrines in the house, and derive their peculiar form from the fact that the Romans believed that life resided in the head and chest. At first accuracy was not essential, and any bust could represent the dead man, but contact with the Greek kingdoms of the east where rulers were honoured with lifelike statues soon changed Roman fashions. Furthermore Greek idealism was also an important factor in creating the great late republican portraits both in the round in stone and on
26, 286 coins. That both public figures like Caesar and Cicero and unknown people are represented in the statues indicates that men honoured both their ancestors and their political leaders in the same way.

Few reliefs survive, but here too great strides must have been made since the days of the early terra-cottas. A large plaque in the Capitoline Museum shows a Roman consul appeasing the gods by riding his horse into a chasm that had opened in the Forum. What has been lost can be reconstructed from the development of coinage from an early conservatism based on Greek chariot types to an imaginative recording of such historic and mythical events as the Trojan War, the Rape of the Sabine Women and Caesar's triumph over the Gauls. Each of these subjects might have been the theme for painting or sculpture kept in private houses or carried through the streets to celebrate the victories of a great general.

The Greeks had lived an open-air life and their houses were simply furnished. The Roman house was far more important. Ideally it was in the countryside, but then, as now, most people had to be content to live in towns, so a spacious, centralised style was evolved. In, for example, the
42 House of the Vettii at Pompeii various rooms radiate off the vestibule, but the most important would be situated around the second courtyard, which is much larger and contains a garden surrounded by a peristyle or cloister

26
CICERO
c. 50–40 BC
h. 29 in (74 cm)
Uffizi Gallery, Florence
In the portraits of the late republic, artists tried to fuse accuracy of detail and psychological insight with Greek idealism. The thoughtful face expresses the gravity and vigilance proper to a Roman orator and statesman. However, the perfect features suggest the Greek theory that moral fortitude should be matched by physical beauty. It is possible that this head is a late first-century AD copy which belonged to an admirer of Cicero and the ideals he represented. The head and neck have been set in a modern bust.

27

A GORGON'S HEAD

c. 500–490 BC
painted terra-cotta, h. 7 in (18 cm)
Museo Nazionale, Syracuse

The roofs of Sicilian temples were decorated with moulded plaques frequently in the form of a gorgon's head. The hideous monster was doubtless introduced into the archaic Greek world from the near east. This late example was found near the agora of Acradina, Sicily; its features are becoming more human, although it still retains the monstrous fangs of a beast usual in earlier examples. It was not until later in the fifth century that the gorgon was represented as a beautiful woman.

28

THE TEMPLE OF HERA

c. 460 BC
limestone
Paestum

This temple was actually dedicated to the goddess Hera, although today it is known as the Temple of Neptune. It is one of the best-preserved Doric temples in the world and the only one in which two tiers of columns stand unrestored inside the central shrine. Like many Greek temples (and unlike Roman ones) it is designed to be viewed from any angle. The columns of the peristyle run all the way round, each one harmoniously fluted, their beauty further enhanced by the rich honey-coloured limestone.

29

KOUROS
c. 550–540 BC
Aegean marble
h. 47 in (119 cm)
Museo Nazionale, Syracuse

In sixth-century free-standing sculpture, gods and men were represented as standing or striding naked youths. This statue, found at Megara Hyblaea, is inscribed on the right leg, 'of Somrotidas the physician; son of Mandrocles' and was probably commissioned in honour of a famous doctor. The inscription was executed in the west, but the statue itself was almost certainly produced in Greece at Naxos.

30 *below left*

APULIAN CRATER
fourth century BC
red-figure ware
h. 13·5 in (34·2 cm)
Museo Archeologico di Pegli, Genoa

Although the vase painters of Italy lacked the discipline of the Athenian masters, they often produced works of great charm. This south Italian red-figure crater, found at Gnathia near Fasano in Apulia, shows a young athlete resting in a gymnasium while a female acrobat turns somersaults. The social status of the youth is evident from his diadem, while the bangles the girl wears shows that she is probably a slave.

31, 32

DORIC TEMPLE
fifth century BC

HELLENISTIC THEATRE
third century BC and c. 100 BC
Segesta

Although the native people of western Sicily were bitterly resentful of the presence of such Greek cities as Selinus and Syracuse on the island, they were quick to adopt Greek customs and Greek architecture. The Elymians at Segesta reached a high standard of culture. They built a theatre at a time when theatres were practically confined to Greek-speaking cities, and they achieved in this temple an impressive harmony of proportion.

33
ANTINOUS
second century AD, Greek marble
78·75 in (200 cm), Museo Nazionale, Naples

The stance is derived from Greek statues of the fifth and fourth
centuries BC, but the expressive head reveals an intensity of
feeling which is completely original. It is a portrait of a man who
has become a god. The cult of Antinous spread widely in the
Roman world (and especially in the east) and heralded the
personal approach to religion that culminated in the mystery
cults of late antiquity.

34

THE TEMPLE OF VESTA

c. 80 BC
Tivoli

This little temple is an excellent example of the fusion of Roman
and Hellenistic ideas. The high podium and the rough wall reveal
the Italian love of heavy masses, but the most notable feature is
the screen of fine marble Corinthian columns supporting an
elegant frieze of garlands and ox-skulls which is derived from the
architecture of the Greek east. The dramatic positioning of the
temple suggests a growing awareness of the relation of buildings
to landscape.

ITALIA AND HER CHILDREN

13–9 BC
marble, h. 61 in (157 cm)
Rome

This relief panel from the south side of the enclosure wall around Augustus's Ara Pacis demonstrates confidence in the establishment of a new golden age. The figure of Italy, or Mother Earth, sits amongst rich foliage and animals with her children. On one side of her reclines a representation of air and on the other water – a reference to the geographical situation of Italy. The altar was commissioned by a vote of the senate on 4th July 13 BC and was finally dedicated in the Campus Martius in 9 BC.

36

LAOCOON

first century BC
Greek marble
96 in (242 cm)
Vatican Museums, Rome

This famous work is possibly by the three Rhodian sculptors, Agesandrus, Athanodorus and Polydorus. The three strangely contorted bodies and the agonised expression on Laocoön's face are typical of Greek art in the first century BC, and appealed to one aspect of Roman taste in the early empire. The statue was rediscovered in an imperial palace on the Esquiline in 1506 and thereafter had a profound influence on the Renaissance.

walk. From the dining room, the plants and statues of the formal garden could be appreciated. If it had a mosaic in the centre of the floor it would probably be small, although a few early mosaics (for example the pavement showing Alexander at the Battle of Issus) were larger. Wall painting, too, was simple for the most part and only later in the first century BC did figured friezes come to replace simple squares of imitation marble. **52**

The emperors

The Roman republic came to an end in the middle of the first century BC when Julius Caesar defeated Pompey at the Battle of Pharsalae. Although there had been 'war lords' like Marius and Sulla before, Caesar's victory in some way confirmed the need for a single undivided rule in Rome, a need which even his assassination and the resultant civil war did not deny. The art of the empire owed its character to the central direction of taste which encouraged new fashions to spread with great rapidity amongst the courtier class and beyond to the country squirarchy and small town parvenu. It is misleading to label it as grand or formal or vulgar, for just as political policies changed from one reign to another, so did architecture and painting. Thus Augustus conserved and strengthened the Hellenising tendencies of the republican period; under the patronage of Nero daring experiments in perspective were made; while Hadrian attempted to revive Greek sculpture and to perfect a new and eccentric architecture.

Reign by reign the character of the Roman empire changed. At first it was merely the old system with the addition of a supreme magistrate, but in the pages of Tacitus and Suetonius we read of how the nobility declined both in power and in political capacity. The vicious world of scandal and make-believe that surrounded the court of Augustus and his successors has deprived us of reliable witnesses, but it is certain that the emperors themselves were not the bloodstained tyrants or debauched libertines of legend. They were the victims of circumstances, and were unable to resist replacing the crumbling power of the republican magistracies with an extension of their own authority, supported by military and financial advantages which the nobles did not possess.

The Primaporta statue of Augustus shows him in his character of **44** 'imperator', an acclaimed general. The Greek idealisation of his features suggests that he was seen as greater than other mortals. To some extent this was ironic as he was naturally conservative and set great store on the past. A fitting symbol of his reign is the Ara Pacis, an altar dedicated not to victory **35** or power but to the peace which Augustus had established in the empire. The frieze which runs along the long sides of the precinct wall emphasises family life – in particular the life of the imperial family. They are shown talking informally, waiting to celebrate the return of Augustus to Rome in 14 BC. The dangers of war are over and on the short sides of the monument we see the goddess Tellus, who represents the fertility of Italy, and Aeneas sacrificing a white sow to the domestic gods, who keep peace in the home. Below the friezes, luxuriant foliage inhabited by birds, lizards and insects reflects the peace of nature. The Ara Pacis is undoubtedly one of the most beautiful monuments in the entire history of art. In it man is in harmony with the gods, inhabiting the same world and not tragically remote from them as he was amongst the Greeks. Yet the freedom depended on a man, Augustus, who had brought the gift of peace. The poet Ovid, in reference to this monument, wrote: 'Pray that the house which secures our peace may itself flourish in peace.' And under later emperors the imperial house had an almost divine sanctity.

Augustus was a lavish builder who claimed that he had found Rome made of brick, but left her made of marble. Parts of his forum, the Theatre of Marcellus and several temples survive in Rome, while elsewhere in Italy triumphal arches at Susa and Aosta, the walls and gates at Turin and the theatre at Aosta bear witness to the achievements of Augustus's reign.

In the reigns of his two successors Tiberius and Gaius Caligula appear the beginnings of a mania for palace building which would culminate in the third and fourth centuries in the 'sacred palace' of emperors who no longer lived as ordinary mortals. The portraits of Tiberius show a shy, reserved aristocrat who hated Rome and spent much of his reign on Capri. Although he built himself splendid clifftop residences there, they do not depart from the traditional idea of the Roman country house. Lucullus had constructed such a lavish palace for himself on the coast near Naples that he had been compared to a Persian king, and Pliny the Younger left vivid and detailed descriptions of his own splendid villa which stood at Laurentum on the coast of Latium. A seaside palace required sun terraces, fine rooms, baths and gardens; it would have been furnished with mosaic floors, wall paintings and statues, probably much more magnificent than the relics from Pompeii, Herculaneum and Stabiae. At Sperlonga, south of Terracina, a cave containing a number of statues has been found which was once attached to such a palace.

The reign of Caligula was very brief, but it saw even more grandiose plans for the heart of Rome itself than those of Tiberius. While the earlier emperors had lived relatively modestly, Gaius Caligula attempted to behave like a monarch and was anxious to impress his dignity on visitors. Very little of his palace survives, but a precedent had been set for Nero and Domitian. Although both of these emperors were hated by the senate and appear in the history books as bad emperors, as art patrons they vie with the greatest princes of the Renaissance, and at their courts all the arts flourished.

Nero, the last emperor of Augustus's family, appears on portrait sculptures and coins as an adolescent trying to cultivate sophistication and elegance. His expression is serious and his hair carefully crimped but he is rather fat and must have found his athletic posturings very awkward at times. He had tried his hand at sculpture, painting, music, acting and chariot racing but had only scandalised Rome and been called a bad lyre player for his pains. Cultured Greeks were delighted with him, however, and his memory was cherished by them for centuries afterwards.

The coins which circulated at this time achieved a higher standard of excellence than had been reached since the heyday of Syracuse, and their originality in the depiction of buildings and events is remarkable. Painting shows a baroque virtuosity, and, although the best examples now preserved **41, 51** were found in Pompeii, the surviving decorations of Nero's palace, the Golden House, indicate that it must have been magnificent. The finest sculptors of ancient Greece, and the best of his own day (including Zenodorus) were represented in the collection which graced its rooms. Following the builders of rural retreats, Nero had rooms for summer and winter, courtyards and grounds, extending over a large area of Rome. The Colos-**55** seum, finished by Domitian, stands on the site of a lake in the grounds. The cult of individuality which Nero fostered reveals the pathos of a boy unfitted to rule, using his power for personal ends. Yet his mechanical toys and self-glorification resulted in a great extension of artistic patronage. Nero spoke his own epitaph in the countryside near Rome where, after the Praetorian guards of Rome rose against him, he took his own life: 'How great an artist perishes in me.'

35 The calm of the Ara Pacis was giving way to a mood of restlessness. **38** In his arch, Titus appears in a great triumphal carriage amidst the bustle and acclamation of the crowd, while the spoils from the Temple of Jerusalem

37
DOMITIAN GREETING
VESPASIAN
AD 81–96
Carrara marble
81 in (206 cm)
Vatican Museums, Rome

This is one of two panels sculpted in honour of the Emperor Domitian. It shows the young Domitian welcoming his father Vespasian who had made himself master of the Roman world. The youth on the extreme left and the two headless figures on the right are part of the emperor's bodyguard. In the background two men represent the Roman people and the Roman senate. Originally the scene was crowned by a Victory holding a laurel wreath over Vespasian's head.

38

THE ARCH OF TITUS

relief from south jamb of the passage way
c. AD 81
78·75 × 151·5 in (200 × 385 cm)
Rome

The Arch of Titus at the eastern end of the Roman Forum was erected by the Emperor Domitian as a memorial to his brother. Both sides of the passage way are decorated with scenes from Titus's great triumph over the Jews after the destruction of Jerusalem in AD 70. This one shows the great seven-branched candlestick and ceremonial trumpets from the temple at Jerusalem being carried through the streets of Rome. The crowding of the figures contrasts with the calm of the Ara Pacis.

39

TRAJAN'S COLUMN

c. AD 106–113, marble
h. of each band c. 36 in (91 cm)
Trajan's Forum, Rome

This is the supreme example of Roman narrative art: a pictorial account of Trajan's conquest of Dacia based on the eye-witness sketches of official war artists. In form the relief can be regarded as an unwound scroll, and appropriately the column was placed between the two libraries which the emperor erected in his forum. From each floor different levels of the column would have been visible. This detail shows three extracts from the beginning of the campaign.

are borne along on the backs of soldiers. On some reliefs made to honour Domitian and Vespasian, it is Domitian himself who is being guided by gods and representatives of the Roman people. On one of the plaques he appears as a nineteen-year-old youth, not timid and repressed as he was in reality at this time, but as an equal to his father. The great state reception rooms of the palace which Rabirius built gave Domitian a retreat in Rome itself and a life of ritual in which to escape from his own loneliness. Martial and Statius wrote poems which glorified his family and allowed him to maintain a mask of quasi-divinity. Naturally many people were offended, and his sensitive nature slowly transformed a handsome intelligent ruler with a conscientious approach to government into a tyrant. After his murder in AD 96, the senate ordered his statues to be destroyed, so his portrait is seldom to be seen except on coins. **37**

In the second century the position of the emperor was more stable. His powers were greater than those of Augustus but he endeavoured to avoid private extravagance in Rome itself. Trajan was a soldier but his artistic judgment was shrewd. Like Augustus he aspired to be the father of his people and on his arch at Benevento we see him distributing alms to poor children, founding new towns or colonies and recruiting troops. In Rome he built baths, and under the masterly direction of Apollodorus of Damascus a fine new market and a forum were added to the growing complex of official buildings in the centre of the city. The two libraries containing Latin and Greek books which stood on each side of his forum faced out onto the largest picture book ever made, Trajan's Column a hundred Roman feet **39** high, showing scenes from the Dacian War. The emperor himself is seen leading his troops through many dangers to final victory.

The triumphs of Trajan were followed by the golden reign of Hadrian who profited by the enlightenment of the age and his own intelligence to open Rome again to Greek influences. In the artistic milieu of the capital, Greek classical art of the fifth century vied with more recent Hellenistic work. Hadrian's ideal lay in the earlier period when the power of Athens was great, and it is characteristic that some of the finest sculpture and architecture of his reign is to be found in Greece, not in Italy. Coinage, sculpture and mosaic all demonstrate the importance of older models in his reign. It can, however, be illustrated best in the statues of Antinous. **33**

Like many emperors, Hadrian had a favourite, but his was unusual both for outstanding beauty and goodness. The relationship of Antinous and Hadrian was truly platonic and culminated in an act of heroic self-sacrifice which had a profound effect on the art of the age. Superstitious rumours that Hadrian would die unless someone was prepared to go to the underworld as a substitute worked on the mind of the impetuous Antinous, who drowned himself in the Nile. Hadrian was broken-hearted and the Roman world was united with him in his grief. For the last time the Greek ideals of beauty, both physical and spiritual, produced an artistic type. As Bacchus god of wine, Silvanus gentle god of the countryside, Mercury guardian of the souls of the dead or as the Egyptian Osiris, Antinous occurs again and again. All the statues have the same melancholy and reflective gaze – boy and god; Greek beauty and the spirituality of the Middle Ages meet.

Hadrian's private palace at Tivoli expressed the same Greek tastes, and **48** his island pavilion, colonnades and statues are reminiscent of work of the fifth century BC. However, this palace is no mere pastiche of rich man's residence and Greek shrine, for many of the elements – domes and pavilions – were decidedly original. The finest dome in Roman architecture is to be seen in a remarkable temple that Hadrian erected in Rome. Although it is one of the most important buildings to have survived from antiquity, the

Pantheon is not a work of self-glorification; indeed Hadrian did not place **40** his name over the porch, but that of the patron of an earlier building, Marcus Agrippa. Mastery of building materials and techniques allowed the architect, perhaps Hadrian himself, to erect the marvellous vault which symbolises the canopy of heaven and the divine harmony of gods and men.

The high seriousness of Hadrian's time was maintained by his successors, Antoninus Pius and Marcus Aurelius, yet the golden age was ending and both military and economic evils were pressing down on the empire. The dignified statue of Marcus on the Capitol emphasises his efforts to combine the philosophy of a ruler with the efficiency of an autocrat. On the base of the now-vanished column of Antoninus Pius and on the column of Marcus Aurelius there is a new formality. The size of the figures is reduced, and on Marcus's column the emperor is alone and aloof. Soldiers scuttle about, triumphing over the barbarians who are less people than an idea. The gods still protected the Roman armies, but plague and massive depopulation were slowly sapping the confidence of all except the few scholars and aristocrats who could afford to look no further than their country villas.

The arts in everyday life

The life of the people during the early empire can be traced in all forms of literature and through material remains. A few ruins survive in almost every Italian city, however much it has been rebuilt in later centuries. The hub of any Roman city was its forum with the great temple of Jupiter at one end and the town hall or basilica at the other. Social life centred around it, radiating out past the various public baths and temples, shops and warehouses, the residences of both rich and poor, the theatre and the amphitheatre to the dark walls and the tombs beyond. Public baths were necessities without which Roman civilisation would have broken down, for they were centres of social life. The vast halls of the Baths of Caracalla in Rome are by no means the only ones, and all cities attempted to provide facilities for the entire population to bathe daily. Standards of luxury were often very high as the fine marble basins, mosaics, stuccowork and wall painting which have survived testify. Several suites can be seen at Ostia, where the mosaic in the entrance hall of the Baths of Neptune showing the god galloping through the waves is justly famous. Another suite has an equally fine mosaic of men hunting animals through a riot of foliage. At Pompeii the Stabian Baths still conserve much fine stucco moulded into strange baroque forms with hanging swags and architectural vistas. There is also a large swimming bath and an exercise yard where ball games might be played. One of the public baths of Herculaneum had a vast room anticipating the modern bathroom with a blue tank and fish painted on the ceiling. Most remarkable is the 'thermal city' at Baiae, the greatest spa in Italy, with a frontage of 450 metres and a theatre, porticos under which to walk, several great halls and bath suites and a residential quarter.

Theatres and amphitheatres survive in large numbers throughout Italy. Of the former those at Aosta, Fiesole and Verona in the north, Ostia and Pompeii in the centre and Taormina in Sicily perhaps give the best indication of the unified and enclosed nature of a Roman theatre as compared with that of the Greeks. Here were performed the rustic comedies, ballets and mimes which formed the staple dramatic fare, as well as those demonstrations of oratory which were so important to the ancients. The spectacles which took place in amphitheatres appealed to more violent emotions, and as late as the fourth century beast fights would draw large crowds. Great trouble was taken to capture the animals as we can see in mosaics. **49** Men also fought one another or were thrown to wild animals, and the sturdy masonry façades of the Colosseum or the Verona Arena point to the **55**

40
THE PANTHEON
second century AD
Rome

The Pantheon was originally erected by Marcus Agrippa, was later restored by Domitian, and completely remodelled by Hadrian. Behind a conventional façade stands the remarkable circular temple which gives expression to Hadrian's vision of the essential unity of the gods. Although the exterior now appears to be somewhat utilitarian, the brick was once faced with fine marble, and the dome was roofed in gilt-bronze tiles. The obelisk which stands in front of the temple is one of many imported into Italy by Roman emperors fascinated by their antiquity and the strange hieroglyphic inscriptions on them.

41

PERSEUS AND ANDROMEDA

first century AD
wall painting
48 × 39·5 in (121 × 100 cm)
Museo Nazionale, Naples

The work of Greek artists was frequently copied in wall paintings. This is one of two similar compositions from Pompeii showing the hero Perseus freeing Andromeda from the rock to which she has been chained by a monster. Perseus holds the Medusa head, which has the power of turning his enemies to stone, in his left hand, and with his right he gently touches Andromeda's arm. His dark skin contrasts with the delicate tones of her body and drapery.

42

THE HOUSE OF THE VETTII

AD 62–79
Pompeii

The two rich brothers who lived in this house could look out from their dining room onto a beautiful garden, full of statues and marble basins brimming with clear water. Even in the hottest weather the surrounding colonnade provided shade and a place in which the owners of the house or their guests could relax in informal surroundings. Here is the Roman ideal of countryside within the town.

true functions of these buildings. They are finished in rusticated masonry and not faced with marble, as if to highlight the savagery which was to be seen inside. At Pozzuoli (Puteoli) and Syracuse the chambers which held the mechanism for raising cages through the floor can still be examined, while in the Colosseum itself an even more bewildering array of tunnels beneath the arena were necessary for the naval battles sometimes staged there.

Houses were often of great magnificence both in country and town. Pliny's description of his villa shows a love of landscape architecture which is also attested in wall paintings from Pompeii and Rome. Pliny's villa was an early attempt to create that variety which Hadrian achieved so magnificently inland at Tivoli and to which the builder of Piazza Armerina aspired two hundred years later. Today the remains of a large villa at Sirmione on the site of Catullus's house on the southern shore of Lake Garda and the imperial villas on Capri may be taken to represent the picturesque approach to living that was denied to town dwellers.

A great variety is manifested in the residences of rich and poor at Pompeii, Herculaneum and Ostia. Here not only the plans, but mosaic floors, walls and even ceilings survive; and from them we gain much of our knowledge of Roman taste. The art of wall painting probably merely required an ability to copy, for the best work of the age according to writers was consigned to temples and public places. Nevertheless a wide range of subjects are represented; these include the three Graces, Venus and Mars, **41, 51** and scenes from the Iliad and the Odyssey. In the age of Nero, fantastic theatrical compositions of columns and drapery and receding perspective become popular. The sumptuous dining room (triclinium) of the House of the Vettii at Pompeii with its decorative cupids and bolder allegorical panels in a sober framework is typical of the approach which prevailed at the time of the destruction of the city in AD 79.

The furnishing of Roman houses was often elaborate. Statues bear witness to the mania for collecting, which led to a host of copies of Greek statues and even originals being conserved on Italian soil. Marble and bronze tables, wooden beds and lamps have also been found in Herculaneum and Pompeii. Smaller items include the magnificent silver dishes, saucepans and bowls from the House of Menander in Pompeii (now in the Museo Nazionale at Naples) and the ubiquitous red pottery from northern Italy and Gaul. We must also envisage a host of bronze figurines which may have stood in little shrines with the lares and penates, the household gods. This simple piety extended to the person, and finger rings containing engraved gems showing cupids, or Fortune or some god are often found.

The spirit of the Etruscan tombs lingered on. Preoccupation with death was also a Roman characteristic, and time and again a skeleton appears on a silver cup or on a finger ring to remind the owner of the other city outside the town. Cemeteries lay apart from human habitation, along the roads **46** leading from the city gates. Good examples may be seen outside Pompeii and Ostia, but the best ones are in Rome. At one end of the scale, the imperial mausolea of Augustus and Hadrian can only be compared to the tombs of eastern potentates, although smaller circular structures like the tomb of Caecilia Metella on the Via Appia demonstrate that the prototype lay in the similar stone-faced tombs of Etruscan Cerveteri. The strange tomb of Eurysaces the baker is shaped like a bread oven. Its sculptured reliefs show the process of breadmaking. Though this type of subject was a notable departure from the practices of other ancient peoples, it can be paralleled hundreds of times in Italy and elsewhere. In the Vatican Museums there are grave reliefs showing cobblers and knifesmiths. Trimalchio, the parvenu who appears in Petronius's novel the *Satyricon,* ordered that his monument should show him as a magistrate sitting on a platform in the hope that, thanks to the skill of an artist, he 'would be able to live after his death'.

Decline of the empire

The third century was an age of decadence, although this is less obvious in Italy than in the Roman provinces where the destruction wrought by barbarian tribesmen was more severe. The emperors were lavish builders and sought to bolster their falling prestige and vulnerability in face of civil unrest and barbarian invasion by a policy of public works. Size, which had been long valued for its own sake in the east, now became the passion of architects in Italy. Standards of decoration dropped as craftsmen found it easy to bore deep grooves in the stone with a bow drill and then to add extra detail in stucco. Neither in the great halls of the Baths of Caracalla nor
54 on the feeble reliefs on the Arch of Constantine does official art achieve true inspiration. The emperors at the time, seized, in the words of the fourth-century emperor Julian, 'by purple death and unavoidable fate', had no chance to initiate fashion. Only in portraiture did the need for the emperor to be recognised by his subjects ensure continuity of standard. Even so, the portrayal of the shifty appearance of Caracalla and the haggard wakefulness of Philip the Arab is a symptom of the change from summer to autumn in the empire. Finally even portraiture became stereotyped and the porphyry statues of Diocletian, Maximian, Galerius and Constantius I in St Mark's Square in Venice are merely puppets. From here it was a short step to the monumental head of Constantine, more divine than human, in the Palazzo dei Conservatori, Rome. From humanist culture man turned to religion and found in strange Egyptian or Syrian gods the humanity which the civil state no longer afforded him. The temples of Mithras in Rome and Ostia are forerunners of the triumph of the Christian church in the fourth century.

At Ostia a number of houses of the third and fourth centuries survive with their elegant marble-lined rooms and cool courtyards. The finest symbol of aristocratic defiance is, however, to be found in Sicily at Piazza Armerina. The palace is spaciously planned with peristyle courts and a bath
43, 49 suite. The brightly coloured mosaics on the floors show hunting scenes, chariot races, athletics and incidents from mythology. Opulent and agitated they reveal serious changes within the Roman world. The mosaics are too overpowering in their effect to have graced private houses of the early empire. The flamboyance is that of a great aristocrat, or possibly a civil servant. This veneer of prosperity on a weakened empire begs many questions. The beast-catching expedition in Africa shown in the hunt rooms is taking place in a province racked by division. When will the hunting come to an end? Where are the other late Roman houses in Sicily, those of the middle classes and the artisans? For most people the late empire was a time of poverty and struggle in a shattered world.

The ancient world took a long time to die. As late as the sixth century an imperial palace was built at Constantinople with very classical mosaic floors, and philosophers were teaching diminishing numbers in the university of Athens. The end of Roman civilisation as manifested by its art came sometime between the end of the second century and the late fourth century, as one form changed into another, as idealisation turned into stylisation and sculptors bored deep grooves into their sculptures to throw long menacing shadows. No more revealing story exists than the visit of Constantius II to the Forum of Trajan which he felt unable to copy. The little man of the new age stood facing the mighty achievements of the past. The lines of Rutilius, 'Fairest queen of the world . . . the mother of men and mother of the gods', speak of Rome in the tone of an epitaph.

Martin Henig

43
THE LITTLE HUNT *detail*
mid fourth century AD
mosaic
Villa Imperiale, Piazza Armerina

Unlike the corridor mosaic of the Great Hunt (plate **49**), this is concerned with hunting as a recreation. The animals pursued are those of Europe – hares, wild boar and deer – and they are destined for the table rather than the arena. The rich clothes of the huntsmen proclaim their aristocratic rank, and it is possible that the pavement commemorates a particularly successful day's hunting by the owner of the palace and his family.

44 *right*
THE EMPEROR AUGUSTUS
c. AD 14
marble
h. 79·5 in (202 cm)
Vatican Museums, Rome

This statue was set up by Livia in the garden of her villa at Primaporta as a reminder of her dead husband. It is based on a fifth-century masterpiece by the sculptor Polyclitus, but, whereas the Greek work showed an athlete, this portrays a Roman general addressing his army. His breastplate celebrates one of his victories; his god-like stance is fitting for a member of a family which claimed descent from Venus.

45

THE TEMPLE OF SATURN IN THE FORUM AND THE TEMPLE OF VESPASIAN

Rome

Although the Temple of Saturn (which stands on the western side of the Roman Forum) was founded early in the fifth century BC, the surviving remains are considerably later in date. Ionic columns support an architrave upon which an inscription records a restoration following a fire in the third or fourth century AD. The Temple of Vespasian, of which three fine Corinthian columns and some of the entablature survive, was erected by Titus and Domitian in honour of their father.

46 *bottom*

A BATTLE SARCOPHAGUS

AD 150–160, marble,
h. 49·25 in (125 cm) Palazzo del Museo Capitolino, Rome

In the second century AD, inhumation of the dead began to replace cremation. This created a market for carved sarcophagi which would stand prominently in family mausolea and serve as both coffins and memorials. Although almost the entire Celtic world has been conquered by the end of the first century AD, this scene of Romans fighting Gauls is accurate and convincing. It is an example of Roman antiquarianism at its best.

49 *below right*
49 *below right*
THE GREAT HUNT *detail*
mid-fourth century AD, mosaic, Villa Imperiale, Piazza Armerina

The rich mosaics of Piazza Armerina reflect the conservatism of the Roman aristocracy in the fourth century. Since the first century BC great numbers of wild animals had been caught in north Africa for the amphitheatres of Italy. In this detail the artist is more concerned with exhibiting the savagery of a leopard and a lion in their natural environment than with actual details of the hunt. It shows a coarse and blood-thirsty taste far removed from the finest aspirations of late antiquity.

47
THE TEMPLE OF FORTUNA VIRILIS
first century BC, Rome

This is one of the best-preserved of Roman temples in the Ionic order, but it owes its survival to the fact that it was converted into the church of Santa Maria Egiziaca. The temple stands on a high podium; the steps in front are in marked contrast to the sacred buildings of the Greeks which could be approached from all sides.

48
THE ISLAND PAVILION
Hadrian's Villa
c. AD 126–134
Villa Adriana, near Tivoli

The choice of the Ionic order, which was frequently used for libraries, suggests that this island was a place of study rather than a theatre or secluded room for merry-making. The living area is small, most of the island is taken up by four large niches, and so would really have been only suitable for one man. Hadrian may very well have suggested the plan himself.

50 *bottom*

GARDEN SCENE

The Villa of Empress Livia
c. 38–25 BC
232 × 118 in (590 × 300 cm)
Museo Nazionale Romano, Rome

The Romans followed the Etruscans in their appreciation of natural beauty, and a number of frescos and mosaics show trees and flowers. The anonymous artists who worked for the Empress Livia at her country villa at Primaporta near Rome produced what must be one of the world's greatest nature paintings. The composition is full of beautiful detail; and many of the trees, flowers and birds can be identified.

51

THE SACRIFICE OF IPHIGENIA

first century AD
55·5 × 54·5 in (141 × 138 cm)
Museo Nazionale, Naples

This painting from the House of the Tragic Poet at Pompeii may be a copy of a work by the fourth-century artist Timanthes. He is reported to have executed a work on this theme and to have been so overcome with grief that he could not paint the face of Agamemnon. King Agamemnon weeps at the prospect of sacrificing his eldest daughter Iphigenia. Above, the goddess Diana is about to substitute a hind and to carry Iphigenia to safety in Tauris.

52 *bottom*

THE BATTLE OF ISSUS

c. 100 BC
mosaic
134·5 × 233 in (342 × 592 cm)
Museo Nazionale, Naples

The great paintings of Greece have all been lost, but copies of a few of them survive in Roman mosaics and wall paintings. This magnificent mosaic may have been based on a late fourth-century painting by Philoxenos of Eretria. It originally graced the floor of a niche which opens onto one of the courtyards in the House of the Faun at Pompeii. It shows the decisive confrontation of Alexander the Great and the Persian king Darius in 333 BC.

53

FRIEZE

early sixth century BC
terra-cotta
9·5 × 23·5 in (24 × 59 cm)
Antiquarium Communale, Rome

This plaque, found on the Esquiline Hill, Rome, was doubtless used in the decoration of a temple. The repetitive nature of the frieze and the orientalising appearance of the animals are typical of archaic Etruscan work. Early Roman art was closely linked to that of Etruria and at the end of the sixth century BC, the great sculptor Vulca came from Veii in order to provide terra-cotta decoration for the Temple of Jupiter on the Capitol.

54 *bottom*

THE ARCH OF CONSTANTINE

c. AD 313–315
Rome

Traditions of public building had been all but forgotten in the invasion and civil strife of the third century. Constantine had high aims, but he was unable to create a new Augustan age. The finest reliefs which adorn the arch he erected to celebrate his victory at Milvian Bridge in AD 312 were looted from second-century monuments. The contemporary work is poor, although the friezes above the side passageways foreshadow the narrative style of Early Christian sarcophagi and mosaics.

55

THE COLOSSEUM

dedicated AD 80
Rome

Despite the considerable ingenuity of its architects, who used three orders of columns and one of pilasters on its façade, this amphitheatre is chiefly notable for its size and vulgarity. It was erected by the Flavian Emperors (Vespasian, Titus and Domitian) on the site of a lake in the grounds of Nero's Golden House as an attempt to convince the Roman people that the new dynasty had their interests at heart. It could, indeed, provide bread and circuses for 45,000 of them.

56
IDEALISED HEAD
probably first century AD
marble
Museo Civico, Piacenza

The portraiture of the Augustan age often succeeded in combining the forthright realism of late republican art with the harmonies of Greek style. This is a version of the type of head shown in the processional friezes on the north and south sides of the Ara Pacis, and it is possible that it was taken from a large relief of this sort which ornamented some monument of Roman Piacenza. The hair is not as finely cut as on the best Roman monuments, the leaves of the wreath are too wide, but the strong Italian features of the face (if not the result of Renaissance recutting) are a remarkable achievement for a local craftsman.

The heart of the seemingly invincible Roman empire, the home of deified emperors and numerous other gods was one of the earliest centres of the Christian faith. From the time of the first disciples the new religion grew steadily in Rome in the face of all difficulties. By tradition, the Christians were systematically repressed for two hundred years but, in fact, the persecutions of Nero, Marcus Aurelius and Diocletian were exceptional in their completeness and savagery, and all three emperors seem to have used the Christians as scapegoats for their personal mistakes and misfortunes. Yet it was obviously imprudent to flout imperial authority at all at this period and to practise Christianity in public. In any case, the first followers of Christ foregathered principally to celebrate the Eucharist and they had little need of a church as such. The simplicity of their houses of worship must have contrasted strongly with the altars and pagan monuments of imperial Rome.

Early Christian art

For the Christians who often lived so near to death it is perhaps fitting that such art of the period that has survived is of a funerary nature. The Romans practised cremation, but, as passionate believers in the Resurrection, the Christians chose to bury their dead. After his martydom, St Peter was supposed to have been entombed in a subterranean chamber on the Appian Way, so whenever possible his followers elected to be buried in the same fashion. These tombs were proclaimed inviolate under Roman law, and the catacombs on the outskirts of Rome provide the historian with a unique repertoire of Early Christian iconography. These underground burial chambers form a honeycomb network of immense complexity, with passages at many different levels. Bodies were placed in semicircular recesses or small rooms off the main corridors, and paintings decorated areas of the walls and ceilings. The catacombs, some to the north and others to the south-east of Rome, were begun even before the days of Christianity and remained in use until well into the fifth century.

Dating of the various parts must rely on certain inscriptions and on a comparison of iconography and style. During the second and third centuries most of the narrative scenes had a Christian theme, although the decorative motifs of birds and dolphins, masks and garlands are exactly like those in Roman and Pompeian pagan houses of the same date. The historical importance of the catacomb paintings outweighs their artistic merit, for they were probably painted by amateur members of the Christian community who based their art on the current style of professional Roman decorators. Yet the inventiveness of these devout people must be acknowledged, for here in the catacombs are the first representations of the Madonna and Child (Catacomb of Priscilla), of Christ the Good Shepherd (Catacomb of Calixtus) and many of the bible stories.

From an artistic point of view the earliest Christian sarcophagi are more successful, for they must have been commissioned from professional sculptors who were probably unaware of the significance of the subject matter. Often, the symbol of the cross or the sign of a fish sufficed to indicate the allegiance of the patron. The representation of the celebration of the Eucharist and the Jonah story on the so-called Sarcophagus of Baebia Hermophile in the Museo Nazionale in Rome is unequivocally Christian in subject matter. The quality is good and certainly from the hand of a professional artist. Perhaps the finest example of Early Christian art that is usually dated before the Constantinian era is the marble statue of Christ the Good Shepherd. This was a favourite subject among the persecuted sect, for if questioned, it could be passed off as a pagan statue of a worshipper bearing his sacrificial offering, yet it could also be interpreted as 'the pure

The First Centuries of Christianity

c.300–1100

57
CATACOMB PAINTING
fourth century
Catacomb of Thraso, Rome

The representation of a figure with arms outstretched in an attitude of prayer was a popular subject in catacomb decorations. Often it was an attempt to portray the patron of the burial chamber. This woman from the Thraso (or Vigna Massima) Catacomb is shown as an elegant matron with an embroidered robe and jewels at her throat and wrists.

58

THE LAZARUS CUBICULUM

fourth century
Catacomb of the Jordani, Rome

Except, perhaps, in times of violence, the Early Christians did not assemble in the catacombs, but only made occasional visits to celebrate the anniversary of a particular martyr and for the purposes of burial. This general view shows that a catacomb chamber was too small to permit gatherings of more than a few people at a time. The wall paintings portray the Raising of Lazarus on the left and the Good Shepherd on the right.

59

SANTA COSTANZA

interior
early fourth century
Rome

The centrally planned church of Santa Costanza is thought to have been built by Emperor Constantine to house the sarcophagus of his daughter Constantina. The delightful mosaic decoration of the ambulatory may be interpreted either as pagan or as an enigmatic Christian allegory. The apsidal mosaics are perhaps a century later.

shepherd with all-seeing eyes, who feeds his flock upon the mountains and the plains'.

The final attack on the Christians was by far the most violent and most sweeping. It was carried out by Diocletian in the last years of his rule. He first demanded that all Christians return to the religion of their forefathers on pain of the loss of civic rights. This order failed and, finally, he issued the Fourth Decree by which the Christian was to sacrifice to the emperor or die. Thousands of men died for their belief and others recanted, yet the religion seemed to gain strength in its adversity and its very tenacity was soon to be rewarded by recognition. At the end of 305, Diocletian abdicated to retire to his palace at Split.

Constantine and Christian Rome

His successors quarrelled among themselves until the appearance of the forceful young Constantine, who was eventually to become emperor. On the 30th of April, 311, Constantine issued a decree of toleration that put an end to the persecution of the Christians and gave them freedom of worship. Two years later, he went north to Milan, where a second edict restored the property of Christians to them and gave them full legal rights.

It is difficult to judge Constantine's personal acceptance of Christianity. His biographer Eusebius stated that he was converted before his decisive Battle of the Milvian Bridge (310) by a sign of the cross in the sky, but, in fact, he did not publicly show his allegiance to the faith for another sixteen years. Although Constantine's main preoccupation was with the establishment of a new Rome on the shores of the Bosphorus, the creation of Constantinople did not preclude further interest in Rome itself. It was entirely due to the emperor's patronage that the great Early Christian basilicas were built there. The first of these was the cathedral of the Saviour, now known as San Giovanni in Laterano, this was followed by St Peter's and San Paolo fuori le Mura. All three churches have been rebuilt many times since their foundation, but until the Renaissance St Peter's, the most venerated of all, remained unchanged. St Peter's took the form of an aisled basilica, based perhaps on the type of Roman assembly halls that may have been still standing, with an apsidal east end and a transept in which the shrine of St Peter stood. It was preceded by an enclosed forecourt and an atrium reached by steps. Inside, the walls of the nave were supported on rows of columns which carried a flat entablature. Many of the columns were taken from pagan temples. These large-scale buildings set the pattern for cruciform churches for a thousand years. In contrast, Santa Costanza has an **59** ambulatory that encircles the central area and is the Constantinian statement of a centrally planned church. Santa Costanza remains today both the most complete monument of his era, and, with its mosaics in the vault of the ambulatory, one of the finest. How far Constantine himself was involved in the designs of these basilicas is not clear, but he certainly expected them to reflect his own power and dignity. On one occasion his orders to a group of bishops were that they were to plan a church 'worthy of my generosity and worthy of the catholic and apostolic church'.

Despite the easing of pressure on the Christian community, the catacombs were still favoured burial grounds, and much more painting was being done in them. Fourth-century works can be distinguished by the increasing complexity of the subject matter and its strongly didactic overtones. An example of the contrast can be seen in the Catacomb of Domitilla by comparing the third-century idyllic, Pan-like figures of Christ among the animals with the fourth-century lunette of Christ among his apostles.

The principal sculptural undertaking in Rome at this time was the triumphal Arch of Constantine, which was erected by the senate not long **54** after the Battle of the Milvian Bridge. Certain stylistic similarities can be seen between this pagan arch and the carved sarcophagi of the Christians. As on the Arch of Constantine, the figures on the Sarcophagus of Claudianus in the Museo Nazionale completely fill the allotted space.

The variation in the type of decoration on fourth-century sarcophagi can be broadly divided into four groups. Firstly, there was plain frieze carving like that on the Claudianus Tomb. Secondly, scenes were separated from one another by the use of attached columns as in the monument in the crypt of St Peter's to Junius Bassus, a prefect of the city, who died in 359. It has a very fine sequence of reliefs depicting scenes from the life of Christ with related Old Testament events each enacted within a classical niche. A third group, known as the City Gate type, with a continuous narrative taking place before an architectural setting, is exemplified in the Sarcophagus of Gorgonius at Ancona Cathedral, where Christ the Lawgiver is seen with his apostles. Less elaborate stone coffins decorated with waved fluting and simple Christian monograms were also popular.

No doubt the first Christians to enjoy freedom of worship were apprehensive, for some must have remembered the terrible purges of Diocletian and feared a reversal of their fortunes after the death of Constantine. But this time they were not to be disappointed and, with the exception of Julian the Apostate, all later emperors were Christian in name at least. Although Christianity did not become the state religion until 380, the church flourished in a peaceful atmosphere and became the principal patron.

Once Christians were free to worship, Rome ceased to be the only focus of Christian art in the west. Indeed it lost much of its political status while Trier and Cologne in Germany and Milan in Italy gained in stature as imperial residences and as ecclesiastical sees. Subsequently these capitals became leading artistic centres.

With the establishment of the church and an organised liturgy, the need arose for small devotional objects such as icons and diptychs for personal prayer and for decorated church furnishings. Such small items made of silver and carved ivory often escaped the notice of vandals and iconoclasts and provide the present-day historian with a wealth of carving and sculpture. For instance, an early fifth-century silver reliquary finely worked with biblical scenes was found beneath the high altar of San Nazaro Maggiore, Milan, where it is now on view. The stylistic origins of such delicate work are unknown, but it is likely that the carvers and silversmiths had some knowledge of the refined work that was then in fashion in Alexandria and Antioch. The Lipsanotheca Casket now in Brescia, and the exquisite votive plaque of the Three Marys at the Sepulchre in the Museo dello Castello Sforzesco, Milan, may have been Milanese in origin.

The greatest surviving series of Early Christian mosaics in Rome, which date from the papacy of Sixtus III (432–440), are to be found in Santa Maria Maggiore. Later alterations to the church fabric in no way lessen the impact of the scenes along the walls of the nave and over the triumphal arch. Stories from the Old Testament and from the life of the Virgin are told with great attention to detail. Each episode is set against a naturalistic background, but the whole cycle takes on the proportions of a heroic saga, an epic with an underlying didactic purpose.

Ravenna, a Byzantine capital

Even at the time of the Emperor Augustus, Ravenna was an important seaport of Italy, a gateway to the eastern Mediterranean, but after the sack of Rome by the Goths in 410 it became for a time the official residence of the western empire. Later the Ostrogothic kings made Ravenna their capital, only to lose it in their turn to the Byzantine general Belisarius and

60

CHRIST ENTHRONED
early fifth century
mosaic
Santa Pudenziana, Rome

Although the apse mosaic of Santa Pudenziana is much restored, it retains the impression of the didactic fervour of Early Christianity. The majestic figure of Christ is enthroned before the city of Jerusalem with apostles to either side of him. In the sky are the four symbols of the Evangelists.

61

SARCOPHAGUS OF JUNIUS BASSUS
c. 360
St Peter's, Rome

Junius Bassus, prefect of the city of Rome, was buried in a splendid sarcophagus that openly proclaimed his allegiance to the Christian faith. The carving of the individual scenes, which show episodes from the life of Christ and related Old Testament events, is of the highest quality and reveals the sculptor's debt to the stylistic traditions of his pagan forerunners.

his emperor Justinian. The period between the fifth and seventh centuries saw major creative activity in all fields of art, and Ravenna became a city worthy of the imperial household. So much of the glory of the city survives today because, after the coming of the Lombards in 741, Ravenna declined and there was little large-scale rebuilding.

78   The first important monument is the so-called Mausoleum of Galla Placidia which contains sarcophagi traditionally thought to be those of Galla Placidia, her husband Constantine and her son Valentinian. It is a small cruciform building with mosaics contemporary in date with its construction, *c.* 450. The east-west axis of the vault is decorated with roundels and stars on a deep-blue background, whilst the transepts have vine scrolls and deer in the lunettes. The main lunettes at the east end and above the entrance are filled with scenes of the martyrdom of St Lawrence and an idyllic interpretation of Christ the Good Shepherd with his sheep in a pastoral landscape. The overall effect of the mausoleum is most impressive and the colours seem to glow with a vibrant warmth.

Almost contemporary with the Galla Placidia mosaics are those in the cathedral baptistery, otherwise known as the Baptistery of the Orthodox or as the Baptistery of Neon, who was bishop of Ravenna from 451 to 473. In the apex of the dome a mosaic of the Baptism is surrounded by the twelve apostles in procession. Although the figures are again set against a background of dark blue, a variety of brilliant colouristic effects distinguishes it from the unity of Galla Placidia, suggesting completely different artists.

Throughout the fifth century the city of Rome declined in power and prestige, so that even before the deposition of the pathetic puppet emperor Romulus in 476 the western empire was a shadow of its former self, and names like Alaric, Attila the Hun and Theodoric the Ostrogoth replace those of the Romans. However, many of these so-called barbarians were devout Christians and it was a period of considerable cultural activity. For example, Boethius, a master of the offices in the court of Theodoric during the late fifth century, has become immortalised through his writings on logic, mathematics and music.

When Theodoric finally gained control of Italy in the last years of the fifth century, he chose Ravenna as his capital. He improved the city by repairing Trajan's aqueduct and built himself a palace, which is illustrated with some artistic licence in the mosaic frieze of Sant'Apollinare Nuovo, one of the churches built during his rule. Panels of mosaic above the windows of the nave tell stories from the life of Christ with a simple directness. In contrast to Santa Maria Maggiore in Rome, a minimum number of large hieratic figures staring out of the picture is used in each scene. Below the windows, a procession of holy virgins and martyrs make a mosaic counterpart to the colonnade of columns leading up to the altar.

As after Theodoric's death in 526 Italy lacked a powerful leader, the emperor of the east, Justinian, took the opportunity to try to reunite the two halves of the Christian empire, divided since the death of Constantine. To this end he sent his general Belisarius, who fought throughout the length of Italy. Despite his legendary fame, Belisarius was but partially successful in his campaign, holding only Pavia and Ravenna. During his years as emperor, Justinian made Constantinople a worthy capital of an empire that stretched across Europe from Spain to Syria. Second only to Constantinople, Ravenna survives today as a lasting memorial to the genius of Justinian. His finely characterised portrait faces that of his wife
79, 63   Theodora across the chancel of San Vitale. The quality of these mosaics in execution and design leaves no room to doubt that Byzantine artists were imported to carry out the imperial commissions which included San Vitale,

With her husband Justinian, the empress Theodora played an important role in the political and artistic ascendancy of the Byzantine world. Among the churches they commissioned in Ravenna is the magnificent San Vitale. In the sanctuary are mosaics of Theodora and Justinian with their court, which are remarkable examples of realistic portraiture.

Sant'Apollinare in Classe and the later work in Sant'Apollinare Nuovo.

San Vitale has a complex plan, but faced with the breath-taking display **62, 77** of mosaics that adorn the walls of the church, the architecture and sculpture fade into second place; an imaginary world is easily created by the coloured surfaces of the wall. The chancel apse is filled with a youthful Christ enthroned on the orb of the world and flanked by angels who present St Vitale on one side and Bishop Ecclesius (donor of the new church) on the other. The surround of flowers and plants seems to set the ethereal figures in a garden of paradise. Stylistically, the use of gold rather than blue backgrounds is the most important change from the earlier mosaics. Sant' Apollinare in Classe was dedicated two years later than San Vitale, and in **76** contrast is a simple aisled basilica of conventional form. Large windows flood the wide nave with light that orchestrates the colour of the mosaics, leading the eye towards the apse. In colours of purple and gold, two angels guard the entrance to the shell of the apse, where the patron saint stands, his arms outstretched in prayer. Above, the cross, as a symbol of the Transfiguration, glitters on a turquoise-coloured sky.

The archbishop's palace in Ravenna may not be the work of Justinian's architects, but, despite later restorations, it gives an idea of the grand manner in which the Byzantine rulers lived. The excellence of the ivory throne of Maximian, bishop of Ravenna during Justinian's reign, is un- **68** questioned, although its origin is disputed. The chair is made up of a number of panels whose style differs from the work of Alexandria, Syria, Anatolia or Constantinople, all of which have been suggested as its possible source. As soon as Justinian's patronage was ended, a decline in the quality of **75** artistic craftsmanship set in. Other works in the Byzantine manner were made, but the high point of Justinian's achievement was never matched.

Carolingian and Ottonian supremacy

Throughout the seventh and eighth centuries Italy was more or less in the control of the 'unspeakable' Lombards, whose art was confined to a few decorations and an ubiquitous flat interlacing pattern. At the insistence of the pope, the Franks were called in to expel the Lombards, but it was not until Charlemagne became the Frankish leader that they were finally ousted. In forty-six years of incessant fighting, Charlemagne was to create a unified empire stretching from the Danube to the Pyrenees. On Christmas day 800 he was crowned holy Roman emperor in the basilica of St Peter's, thus creating a new western empire free from Byzantine authority. As its head Charlemagne tried to surpass his Byzantine counterpart, modelling himself on the great Caesars of Rome and showing a conscious desire to revive the antique. He gathered round him numerous advisers, scholars and artists whose work presented a synthesis of different influences. The Carolingian style was not bounded by the present-day frontier of any one country, but was a European art. Mainly concerned with the north of his empire, Charlemagne based the court at Aachen and delegated the government of Italy to others. But Rome and Ravenna had made a lasting impression, so when the Palatine Chapel was built at Aachen, it was based on the design of Justinian's San Vitale and columns were transported from the archbishop's palace for use at the Frankish court. Little Carolingian architecture survives in Italy, but a few wall paintings and mosaics, some manuscripts and a number of small objects worked in metal and ivory remain to give an idea of this international style.

Santa Prassede in Rome was built under the personal patronage of Pope Paschal I (817-824), and its mosaics typify the best work of the ninth **72** century, with the large, stiff figures in the apse and the schematic abstraction of the decoration in the chapel of San Zeno. At Castelseprio near Milan, the

64 tiny chapel is decorated with frescos of the childhood of Christ. Their date is unknown and different schools have been proposed, but the paintings have an antique flavour that suggests the classical revival of Charlemagne. Despite the faded colours, the frescos of Castelseprio seem to be the work of an original and gifted artist whose dynamic narrative abilities are obvious.

72, 73 That artists of this time drew on a variety of sources is best illustrated in ivory carvings and metalwork. The high altar of Sant'Ambrogio in Milan is a sumptuous work covered on all four sides with precious metals, each panel having work of the highest quality that reflects the illusionistic style of manuscripts from the Carolingian scriptorium at Rheims. In contrast, the carved ivory book cover of the Lorsch Gospels in the Vatican Library has **68** that same rhythmic modelling as panels on Maximian's chair, whilst a diptych at Monza showing King David and Pope Gregory must be based on a fifth or sixth-century pagan diptych.

70 Ivories and small-scale objects are easily portable, so it is difficult to judge the extent of the Italian element in any of these treasures. Certainly **65** the Bible of St Calixtus in San Paolo fuori le Mura, Rome, was brought to Italy from Rheims by Charles the Bald. It is a strange manuscript as some of the illuminations seem to have been pasted in and it may not have been made in one single scriptorium, but as such it presents an interesting anthology of Carolingian illuminations.

Soon after the death of Charlemagne, Italy once again became a number of separate warring states. It was attacked and appropriated on all sides, most notably by the Saracens who overran Sicily and developed Palermo into a prosperous trading city that remained in the Moslem faith until the coming of the Normans in the eleventh century.

The German emperor Otto I and his successors of the same name sought a close political association with the pope, and thereby introduced their art into Italy. To mark Otto II's state entry into Milan in 980, a number of ivory carvings were made. They include a panel of the emperor and his family adoring Christ now in the Museo del Castello Sforzesco, Milan, and a ceremonial ivory stoup in Milan Cathedral. Both these relate to the more impressive ciborium which stands today at the entrance to the chancel of Sant'Ambrogio, Milan. The Ottonian style, though non-Italian, was strongly influenced by the Early Christian art carried across the Alps by pilgrims returning from Rome.

The only indigenous Italian school that existed at this time was in the north. One of the most impressive monuments of early medieval art is the apsidal painting in the little church of San Vincenzo at Galliano near Como. A conclusive date of 1007 is given to this work which consists of a large standing figure of Christ in a mandorla accompanied by archangels. These large monumental figures are swathed with deliberately stylised draperies that look ahead to the art of the twelfth century rather than back to the earlier art of the Carolingian or of the Byzantine school of Constantinople.

Throughout the era of the Carolingian and Ottonian supremacy, the figurative arts of Italy were to a large extent reliant on styles worked out and elaborated north of the Alps, but in architecture Lombardy played a role of supreme importance. Despite their warlike character and their 'barbaric' behaviour the Lombards were renowned as builders as early as the seventh century when their king Rotharis registered a guild of builders. A good example of their achievement may be seen in the church of San Vincenzo in Prato. The Lombard heritage played an important role in the history of Italian Romanesque architecture for it was in the north of the country that the major technical advances were made.

Sabrina Mitchell

64

THE JOURNEY TO BETHLEHEM
ninth or tenth century
fresco
Castelseprio

The walls of the tiny chapel at Castelseprio are adorned with a striking cycle of frescos. Their date is unknown, but it is clear that they are the work of someone highly gifted. It has been suggested that they may have been painted by a Byzantine artist, for the composition of the figures and the facial types are handled with great sensitivity.

65

GENESIS

The Bible of St Calixtus
c. 870
San Paolo fuori le Mura, Rome

This bible was commissioned by Emperor Charles the Bald and was probably brought to Italy as a gift from him to the pope. The simple illustrations of the Genesis scenes are arranged in narrative strips, a formula that was much favoured by late classical artists, and it seems that the artist may have had an antique model to work from.

66

THE GOOD SHEPHERD

late third or early fourth century
Museo del Laterano, Rome

Although statuary was so popular in
pagan Rome, it was rarely used by the
Early Christians. This fine statue which
clearly represents Christ the Good
Shepherd is therefore doubly remarkable
for its iconography and for the skill with
which it was made. At a time when
Christianity was generally forbidden, very
little artistic creation aspired to such high
standards.

67 *bottom left*

THE LIPSANOTHECA CASKET

fourth century
ivory
10 × 13 × 11 in (25 × 33 × 27 cm)
Museo Civico Età Cristiana, Brescia

The Lipsanotheca is one of the finest
examples of an Early Christian ivory
casket to have been made in Italy. One
master carved the entire work, covering
the sides and the lid with beautifully
composed scenes from the Old and New
Testaments. Around the sides of the lid
are heads of saints and apostles.

68

THE THRONE OF MAXIMIAN

546–c.556
ivory
59 × 26 in (149 × 66 cm)
Museo Arcivescovile, Ravenna

In Justinian's Ravenna, Bishop
Maximian was the effective head of the
eastern church in Italy. This magnificent
throne, which is made up from a number
of ivory panels, is the work of various
different artists and may have been
brought from Constantinople.

70
THE IRON CROWN OF LOMBARDY

tenth century
Cathedral Treasury, Monza

Although the Iron Crown of Lombardy is traditionally connected with Charlemagne, it is in fact a work of the tenth century. The crown is made of gold and inlaid with enamels and precious stones, but inside a strip of iron, said to be one of the nails from the True Cross, gives the crown its name.

71
SANTA SABINA

fourth or fifth century
Rome

During the seventeenth and eighteenth centuries the old churches of Early Christian Rome were masked with a covering of elaborate Baroque ornament, but now they are gradually being restored to their original state. Santa Sabina is a typical basilican church, with parallel rows of reused antique columns, here spanned by an archivolt that supports the walls above.

72 *right*
RELIQUARY OF THE TRUE CROSS

ninth century
10.5 × 7 in (26 × 17 cm)
Vatican Museums, Rome

The small crucifix is decorated with scenes from the early life of Christ and is inscribed with the dedication of Pope Paschal I, one of the principal patrons in Rome during the ninth century. The cross is probably the work of a Roman artist for there are stylistic connections with Paschal's commission for Santa Prassede.

69
FEMALE SAINTS

probably c. 762–776
Tempietto, Santa Maria, Cividale del Friuli

The little church of Santa Maria at Cividale in north-eastern Italy is generally considered to be a unique example of architecture dating from the time of the Lombard supremacy. On the interior wall above the entrance a frieze of six stucco figures is placed above the richly ornamented doorway. The figures are beautifully made, and it has been suggested that they are the work of a Byzantine expatriot fleeing from the Iconoclasts.

73

THE ALTAR

c. 835
silver, gold and enamels
Wolvinus Magister
Sant' Ambrogio, Milan

The magnificent altar of Sant' Ambrogio
was the gift of Angilbert, bishop of Milan.
It is a sumptuous work wrought in silver
and gold and ornamented with filigree
and enamels. The panels containing
narrative scenes are of the highest artistic
achievement, and it is generally thought
that Wolvinus, who signed the altar, must
have received his training in the courts of
Charlemagne.

74, *bottom right*

THE CRUCIFIXION

586
*Biblioteca Laurenziana, Florence (MS Plut
I 56c)*

The book known as The Rabbula Gospels
was made at Zagba in eastern Syria. It is
one of the earliest manuscripts with
illustrations of Christian themes that has
survived. The gospels did not come to
Italy until a later date and were principally
influential in eastern Europe. Below the
crucifixion is a scene showing the empty
tomb and the appearance of Christ to the
three Marys.

75

CROSS OF GALLA PLACIDIA
detail

probably mainly sixth century
Museo Civico Età Christiana, Brescia

The crucifix traditionally known as the
Cross of Galla Placidia was given to a
Benedictine monastery in Brescia by
Desiderius, king of the Lombards, in the
eighth century. It was probably made in
Ravenna by Byzantine craftsmen. In the
central part there is a contemporary
figure of Christ the Redeemer.

76
ST APOLLINARE

533–549
Sant' Apollinare in Classe, Ravenna

Like San Vitale, Sant' Apollinare in Classe
was built by the Emperor Justinian. By
contrast it is a simple basilican church, but
magnificent mosaics adorn the apse. Set
against a delightful background of
landscape motifs, hills, trees and flowers,
the twelve apostles, shown as sheep, stand
around the central figure of the patron
saint. Above is a symbolic representation
of the Transfiguration.

77 *centre right*
DETAIL OF ARCADED OPENING

c. 547
San Vitale, Ravenna

The overall impression of sumptuous
decoration at San Vitale is attained by a
careful attention to every detail in the
design. In a single arcaded opening the
spandrel may be filled with geometric and
foliate patterns of mosaic rising above
exquisite capitals. The capitals are deeply
cut to allow the upper surface to stand
out like applied filigree.

78
THE MAUSOLEUM OF GALLA PLACIDIA

c. 450
Ravenna

The little Mausoleum of Galla Placidia
still houses the sarcophagi of Honorius,
the first emperor to settle in Ravenna; of
his sister Galla Placidia, who governed for
twenty-five years for her son; and of her
husband. It has rich mosaic decoration on
all the upper walls and the ceiling, with a
background of dark but intense blue
dominant. On the eastern wall the mosaic
depicts the martyrdom of St Lawrence,
with apostles placed on either side of the
window of the raised crossing.

79 *far right*
JUSTINIAN AND HIS COURT

c. 547
mosaic
San Vitale, Ravenna

The mosaic showing Justinian and his
court, which graces the left-hand wall of
the apse in San Vitale, is an everlasting
reminder of the emperor's stature as a
ruler and as a patron of the arts. The style
and craftsmanship is of the highest quality,
with a fine characterisation of Justinian
himself enhanced by the individual
portraits of his followers.

80

THE PORT OF RAVENNA

early sixth century
mosaic
Sant' Apollinare Nuovo, Ravenna

This detail from the mosaic decoration of Sant' Apollinare Nuovo represents a boat outside the city walls of Ravenna. It is part of a larger panel containing the palace of Theodoric, which enables the historian to gain information about the city as it was at the time.

The eleventh century in Italy was dominated by the struggle for power between the papacy and the emperors. Papal activity in the arts was thus minimal, and it was the individual towns and cities and the rise of the monasteries which played major roles in producing the outstanding monuments of the day. The Norman invasion of Sicily and the south of Italy and trade links with Byzantium through Sicily, Venice and Pisa led to foreign influences in these areas, but, despite continuing political pressures from abroad, art in the eleventh century became more positively nationalistic and made an individual contribution to the Romanesque style.

Northern Italy

The period saw great advances in the technique of building in stone and brick with Lombardy playing an important role. The valley of the river Po is an agriculturally fertile area, and the river provided a navigable trade route across the greater part of northern Italy. Along the Po a number of prosperous cities grew. During the twelfth century the citizens formed trading confraternities and guilds, so that they became self-governing municipalities, to a large extent independent of papal control or imperial power. Indeed the so-called Lombard League successfully repulsed Frederick Barbarossa. In Italy any city of importance was the see of a bishop and, although the bishop played a lesser role in these northern cities than elsewhere, the present-day provinces of Lombardy and Emilia are richly endowed with fine cathedrals dating from this period of wealth.

San Pietro at Agliate near Monza was built as early as the ninth century, yet it contains most of the formative elements of the new style. Its sanctuary is covered with a stone barrel vault, while the corresponding bays in the side aisles have groined vaults. Outside, the apse is ornamented with unbroken pilaster strips and a series of niched recesses beneath the cornice. Here the exterior is not particularly striking, but it was to become one of the hallmarks of the so-called First Romanesque that spread from Lombardy to Germany, France and Spain. At Como, Sant'Abbondio, San Fedele and San Giacomo give a good idea of Lombard Romanesque architecture. The masons of Como were renowned for their fine work and their travels abroad created an interchange of ideas. Sant'Abbondio, consecrated in 1095, has the Germanic arrangement of towers beside the apse and decoration around the apsidal window that is related to the great cathedral at Speyer. San Fedele has a trefoil-shaped eastern complex that is only found elsewhere in St Maria in Kapitol, Cologne.

One of the most splendid of all Romanesque buildings is the church of Sant'Ambrogio at Milan. During the eleventh and twelfth centuries, western architects were much preoccupied with the problems of stone vaulting. A barrel vault was the first solution, but its heaviness called for massive supporting walls. Logically, the next step was the groin vault produced by the intersection of two barrel vaults at right angles to each other, but when applied to a large span it tended to sag. Far more important was the decision to construct ribs whose arched supports could carry the actual vault. This innovation was to have far-reaching consequences in the development of the Gothic system, and Sant'Ambrogio has been claimed as the earliest building in which it was used. No conclusive evidence is available, but this must rank with Durham Cathedral as an early example.

The towns of the province of Emilia (Ferrara, Cremona, Piacenza and Modena) have a number of important churches whose architecture and sculpture is related to the Lombard style, although they differ in some important respects. Modena Cathedral was begun in 1099 by Lanfranco, the architect whose name is commemorated in the apse. On the façade, an inscription states clearly that Wiligelmo was the sculptor. Almost for the

81

AN ANGEL

1143–51
mosaic
Martorana, Palermo

The Martorana, otherwise known as Santa Maria dell' Ammiraglio, was built and decorated for Admiral George of Antioch in the reign of King Roger II. The mosaic decoration is particularly fine, and the figures are handled with a delicate sensitivity that suggests the presence of eastern artists, possibly from the patron's native lands.

82

MODENA CATHEDRAL
twelfth century

Although the principal point of interest in the façade of Modena Cathedral is the sculptural frieze by Wiligelmo, the general view gives a clear indication of the quality of the whole building. The architect Lanfranco designed the building at the end of the eleventh century and his plans were closely adhered to, apart from the introduction of the rose window in later times.

83

ADAM AND EVE
c. 1110
Wiligelmo
Modena Cathedral

The name of Wiligelmo, inscribed on the façade, is linked with the four carved panels on the west front of Modena Cathedral. Each panel contains stories from the book of Genesis, told with a charmingly direct approach. The literal interpretation of biblical stories is one of strong points of Romanesque figurative art.

first time named artists emerge, but in the case of Modena the inscriptions only put a single name to a group of artists, and give no indication of date, which must be assessed purely on stylistic grounds. Inside, the nave of the cathedral is broken up into bays by means of diaphragm arches, each bay having a triforium set beneath a sub-arch and clerestory opening. A large crypt set almost on ground level raises the chancel. Rather than earlier Lombard elevations, the interior of Modena recalls the abbey church of Jumièges in Normandy built by William the Conqueror. This is a link that exemplifies the spread and diffusion of ideas in western Europe either through itinerant architects or travelling churchmen.

The development of sculpture

Wiligelmo's sculpture at Modena consists of panels on the lower part of **83** the façade, the jambs of the main portal and two reliefs of cupids with lowered torches. The appearance of such an elaborately decorated façade was quite new in Italy and one must look to Santiago di Compostella in Spain or to St Sernin at Toulouse for its closest prototypes. Yet the continuous narrative and the handling of the figures, particularly the nudes, shows that Wiligelmo must have also been aware of the carving on Roman sarcophagi. Two side portals at Modena are of slightly later date than the work of Wiligelmo; the Porta della Pescheria has a scene from Arthurian legend on the archivolt, suggesting a definite connection with the French Romance cycle which was probably made known by lay singers on the pilgrimage routes, while the Porta dei Principi has the life of St Gimigniano. A continuous moulding of stringy interlacing inhabited by storks, foxes, fabulous beasts and men engaged in their crafts decorates the jambs and archivolt. Wiligelmo seems to have worked at Cremona as well; there four large figures of prophets are set two on either side of the main doorway. These are on a much larger scale than anything at Modena and must play a part in the origins of the column statue.

Niccolo, a sculptor who worked at Ferrara and Verona, inherited the basic conception of Wiligelmo, but transformed his predecessor's work by a closer union of architecture and sculpture. The conception of the main doorway of the cathedral at Ferrara has been carefully thought out and is much more like a French doorway, for Niccolo had certainly visited France at least once. The jamb figures, although by no means column statues, form an integral part of the column and harmonise with the other decorated half-columns and pilasters. The tympanum is filled with St George and the

dragon; the architrave shows a touching series of episodes in the early life of Christ. This sculptor went from Ferrara to Verona, where the doorway of the cathedral has many similarities with Ferrara. A later inscription also connects Niccolo with the church of San Zeno in Verona, where renova-
90 tions took place in 1138. The principal door of San Zeno is covered by a projecting porch with two columns resting on lions and with caryatid figures above the capitals. St John the Evangelist and St John the Baptist stand on the gable. Beneath, the doors are set in a plain architrave, but elaborate sculptures decorate the tympanum and reliefs on either side of the doorway. Niccolo's hand may be detected in some places, for instance in the Creation scenes on the right-hand relief, but he obviously had assistants working with him, one of whom, Guglielmo, made the New Testament reliefs. Guglielmo's delight in movement and gesture contributed to a far more painterly style than Niccolo's.

At the risk of leaping too far ahead in time, it is opportune to mention here the work of Benedetto Antelami, whose principal sculptures can be seen in Parma. A relief of the Deposition that is now set into the wall of the transept in the cathedral was probably an altar frontal. Solemn dignity befitting the subject is enhanced by a processional arrangement of cere-monial figures which stand rigidly against the flat background. Nothing is known of Benedetto the man, but he was certainly working at Parma in 1196. He would seem to have been trained in Provence at Saint Gilles or at any rate to have been familiar with its art. Apart from the cathedral at Borgo San Donnino and the bishop's throne in Parma Cathedral, his principal task was the decoration of the Parma Baptistery. A comprehensive sculptural programme was devised which included three deeply recessed niches and a continuous animal frieze running round the building one third of the way up. This has a variety of real and fabulous beasts more often found in a bestiary. The fleshy acanthus foliage that is used was often finished with tiny drill holes, a hallmark of the Provençal style which was
86 to appear again at Pisa.

The Tuscan cities
The countess of Tuscany, Matilda, an energetic political figure, was an active patroness of the arts throughout the second half of the eleventh century, and the Romanesque style in her provinces greatly benefited from her encouragement. Although Florence prospered under her rule, practically nothing of her influence remains today, though the present-day appearance of the cathedral baptistery is probably a result of building at this
5, 95 period, and San Miniato al Monte, the most remarkable surviving Floren-tine basilica, was essentially complete by 1062.
94 Except for Pisa Cathedral and the buildings put up in emulation of it, Romanesque Tuscan architecture is far more conservative than any in Lombardy or Emilia. As in Rome, the classical tradition of church archi-tecture was a formative element calling for a simple plan, a straightforward elevation and little interest in stone vaulting. Typical examples can be seen in San Piero a Grado and the cathedral at Carrara. Diaphragm arches were
95 used at San Miniato al Monte in Florence, but the arcade of columns is sup-ported on Corinthian capitals like those in Santi Apostoli, also in Florence.

Near Siena, the abbey church of Sant'Antimo provides an interesting contrast to the normal type of Tuscan architecture. Begun in the early twelfth century it must have been built under French supervision, for the apse is surrounded by an ambulatory with radiating chapels and there are indications that the original intention was to vault the whole church. Obviously these unknown Frenchmen, rather than local tradition, are behind the unusual design of Sant'Antimo, and its building did nothing to

84
LUCCA CATHEDRAL
c. 1200 and later
The cathedral of San Martino is one of the three churches in Lucca to have been built in emulation of Pisa's cathedral. The interior of the church is in the Gothic style, but the west front is decorated with three registers of colonnaded arcading and is a modest version of the Pisan west front.

85
SAN MINIATO AL MONTE
1018–62
Florence
The Benedictine San Miniato al Monte is one of the earliest churches surviving in Florence. Instead of using the decorative effects of sculpture, so popular in Lombardy and Emilia, the architects chose to use a variety of colours in the marble veneers of the wall surfaces. This type of geometric decoration remained popular in Tuscany until the fifteenth century.

change the style of Tuscan churches, which continued to be built as before.

When the great cathedral of Pisa was seen, neighbouring cities such as Arezzo and Lucca tried to outdo the Pisan masterpiece. Pisa's cathedral was founded in 1063 as a manifestation of civic pride in celebration of the massive defeat of the Saracen fleet near Palermo, which enabled Pisa to gain control of Sardinia and Corsica. Changes in plan, however, meant that it was not completed until the thirteenth century. It was originally placed on an open site, but now with the baptistery, the campanile and the Camposanto (burial ground) it forms the centrepiece of a splendid architectural complex. Apart from the sheer size and quality of the design, the most distinctive feature of Pisa Cathedral is the treatment of the exterior arcading. Each face is dressed with marble panelling, with arcading and free-standing colonnades which are highly decorative, and yet, unlike the Lombard arcading, they are perfectly related to the architectural construction of the interior. Pisa's importance as a great commercial and mercantile city brought her into contact with the cities of the east and must account for the non-Italian elements in the architecture of the cathedral. For instance, old Roman gravestones and pagan altar tables are ranged around the inner walls of the nave in the Byzantine manner, and the dome of the baptistery has a profile related to the rotunda of the Anastasis in Jerusalem. Pisa also had colonies in Provence, at Narbonne, Montpellier and Saint Gilles, and it seems likely that many of the sculptors working on the façade of the cathedral were at least trained in Provence. The main columns on the west front of Pisa Cathedral and the baptistery doorway have their surfaces carved with fleshy acanthus foliage, with classical nymphs and other figures introduced into the decoration, suggesting a conscious imitation of Roman sarcophagi. The famous campanile, better known as the Leaning Tower of Pisa, at the eastern end of the cathedral, was not begun until 1174, yet its decoration harmonises perfectly with it.

86

ACANTHUS DECORATION
late twelfth century
Pisa Cathedral

From a distance the decorative effects of Pisa Cathedral appear to rely on an architectonic scheme rather than sculptured ornament. Yet the pillars of the west front are in fact richly carved with acanthus foliage, which is deeply incised and heightened with drill holes in the antique manner.

Rome in decline

In contrast to the prosperity of Pisa, during the late eleventh and early twelfth centuries Rome was the scene of an almost continual series of pillages and sieges resulting from political struggles between pope and emperor. Little building was done during these years, and from what has survived it is clear that classical tradition was so strong that it resisted the Romanesque style. Often the architects were required to renovate an older church rather than build a new one, so the Early Christian principles were firmly adhered to. Examples of twelfth-century churches in Rome are Santa Maria in Cosmedin, San Clemente and Santi Quattro Incoronati. All these are based on a simple basilican plan, and it is interesting to note that until the excavations of 1860 San Clemente was thought to be a fourth-century church. In decoration, too, the approach was one of calm simplicity. The Cosmati family, who were working in 1150 and after, are the best-known sculptors, and their work is generally in the style of the Roman 'opus Alexandrinum' (geometric patterns of white marble with discs of coloured porphyry and bands of coloured mosaic).

The style of painting in Rome c. 1100 can be seen in the fresco decoration of San Clemente. Here, narrative scenes from the life of St Alexis and the legend of the mass are framed by painted friezes filled with decorative birds and fishes. The frescos of San Clemente form the central core of a group of related works in the region, notably Castel Sant'Elia near Nepi, San Silvestro at Tivoli, and San Pietro in Tuscania. A formalised way of handling the drapery in these paintings, with tiny V folds to indicate depth and the clinging damp appearance of the material, also appears in a number of large bibles written and illustrated in the district. Examples of these

87
WEST FRONT AND CAMPANILE
1063
Abbey church, Pomposa

Built by Abbot Guido of Ravenna in the mid-eleventh century, the abbey church at Pomposa is a fine example of Lombard Romanesque architecture. The tower is divided into nine stages by pilaster strips and arched openings and is ornamented with roundels of geometric design.

88
THE CROWNING OF
ROGER II BY CHRIST
1143–51, mosaic, Martorana, Palermo

Although the crowning of Roger II by Christ takes a prominent place in the narthex of the Martorana, the church was in fact commissioned by a court official rather than the king himself. The figures are shown as serene, hieratic beings, suggesting the hand of an artist trained in Constantinople, rather than in Sicily.

so-called Atlantic bibles can be seen in the Vatican and at Cividale del Fruili. In all these Roman paintings the Byzantine influence is apparent, particularly in the facial types, but it never really stirred the artist.

The monasteries

The eleventh century was a time of reformation in the monastic orders throughout Europe. At Montecassino, birthplace of the Benedictine order, Abbot Desiderius was not only instrumental in reforming the abbey, but also in mediating between pope and emperor. For the rebuilding of his church he sent to Constantinople for the finest artists of the day. How far eastern influences affected the work of painters at Montecassino can be seen in the *Life of St Benedict and St Maur* in the Vatican Library which is illus- 92 trated with over a hundred small scenes from the lives of the saints. Nothing survives of Desiderius's church, but in the church of Sant'Angelo in Formis 93 a cycle of frescos is thought to be based on lost mosaics at Montecassino, although these frescos are by Italian rather than Byzantine artists. A type of manuscript peculiar to south Italian monasteries was the Exultet Roll. This is a long strip of parchment containing the Easter hymn which was sung by the priest during the benediction of the Paschal candle. The roll was unrolled over the lectern, with the illustrations displayed to the congregation, but upside down to the reader.

Southern Italy and Sicily

Owing to special geographical and political circumstances, the south of Italy in the Middle Ages was a region set apart from the main peninsula. In the eleventh century, the Normans invaded southern Italy and Sicily, expelling the Greeks from Apulia and conquering the Moslem Saracens of Sicily. They brought with them new styles of sculpture and architecture. San Nicola at Bari is typical of Romanesque architecture in Apulia, showing a combination of north Italian and Norman influences. It is a Benedictine foundation and was probably a pilgrimage centre, for it housed the relics of St Nicholas of Myra. The cathedral at Trani and the collegiate church of Barletta are two other examples of the San Nicola group of buildings.

The Normans who conquered Sicily in 1061 left monuments of great dignity. In their choice of architecture for secular court buildings, the Normans relied almost entirely on Moslem models like Favara and la Ziza, but in church architecture their selection of prototypes was more varied. The Palatine Chapel at Palermo was built by Roger II between 1132-43 with a western ground plan, Byzantine mosaics, but tall stilted arches and an elaborate wooden roof of Moslem origin. The Sicilian Romanesque style is best seen in the great cathedrals of Cefalù and Monreale. The exterior of 99, 96 Cefalù is covered with a profusion of intersecting wall arcades, quite unknown in Italy and presumably originating in Normandy. The exterior of Monreale is in comparison over-ornate, but the interior of the cathedral with its mosaics is breathtaking.

As active patrons of the arts, the Norman rulers of Sicily called artists from Constantinople to decorate their churches with mosaics. Cefalù 88, 98 Cathedral, built by the Norman king Roger between 1131-48, has magnificent mosaics in the chancel and the apse. A majestic bust of Christ fills the concha of the apse; in his hand is an open bible with the text written in Greek and in Latin. Certainly this is the work of a Greek artist, although Sicilian craftsmen seem to have worked side by side with Greeks in the chancel, and the same sort of collaboration occurs in most of the major decorative schemes of Sicilian churches. At Palermo, the decoration of the Palatine Chapel was begun by purely Greek artists, with the fine technique, subtle gradations of colour and elegant figures characteristic of their style. In contrast, the nave is decorated with scenes of the Creation by Sicilian pupils whose lesser technical skill is compensated by a lively, more direct approach to the narrative. The most extensive cycle of mosaics is to be found in the cathedral of Monreale. Finished before the end of the twelfth century, these represent the culmination of the composite Sicilian style. The narrative panels emanate a dynamic vitality and an undoubted power of expression, but in the colouring and the composition something of the Greek sensitivity is lost.

Much later there was an important if isolated group of artists working in the court of Frederick II in southern Italy and Sicily. Frederick, holy Roman emperor from *c.* 1220 to 1250 and king of Sicily, was a great patron of all branches of the arts and was interested in reviving the antique, perhaps in his desire to emulate the great emperors like Charlemagne and Otto. At his Castel del Monte near Capua he made the gateway resemble a triumphal arch with direct copies of Roman portrait busts and free-standing sculpture to decorate it. He also wrote a very detailed treatise on the art of falconry, *De Arte Venandi*, which today belongs to the Vatican and is illustrated with a series of delightful drawings, possibly from the pen of Frederick himself. The drawings reveal a spontaneous mood far removed from the stylisations of northern and central Italy. Frederick's interest in the antique and a new approach to painting in some way foreshadow the great achievements of the second half of the thirteenth century.

Venice

Venice with its increasingly prosperous trade was one of the first cities of the west to come into contact with Byzantium and accept its artistic tradition. The appearance of her monuments at once indicates the fact that her greatness was founded on her oriental commerce. The most obviously Byzantine building is St Mark's, which was begun in 1063 with Byzantine architects and craftsmen playing a large part in the work. Mosaics of this date survive in the north-east of Italy at Torcello, Murano and in the basilica of St Mark's itself. The mosaics in the apse of St Mark's, among the earliest, reveal a calm formalised narrative rather than the excited attitudes of Sicily. Torcello Cathedral, with its impressive apsidal mosaic and the Last Judgment on the west wall, presents that same collaboration of Greek artist and native school, for while the elegantly proportioned Virgin recalls the best work of Constantinople, the Last Judgment is western.

The Treasury of St Mark's contains a few of the many hundreds of works of art in precious metals and enamel which were brought back as loot from the sack of Constantinople by members of the Fourth Crusade. Byzantine craftsmen must also have come to Venice in large numbers and trained Venetians in the skills. The famous Pala d'Oro has purely Byzantine enamels side by side with Venetian ones which have many similar qualities. This influx of workman and objects reinforced the Byzantine influence which can be seen in the works of early Renaissance Venetian painters.

The failure of the Gothic style

Gothic architecture, as typified in the great cathedral of Chartres, seems to have held no attraction for the Italians, surrounded as they were by a great classical past. No sculptor tried to emulate the portals on the west front of Amiens or Rheims; no illuminator could rival the manuscripts of Paris. All this meant that the so-called Romanesque tradition persisted in Italy far into the thirteenth century. Frescos in the crypt of Agnani Cathedral are mid-thirteenth century and yet in style they hark back to San Clemente, giving no suggestion of the new style about to be born. The Gothic style of Fossanova came directly from France and had little influence on neighbouring architecture.

Sabrina Mitchell

89

THE ABBEY CHURCH OF FOSSANOVA

1197–1208

The abbey church of Fossanova in the Pontine marshes was founded by the Cistercian order at the end of the twelfth century. Its architecture is purely French in conception with a simple elevation and pointed groin vaults reminiscent of Fontenay in Burgundy. The Cistercian churches in Italy are a close approximation to the French Gothic style.

90

BRONZE DOOR

eleventh and twelfth centuries
San Zeno, Verona

The bronze doors of San Zeno, which were installed in the porch carved by Niccolo in the twelfth century, have some panels dating from the century before. These are an early example of a tradition that reached ultimate perfection in the bronze doors of Ghiberti in Florence. At Verona the scenes are restricted to small animated figures against a plain ground. In the scene of the Road to Calvary the Jews are distinguished by their little pointed hats.

91

DE ARTE VENANDI

c. 1240
manuscript
Vatican Library, Rome

This treatise on falconry is generally
thought to have been written by the
emperor Frederick II at his court in
Sicily. Certainly Frederick had a deep love
of nature, for he also wrote a book about
plants. The Vatican copy of *De Arte
Venandi* is illustrated with a series of
drawings that bear out the instructions of
the text, and the sketch of an enthroned
figure may be an attempt by Frederick to
portray himself.

93

APSE PAINTING

1058–73
Sant' Angelo in Formis

In Italy, one of the most artistic
undertakings of the eleventh century was
the rebuilding of Montecassino by Abbot
Desiderius. That church is lost, but the
church of Sant'Angelo in Formis is closely
modelled on it. Thus the rather dramatic
frescos in the apse reflect the lost mosaics
of Desiderius's Montecassino.

92 *right*

LIFE OF ST BENEDICT AND ST MAUR

1057–85
manuscript
Vatican Library, Rome (Lat MS 1202)

The manuscript contains the life of the
founder of the Benedictine order and one
of his principal scholars, St Maur. It was
made at Montecassino during the abbacy
of Desiderius, a dynamic man who
revitalised monastic activity and restored
to Montecassino some of its former glory
as mother house of the order. On the page
showing the dedication to St Benedict
some of the old abbey buildings appear.

94

THE CATHEDRAL, CAMPANILE AND BAPTISTERY

begun 1063, completed in thirteenth century
Pisa

The cathedral, with its related buildings, stands apart from the civic buildings in Pisa, presenting a complete impression of ecclesiastical medieval architecture. It was built at a time when Pisa was a leading mercantile power in the Mediterranean, and its scale and proportions are an expression of civic pride that was emulated elsewhere. The elaborate mouldings and the arcading enhance the exterior of the church.

95

SAN MINIATO

1018–62
Florence

The interior of San Miniato has a raised sanctuary that is reached by steps in the aisles rising on either side of an open crypt. Heavy diaphragm arches divide the nave into a series of three-arched bays and support a wooden roof.

96 *below*

THE CROSSING

1174–90
Monreale Cathedral

Built in the time of King William II, the cathedral of Monreale
has the latest and most complete cycle of mosaics in Sicily.
Every part of the church is adorned with marble veneers or
figurative mosaics. The spandrels of the crossing arch are filled
with figures of angels, whilst underneath are numerous
medallions.

97 *right*

MADONNA AND CHILD

early eleventh century and c.1190
mosaic
Torcello Cathedral

The handsome basilican cathedral of
Torcello was largely built in the early
eleventh century. Originally it seems that
a large figure of Christ filled the arch of
the apse, but, when the cult of the Virgin
became popular in the late twelfth
century, it was replaced by this serene
Madonna and Child.

98 *left*

CHRIST PANTOCRATOR

c. 1148
mosaic
Cefalù Cathedral

The cathedral of Cefalù was built for
Roger, the Norman king of Sicily, and in
both the architecture and the mosaic
decoration there is a mixture of
Romanesque and Byzantine features. The
bust of Christ Pantocrator in the apse is of
very high quality, handled with a
sensitivity that suggests the work of an
artist trained in Constantinople. The open
bible with texts in Greek and Latin seems
to be a concession to the western patron.

99

THE CATHEDRAL

c. 1131–1240
Cefalù

The exterior of the cathedral at Cefalù
reveals the various origins of the Sicilian
style. The interlaced arcade which runs
above the clerestory windows is a hallmark
of Norman architecture, whereas the towers
flanking the façade have a distinctly
Moslem profile. Roger, king of Sicily,
planned Cefalù as the royal pantheon, but
after his death the court transferred its
allegiance to Palermo.

100 *centre left*

BYZANTINE GOBLET

twelfth century
Treasury of St Mark's, Venice

The elegant goblet has its base, handles
and lid made in filigree and ornamented
with enamels and precious stones. Like
many of the treasures of St Mark's, it was
probably brought to Venice as loot after
the sack of Constantinople in 1204.

101 *left*

THE PALA D'ORO

central portion
tenth to fourteenth centuries
gold, silver, enamels and precious stones
Treasury of St Mark's, Venice

The Pala d'Oro was given its present
form in 1345 when the individual
Byzantine plaques, which are of an earlier
date, were set in an elaborate Gothic style.
They were brought to St Mark's as
trophies from successful Venetian raids on
Constantinople during the tenth century
and after the sack of 1204. The central
panel of Christ the Lawgiver is an
imposing work of art.

The year 1250 marks the death of Frederick II, holy Roman emperor and ruler of the kingdom of Sicily. Henceforth, the holy Roman emperor retained no real power in Italy, and the chronicles of the years following 1250 tell of the efforts to rule the kingdom of Sicily (which as well as Sicily encompassed lands in southern Italy). Towards this end Pope Urban IV summoned Charles of Anjou, brother of St Louis of France, to claim the crown of Sicily, but by 1282 Charles had so alienated a part of his people, the Sicilians, that they revolted; the event is known as the Sicilian Vespers. The island of Sicily was then won by the Spanish crown of Aragon, while the house of Anjou kept the part of the kingdom on the mainland.

The claims of the holy Roman emperor did not, however, die out with the presence of the Angevins in Italy, and the struggle between the Guelphs, allies of the papal party, and the Ghibellines, adherents to the imperial cause, continued into the fourteenth century. This system of alliances, although basically tied to pope and emperor, served also to identify local factions and establish foreign policy for the many small Italian states.

In 1305 the archbishop of Bordeaux was elected pope and took the name Clement V. His elevation to the papacy represented a triumph for the king of France, Philip IV, who had been involved for a number of years in a power struggle with the papacy, and the new pope never left his native country for Italy. From 1309 the popes were established in Avignon, not to return to Rome finally until 1378. Thus, for seventy years there was a serious neglect of the arts in Rome, which, without the papal court, had lost its most important source of patronage. Avignon, in its place, became an important focus. Artists were drawn there not only from Italy but from all over Europe. Simone Martini, a native of Siena who also served the Angevins in Naples, was among the many Italian artists who worked for the papal court.

Another important phenomenon of these years in Italy was the rise of the city-state, exemplified by such a city as Florence in Tuscany. The change-over from the feudal system based on an agrarian economy to the communal system where commerce and capital were concentrated in the cities had started long before. The thirteenth and fourteenth centuries, however, saw the commune with its government controlled by merchants and tradesmen firmly established. In Florence, for example, the importance of manufacture and the rise of international banking were significant not only commercially and politically but also for patronage of the arts. There arose a class, best described by the term upper bourgeoisie, which had the money and the influence to commission important works of art.

In northern Italy it was a different matter. Here the cities and their surrounding territory were ruled by tyrants, who were frequently seen as the only substitute for the anarchy created by warring factions. They often succeeded in forming dynasties, and it was in just this way that the Visconti in Milan and the Della Scala in Verona came to power. The smiling Cangrande della Scala is shown sitting boldly in the saddle. He was a wise ruler known to have been an enthusiastic patron of the arts.

The optimism of these years was not, however, unmarred, for in 1348 there occurred the first wave of the Black Death, the bubonic plague that was to decimate cities not only in Italy but in all Europe as well. The visitor to Italy constantly encounters reminders of the dreadful holocaust. The nave of a newer and grander Siena Cathedral was left only partially finished, its workmen struck down, the desire to complete the ambitious project gone. In *The Triumph of Death*, painted by Francesco Traini in the Camposanto at Pisa (the burial ground of the cathedral), there is a horrifying image of three putrefying corpses, a recollection of the dreadful days of

The City-states in the Age of Giotto

1250–1400

102

ST LOUIS OF TOULOUSE

1317
wood panel with painted surface
Simone Martini, c. 1284–1344
78·75 × 54 in (200 × 138 cm)
Galleria Nazionale, Naples

This altarpiece was commissioned from Simone Martini by Robert of Naples in the year of the canonisation of his brother Louis. It demonstrates King Robert's right of succession by showing him being crowned by his elder brother, St Louis, who had renounced the throne. Simone was both knighted by King Robert and in 1317 awarded an annual grant of fifty ounces of gold—a measure of the esteem in which he was held by the court.

103

THE TRIUMPH OF DEATH *detail*

probably 1350s, fresco
attributed to Francesco Traini, active 1321–63
18 ft 5 in × 49 ft 1 in (564 × 1497 cm)
Camposanto, Pisa

During the last war the series of frescos in
the burial ground of Pisa Cathedral were
severely damaged and were detached from
the wall. At this time the underdrawing in
red chalk was revealed. In this detail from
The Triumph of Death a group of nobles
who are out for a day's hunting come
across the corpses of three kings, each in
different stages of decomposition. The
theme of the Three Living and Three
Dead was well established.

104 *above right*

PULPIT

signed 1260, completed 1259
Nicola Pisano, active 1258–78
Baptistery, Pisa Cathedral

The pulpit from the baptistery at Pisa
bears the name of its sculptor, Nicola
Pisano, and the date 1260. Six columns,
three borne on the backs of guardian lions,
support the arches, whose spandrels are
decorated with figures of the evangelists
and a series of Old Testament prophets
and kings. The columns themselves are
topped by sculpted figures representing
the six Christian virtues. The pulpit is
completed by five reliefs representing the
Nativity, the Adoration of the Magi, the
Presentation in the Temple, the
Crucifixion and the Last Judgment.

the Black Death, of which the artist must have had personal experience.

In the life of the Middle Ages religion was of paramount importance.
To the influence of the papacy must be added that of the two religious
orders founded in the early thirteenth century, the Dominicans and the
Franciscans. St Dominic was canonised in 1234, and his order emphasised
orthodoxy and intellectualism. Taking in hand the eradication of heresy,
it grew in importance throughout the century. St Francis, who had lived
a life of poverty, was canonised in 1228 a few years before Dominic, and
his followers, reacting against the worldliness of much of the religion
of the day, emphasised direct emotional experience in their daily worship.
The churches and monasteries of these two orders were to multiply, and the
growth of the mendicant orders had an influence on the art of the time.

Italian art in the thirteenth century, although not unmoved by French
achievements, followed mainly an indigenous tradition, and there are a
number of centres where it shone with particular brilliance. In one city in
Tuscany just after the middle of the century a sculptor was working in a
manner markedly different from that of his contemporaries; the results
were full of innovations, yet linked to the art of antiquity. The sculptor was
Nicola Pisano, and the city was Pisa.

Pisa

Nicola's origins are obscure. He is referred to in contemporary documents
as being from Apulia, and this suggests that he did, in fact, emigrate to
Pisa from southern Italy. The recurring references to classical art, particularly
in his first work in the baptistery at Pisa, indicate a possible training in   **104**
southern Italy where classical art was revived and emphasised during the
reign of Frederick II. Although Nicola's birthdate is not known, by 1250 he
was probably in Pisa where he sculptured the baptistery pulpit around 1260.

Five years later he was working in Siena on the cathedral pulpit. By 1284 he is assumed to be dead. His son, Giovanni, was an outstanding sculptor in his own right and went on to sculpt two pulpits, at Pistoia in Sant'Andrea and

Pisa in the cathedral, in addition to carving a whole series of figures for the façade of Siena Cathedral.

04

Nicola's Pisa Baptistery pulpit, raised on arches supported by columns and decorated with carved panels, is a distinctly Italian type. Northern European artists were not interested in pulpit sculpture, while the Italian

interest is perpetuated into the fifteenth century. In the panel of the Nativity

105
THE NATIVITY
signed 1260, completed 1259
marble
Nicola Pisano, active 1258–78
Baptistery, Pisa Cathedral

This is one of the five relief panels that form the sides of the pulpit sculpted by Nicola Pisano at the end of the 1250s for the baptistery at Pisa. Interest centres on the Nativity in the middle of the panel, but around it cluster subsidiary scenes of the Annunciation, on the left; the Annunciation to the Shepherds, on the right; and the apocryphal Washing of the Christ Child, in the foreground. When first completed the relief was fully painted in the tradition of much of medieval sculpture.

which forms one of the six sides of the pulpit, the truly classical spirit behind Nicola's conception is clear. The Madonna reclines like a matron, her features set in a truly Roman cast, her hair waved after an antique model. The relief field is crowded, for Nicola chose to show not one but four events on the same panel. In addition to the Nativity, the Annunciation, the Annunciation to the Shepherds and the Washing of the Feet of the Christ Child form part of the scene. The crowding of many scenes into one panel is also a late classical motif. These classical quotations are important, especially in Nicola's early work, as they form a touchstone for a recreation of classical art. But Nicola's genius lies in the way he transformed this heritage to achieve an art which was new and never a pastiche of antique sculpture.

The papal court

Before the popes moved to Avignon in 1309, the papal court attracted artists and craftsmen to Rome and Viterbo, where a generally conservative artistic atmosphere reigned. The roundel of Christ Crowning the Virgin by Jacopo Torriti from the church of Santa Maria Maggiore in Rome is executed in a centuries-old technique, mosaic, and still retains the hard, hieratic brilliance that characterised the large mosaic decorations of the first Christian centuries in Rome. The church of Santa Maria Maggiore itself is adorned with fifth-century mosaics, and Torriti's apse mosaic blends well with the earlier decoration. Large mural programmes, whether in mosaic or fresco, have always been part of the Italian artistic scene. The majority of the artists of the thirteenth and fourteenth centuries abandoned the costly and formal mosaic and turned to the more intimate and less costly fresco. The new humanity of the late Middle Ages in Italy called not only for a more familiar approach to the subject, but also for a medium that was allied to this approach. Mosaic was too stiff and formal.

In these same years the sculptor and architect Arnolfo di Cambio was working in and around Rome. Arnolfo's patrons included cardinals, popes, 106 and even the illustrious Charles of Anjou, for whom he carved in Rome in 1277 a statue of the Angevin ruler seated on his throne. Arnolfo's sculptural masterpiece is, however, his tomb for the Cardinal de Braye, not in Rome but in the church of San Domenico in nearby Orvieto. The tomb is placed against the wall with the Virgin and Child on high, flanked by St Dominic and St Mark, who is in the act of presenting the cardinal to the Virgin. 129 Below is a bier bearing the body of the deceased. Two deacons, one on either side, are in the act of drawing the curtains, symbolically bringing the cardinal's life to a close. These figures, with tonsured heads and wearing the robes of their office, are lifelike and animated, exactly observed by the sculptor as if carrying out their duties during the daily service. Besides the immediate delight that one takes in these two small figures, they introduced an entirely new motif into the repertoire of Italian sepulchral art.

Angevin Naples

There was only one other court in Italy which could be set beside that of the papacy with respect to patronage of the arts: the Angevin court at Naples. Charles of Anjou was called to Italy by the pope in 1266 and was succeeded by his son, Charles II, who was in turn followed by his son, Robert. Robert ruled from 1309–43, and it was during his reign that most of the artists with whom we are concerned worked in Naples. Under Robert a royal library was begun. He established a school of miniaturists and calligraphers, and goldsmiths were imported from France. Cavallini, Giotto and Simone Martini were all summoned to Naples to enhance its court. Of the part of the town where the nobility lived, begun by Charles of Anjou with the Castel Nuovo as its nucleus, there remains today not a trace. It was here that the splendid festivals and tournaments staged by the court were held. Many of the great Neapolitan churches came into being at the time of the Angevins, and Santa Maria Donna Regina, Santa Chiara, San Lorenzo and San Domenico Maggiore all owe their inception to Angevin patronage. We know that Charles I used French architects exclusively, and the tradition of French Gothic was always strong in southern Italy. It was particularly allied to Provençal forms, due partly to the fact that the house of Anjou held lands in southern France.

102   The portrait of St Louis of Toulouse by the Sienese Simone Martini must have been one of the particular treasures of the Angevin court. The altarpiece consists of an image of St Louis crowning his brother, Robert, and is surrounded by a frame of gold fleurs-de-lis on a blue background; underneath is the earliest surviving predella with narrative scenes. The whole effect is one of great richness appropriate to court art. Gold is used for the background, its edges tooled with fleurs-de-lis. In this great painting time stands still. The jewels and goldsmiths' work which originally adorned this image undoubtedly increased its hieratic value. St Louis was canonised in 1317, which was also with all probability the year in which Simone painted this altarpiece. The Angevins, eager to add lustre to their house through the acquisition of a saint, wisely chose Simone Martini to create with sinuous line and rich display this supremely graceful yet impressive image.

Assisi and the Franciscans

Despite the attraction that the power and prestige of the court at Naples undoubtedly exercised on artists, important developments were also taking place elsewhere in Italy. The influence of the Franciscans on many aspects of life in the late Middle Ages is significant. The growth of the order resulted in a more personal approach to religion, as emphasised in the teachings of its founder, St Francis. This in turn was reflected in the art of

106
CHARLES OF ANJOU
1277
Arnolfo di Cambio
active during the second half of the thirteenth century
Museo del Palazzo dei Conservatori, Rome

Arnolfo di Cambio is documented as being in the service of Charles of Anjou in 1277 and to him is attributed this formal and powerful portrait of the Angevin ruler. Called to Italy by Pope Urban IV in 1266 to rule the kingdom of Sicily, Charles governed lands beset by strife and insurrection. All this is forgotten in this statue, which presents in stiff and formal pose a forceful representation of Charles.

107
PULPIT
1265–68, marble
Nicola Pisano, active 1258–78
Siena Cathedral

The contract for the Siena Cathedral pulpit is dated 29th September 1265, and in addition to Nicola's name there appear those of his principal assistants Arnolfo di Cambio and Lapo. It was also stated that Nicola's son Giovanni was to be paid as a junior assistant. This work differs from Nicola's earlier pulpit in the baptistery of Pisa in being octagonal rather than hexagonal, and more fully Gothic in style than the classical-influenced scenes at Pisa.

108
THE ALTAR OF SAN JACOPO
detail
1287–fifteenth century
Pistoia Cathedral

This altar, executed in silver for the cathedral of Pistoia, was commissioned in 1287. It was restored and added to throughout the following century by a large coterie of artists and not finally brought to completion until the early 1400s. The central figure is that of St James with Christ in a mandorla surrounded by a choir of angels shown above. The scenes on the altar frontal are from the lives of Christ and St James.

109 *below*

THE UPPER CHURCH OF
SAN FRANCESCO

1228–53
Assisi

The church of San Francesco at Assisi was founded in 1228, substantially completed by 1239 and finally consecrated in 1253. It is a Latin cross in plan, and this view of the Upper Church looking towards the west end shows the aisleless nave, its walls covered with frescos. This plan, which accommodated large congregations, was ideally suited to the preaching that played such an important part in the Franciscan order.

110

INNOCENT III APPROVING THE RULE OF THE ORDER *detail*

c. 1290(?)–c. 1307(?)
fresco
Upper Church of San Francesco, Assisi

The fresco of Innocent III Approving the Rule of the Order comes from the Upper Church of San Francesco at Assisi. It is one of twenty-eight scenes which tell the story of St Francis's life. Fictive architectural and decorative elements, such as twisted columns and mosaic inlay, surround the individual scenes–a scheme made possible by the simplicity of the church with its plain walls and aisleless nave. The frescos were once firmly attributed to Giotto, but it now seems that several masters contributed to the cycle which decorates the nave and entrance walls of the great Franciscan church.

111

THE MAESTA

1308–11
tempera on wood panel
Duccio di Buoninsegna, c. 1255/60–1318/19
83 × 168 in (210 × 426 cm)
Museo dell' Opera del Duomo, Siena

This altarpiece was painted for the high altar of the cathedral of Siena, where it was placed in 1311. The four saints depicted kneeling in the front row are the four principal guardian saints of Siena. In an inscription on the base of the throne Duccio implores the Virgin to grant peace to Siena and long life to the artist who painted her thus.

112

THE KNIGHTING OF ST MARTIN

c. 1330, fresco, Simone Martini, c. 1284–1344
Lower Church of San Francesco, Assisi

The fresco decoration of the chapel of St Martin is composed, apart from some single figures of saints, of ten scenes set in three tiers showing events from St Martin's life. Here St Martin is invested with the spurs of knighthood before the Emperor Julian. The event is accompanied by colourfully attired musicians and watched by a few courtiers on the left.

113

THE LAMENTATION OVER THE DEAD BODY OF CHRIST

1304–13, fresco, Giotto, c. 1267–1337
91 × 79.5 in (231 × 202 cm)
Arena Chapel, Padua

The Lamentation is one of the scenes from the life of Christ which, together with scenes from the life of the Virgin, decorate the side walls of the Arena Chapel. These scenes are surrounded by feigned architectural elements which both form a frame for the narrative and provide a unified decorative scheme for the chapel as a whole. *The Lamentation* itself is highly charged emotionally. Each figure has been carefully studied and responds in a different manner to the death of Christ.

the time. Scenes in which humanity and the emotional responses of man could be displayed were chosen by an increasing number of artists who abandoned the more formal and distant qualities of the art of preceding centuries. The mother church of the order, San Francesco at Assisi, houses many of the treasures of Italian medieval art. It is composed of two churches, one directly above the other. The Lower Church, originally without side

chapels, was planned as a crypt to contain the body of the saint. In the Upper Church the high altar is placed directly above the tomb of St Francis. The architecture is severe; broad expanses of wall, relatively low vaults, and massive forms achieve a feeling of simplicity and strength that is characteristic of much of the Italian architecture of the age. We have already noted how fond the Italians were of mural decoration, and at Assisi artists had the opportunity to cover huge expanses of wall with the stories of St Francis, images of the saints, and religious narratives of all manner and kind. Almost all the great names of fourteenth-century art—Cimabue, Pietro Lorenzetti, Simone Martini—painted there. Giotto's contribution is problematic.

On entering the Lower Church at Assisi the visitor finds on his left the chapel of St Martin with frescos by Simone Martini. In all probability the chapel decoration was financed by Cardinal Gentile da Montefiore's bequest of 1312 (one fresco shows St Martin receiving the cardinal); but the actual date at which it was carried out is problematic, although it was certainly before Simone's departure for Avignon in 1339. The total impression is of opulence. The graceful and decorative frescos are highlighted with gold leaf. The floor and lower wall are covered with real marble, and the windows filled with glowing stained glass. The original effect, when colours were fresh and the gold just applied, must have been dazzling, and this richness is matched perfectly by the frescos themselves. Simone was again working in a courtly ambience, employed this time not by a secular

prince but by a prince of the church. In *The Knighting of St Martin* the artist has made use of the contemporary courtly scene which he knew so well. Minstrels accompany the investiture of St Martin, who appears as a medieval knight. This is a world of fashion, of secular pleasure. The opulence of the decor does not signify, however, the mere addition of one dazzling detail to another, for an organised perspective scheme is used throughout and draws the frescos into a coherent whole. Complete as it is, this little Gothic chapel provides one with a very real glimpse back into the world of the Middle Ages.

Giotto in Padua

A few years before and far to the north, another chapel was built to contain the frescos of one of the foremost masters of this or or of any age, Giotto. This project was conceived not by a cardinal or a king but by a wealthy

citizen, Enrico Scrovegni, the richest man in Padua, who probably erected the chapel to expiate the sin of usury. It was completed between 1304 and 1313. The chapel, not a distinguished piece of architecture in any sense, was built as a private chapel for Scrovegni in the Roman arena at Padua and is sometimes known as the Arena Chapel. The purpose of the architect, who has sometimes been identified with Giotto, was to provide as much wall space as possible. The frescos were not an afterthought to be fitted into the existing architecture, but were conceived as part of the building's decoration from the beginning, just as stained-glass windows filled with glowing figures were an integral part of the Gothic cathedrals of France.

The vault is a starry heaven punctuated by roundels from which Christ and the Virgin, saints and prophets look down. The walls are covered by narrative scenes from the lives of Christ and the Virgin. On the altar wall various scenes complete the cycle, while in the dado on the lower part of

114
SCROVEGNI PRESENTING A
MODEL OF THE ARENA
CHAPEL TO THE VIRGIN
1304–13
Giotto, c. 1267–1337
fresco
Arena Chapel, Padua

The Arena Chapel at Padua was built for Enrico Scrovegni and served as a private chapel for the wealthy citizen and his family. It was founded in 1303 and the consecration held two years later in 1305. Giotto was commissioned to cover the walls of the interior with frescos which outline man's redemption and have their climax in *The Last Judgment* on the entrance wall of the chapel. This detail from *The Last Judgment* shows Scrovegni himself presenting a model of his chapel to the Virgin, who stretches out her hand toward the wealthy benefactor.

115
GIRLS DANCING
detail of plate **125**

the nave wall are grisaille figures of the Virtues and Vices. The Last Judgment unfolds on the entrance wall and even includes a portrait of the patron Enrico Scrovegni, who presents a model of his chapel to the Virgin. 114

Outstanding as Giotto's total scheme is, the chapel's greatest interest lies in the individual narrative scenes. A more personal and intimate approach to art, in strong contrast to the Byzantine-influenced painting of the earlier centuries, arose during these years in Italy. The emphasis on direct emotional experience in religion coming from the mendicant orders, particularly the Franciscans, together with the rise of the city-state where individual enterprise was rewarded, contributed to this mood. Nowhere is it more perfectly expressed than in the art of Giotto, who was probably trained in Rome and came from an artistic background influenced by Byzantium. He created a human and naturalistic art in direct contrast to that of his predecessors. In what way was Giotto different? Looking at *The Lamentation Over the Dead Body of Christ* we see in the lower left-hand corner 113 Christ embraced by his grief-torn mother, who makes a direct appeal to our emotions by the very intensity of her passion. All the participants display their emotions in different ways, and all elements in the composition contribute to the emotional experience. The Arena Chapel is a world away from the stiff poses and frozen emotion of earlier painters. The art of Giotto is part of an age in which the importance of the individual was stressed, and it is appropriate that we should first meet this outstanding artist in a chapel constructed by a businessman of Padua.

Siena

The rise of the communal system and the new wealth which it created have already been remarked on with regard to Florence. Another prominent Tuscan city was the flourishing commune of Siena, where from 1282 a new city centre was planned to take shape around the seat of government, the Palazzo Pubblico. The Campo, which is the city square of Siena, is shell- 124 shaped and sloping, with the town hall equipped with a typically Tuscan tower on the straight side, and private palaces flanking its curved side. It is an ambitious project conceived by a people proud of their city. The whole ensemble is picturesque and colourful, a quality which marks much of Sienese art and architecture.

An important focus of artistic life in Siena was the exotic and beautiful cathedral, built on one of the high points of the city and filled with treasures 126, created for it by its greatest artists. One of the most splendid projects for its adornment was the altarpiece commissioned from Duccio di Buoninsegna for the high altar. A contemporary chronicle tells us that great rejoicing accompanied the completion of the altarpiece in 1311 and that a procession of priests and friars, women and children followed the picture on its way from the artist's studio to the cathedral, ringing bells joyously out of reverence for so noble a work as they went. It must have been a beautiful spectacle, topped by spires and pinnacles, glittering with gold and fresh colours. The front of the altarpiece was occupied by *The Maestà*, the 111 Madonna in majesty with saints. The enthroned Madonna is shown in the centre larger than the flanking saints and angels, because in the hierarchy of the heavens she was more important. This medieval idea of making more important personages actually bigger physically was followed by Duccio, tied as he was in so many ways to the old traditions. Although it was a habit that artists were reluctant to break, it was incompatible with ideas of naturalism and was abandoned by those who accepted the full implications of the painting of an artist like Giotto. The new ideas took a long time to develop, and here Duccio is still firmly in the world of Byzantium. Each angel, dressed in the robes of the imperial Byzantine court, carries a loros

116

A STAG AND A LEOPARD

The Bergamo Sketchbook
Giovanni dei Grassi,
first heard of 1380, died 1398
Biblioteca Civica, Bergamo

On this page from the Bergamo Sketchbook Giovanni dei Grassi has drawn a stag and a leopard, which together with sketches from the other pages form a collection of bird and animal studies of the greatest truth and charm. Giovanni was in the employ of the ruling family of Lombardy, the Visconti, during the 1390s and in addition to illuminating their manuscripts was involved in work on one of the most important objects of their patronage – Milan Cathedral.

(a kind of sceptre). The figures are stiffly posed and ranged in three rows on either side of the Virgin, so that the whole retains the spirit of an icon. This is not to say, however, that Duccio was completely absorbed in the past and unresponsive to the newer developments of thirteenth- and fourteenth-century art. The influence of French Gothic art, to which Siena was particularly susceptible, is felt in the delicacy and elegance with which, for instance, Duccio treats the drapery of St Agnes who stands on the right holding a medallion bearing her attribute, a lamb.

The interior of the Palazzo Pubblico contains many of the treasures of the city. Frescos adorn its walls and point again to the civic pride of the Sienese. In the Sala dei Nove is a series of frescos painted by Ambrogio Lorenzetti during 1338-39 to illustrate the efficacy of good government and the disasters of bad. The Brothers Lorenzetti, Pietro and Ambrogio, of whom Ambrogio was the younger, were heirs to the Sienese tradition of Duccio and Simone Martini but had also been moved by the art of Giotto, and their painting shows a fusion between the linear grace and fantasy of Sienese artists and the solidity and modelling which mark Giotto's art. In *The Effects of Good Government in the City*, which together with *The Effects of Good Government in the Country* occupies one wall of the Sala dei Nove, Ambrogio Lorenzetti gives us a glimpse into the world of fourteenth-century Siena. It might be May Day, for on this occasion every year dancing took place in the streets. Young women are disporting themselves to the beat of a tambourine, and on the right a teacher and a shoemaker carry out their tasks, with the hill town of Siena rising behind them. Surrounded by crenellated walls, all is ordered, serene and secure – the result of good government, an ideal so ardently sought after but so rarely achieved during the tumultuous years of the Middle Ages.

Florence

In Florence the civic virtues present in Siena were also important, and the Florentines, too, sought to express pride in their commune through great public buildings. In 1282 a popular government took over the rule of Florence, democratic in only a limited sense as the wealthy and influential merchants and tradesmen kept the power in their hands. This power was consolidated in 1293 with a constitution which made the seven greater and fourteen minor guilds virtual rulers of Florence. The city was under their sway until the close of the fourteenth century. The cathedral, the Palazzo Vecchio, Santa Croce (the great Franciscan church), and the Badia (a Benedictine abbey) were all begun during the last years of the thirteenth century. The responsibility for the major public buildings lay with the guilds. In 1330 the Arte della Lana, the wool merchants' guild and the richest guild in a city in which the manufacture of cloth was the basis of a thriving economy, took over the supervision of the cathedral begun at the end of the previous century by Arnolfo di Cambio. This guild was not only concerned with the practical problems of construction, such as the hiring and firing of workmen, but also commissioned the works of art that were to adorn the buildings in its charge.

It was for the silk guild, which supervised the nearby baptistery, that in 1330 Andrea Pisano undertook a pair of bronze doors. Andrea's doors were an artistic enterprise of the highest importance. Such an undertaking had not been dared for years, and it was necessary to use the twelfth-century bronze doors of Pisa Cathedral as a point of reference. Bronze casters were brought in from Venice, and the doors, although signed and dated 1330, were finally finished in 1336. Both Giotto and the contemporary mosaics of the baptistery itself were sources of inspiration for Andrea Pisano, and the delicacy with which he handled his reliefs demonstrates a

117
THE PALAZZO VECCHIO
founded 1299
Florence

The Palazzo Vecchio, the town hall of Florence, was founded in 1299. Building proceeded so rapidly that it was ready for the ruling priors by 1302, and the bell tower was completed by 1310. The speed of construction reflects the troubled times when it was necessary to install the rulers of the city quickly and securely in a building which served as much as a fortification as a seat of government.

118
ST JOHN BAPTISING
1330–36
Andrea Pisano, c. 1290–1348 (?)
bronze
south doors, the baptistery,
Florence Cathedral

The bronze doors created by Andrea Pisano for the baptistery of Florence are signed and dated 1330, although they were finally completed in 1336. The commission was undertaken at the request of the silk guild, which supervised the decoration of the baptistery. Scenes from the life of St John the Baptist together with eight Virtues adorn both leaves of the door. Here St John, silhouetted against a rocky landscape, is shown in the act of baptising a member of the crowd which watches on the left.

knowledge, possibly indirect rather than direct, of French Gothic art.

Another great building which was rising during these years was the
134 Franciscan church of Santa Croce, probably designed by the same Arnolfo di Cambio who was responsible for the cathedral. At the east end the architect provided the church with a wealth of little chapels which were destined to receive some of the finest fresco decoration of the fourteenth century. Giotto, Taddeo Gaddi, Maso di Banco, Giovanni de Milano and Agnolo Gaddi all painted in Santa Croce. The Bardi Chapel was frescoed by Giotto as was its neighbour, the Peruzzi Chapel, which belonged to a family who
119 fully equalled the Bardi in wealth and power. *The Apparition at Arles* from the Bardi Chapel follows the Arena Chapel frescos in Giotto's oeuvre and
113 can probably be dated to the years around 1315-20. Where in *The Lamentation* at Padua emotion was intense, here a calmer atmosphere prevails. The figures of the modest friars in their brown Franciscan habits complement the simple architecture, and just such a stillness and simplicity as the event itself suggests is achieved. St Francis raises his arms which, together with the half circle of the arch above, form a huge halo that serves as a foil for the figure of the saint. The massive forms, such as the bulky friars with their backs to us; the modelling with light and shade; the creation of pictorial depth receding from the picture plane – all characteristic of Giotto's work at Padua – are present again in the remarkable frescos at Santa Croce. The remainder of the frescos of the Bardi Chapel continue the story of St Francis, while those of the Peruzzi relate events from the lives of St John the Baptist and St John the Evangelist.

135 In the Dominican church of Santa Maria Novella on the other side of Florence artists were also at work. The Strozzi Chapel, whose decoration was placed in charge of the Brothers Orcagna, is a completely preserved mid-fourteenth-century chapel with frescos and altarpiece still in place.
121 The altarpiece, by Andrea Orcagna and dated 1357, presents a very hieratic vision of Christ and the saints. We feel that we are in the world of thirteenth-century art rather than in a century that had been touched by the genius of Giotto. Here Christ performs the double task of presenting the keys to St Peter on his left and a book to St Thomas on his right. He is surrounded by saints to whom the three predella scenes below the main altarpiece refer. The walls of this family chapel are covered with frescos by Andrea's brother, Nardo di Cione, also dating from the 1350s. They show scenes from the Last Judgment, Paradise, and Hell, the latter a truly Dantesque vision.

133 In the little church of Or San Michele stands a tabernacle begun before 1355 by Andrea Orcagna, whose activities encompassed sculpture as well as painting. The tabernacle was financed by the Compagnia di Or San Michele (one of the many lay fraternities in Florence founded to perform charitable works) in remembrance of liberation from the Black Death and planned as a shrine for the *Virgin and Child Enthroned with Angels*, painted about a decade earlier by Bernardo Daddi. The effect of the tabernacle as a whole is one of richness: the colours are brilliant; inlays of mosaics, gold, and coloured stones are used throughout. Tracery and figures of saints form part of the lavish decoration, and the front is topped by a gable, flanked by pinnacles, with a cupola behind. At the rear of the tabernacle Orcagna
128 carved the scene of the Death and Assumption of the Virgin. Here again, as in the Strozzi Chapel, he created a supernatural event. In the Assumption the Virgin floats in a mandorla supported by angels; a foil for the sculptured figures is provided by a mosaic pattern which forms the background for the scene as a whole.

Orvieto

In the tabernacle of Or San Michele, Orcagna indulged a fondness for

119

THE APPARITION AT ARLES

c. 1315–20
Giotto, c. 1267–1337
fresco
Bardi Chapel, Santa Croce, Florence

The Apparition at Arles was probably painted in the years around 1315-20 when the church as a whole was still under construction. Funds for the decoration of the little chapel, which is covered with scenes from the life of St Francis, were provided by the Bardi, one of the wealthiest families in Florence and bankers to all of Europe. Here St Francis is shown appearing in the midst of the general chapter of the Franciscan order which was assembled at Arles.

120

THE CAMPANILE

1334–50s
Giotto, c. 1267–1337
Florence Cathedral

The campanile of Florence Cathedral, which was founded in 1334 and designed by Giotto, forms together with the baptistery and the cathedral an architectural complex of great beauty. The lower storey was completed before Giotto's death in 1337 and is decorated with a series of reliefs. The upper storeys are pierced with openings and covered with marble inlay typical of much Tuscan architecture of the time.

121

CHRIST IN MAJESTY WITH SAINTS

1354–57
Andrea di Cione, called Orcagna, active 1343–68
altarpiece, 63 × 116 in (160 × 296 cm)
each predella scene, 9·75 × 34 in (25 × 86 cm)
Santa Maria Novella, Florence

Orcagna's altarpiece painted for the chapel of the Strozzi family in Santa Maria Novella still occupies its original site. Extremely formal and hieratic in conception, it shows Christ in Majesty in the centre suspended in a mandorla of seraphim. On the left the Virgin backed by St Catherine of Alexandria and St Michael presents St Thomas Aquinas, the foremost Dominican saint. On the right St Peter is presented by St John the Baptist, while St Lawrence and St Paul stand behind them.

incrustation. The same aesthetic ideals prompted the architect of Orvieto Cathedral, begun in the last decade of the thirteenth century; its façade is covered with mosaic, twisted columns and sculptural decoration, achieving an effect that is extremely colourful and decorative. The cathedral was, in fact, planned as a shrine to hold the Holy Corporal. Thus the precious, finely wrought quality of Orvieto's façade is most appropriate to a building which serves as a shrine for such a holy relic.

Among the chief glories of Orvieto is certainly the sculpture carved by Lorenzo Maitani and his workshop in the years from 1310-30. Scenes from Genesis, the Tree of Jesse, Old Testament Prophecies of Redemption, the life of Christ, Prophets and a Last Judgment occupy the four piers of the façade. The beauty of conception and the fineness of carving are breathtaking. In *The Creation of Eve* two angles float, their beautiful wings, 127 unfurled behind them, detailed down to the last feather.

Northern Italy

At the beginning of this chapter brief mention was made of the tyrant-ruled cities of northern Italy, with special attention paid to the Della Scala dynasty of Verona. Cangrande della Scala who died in 1329 was followed by Mastino II, whose heir was Cansignorio; all of them are commemorated by splendid equestrian sepulchral monuments at the church of Santa Maria Antica, Verona. Mastino and Cansignorio are buried in elaborate mausolea surrounded by marble balustrades and wrought-iron grills. The tomb of the smiling Cangrande is placed over the door of the church. Simpler in 123 conception than the family tombs which follow it, the immediacy of the portrait of the mounted ruler, whose happy countenance reflects confidence in his power, makes a strong and lasting appeal to all who see it.

Milan, as well as Verona, was the seat of a dynasty, the Visconti, which established itself in the course of the fourteenth century. The Visconti ruled Milan with minor interruptions from the end of the thirteenth century, and succeeding generations consolidated this power so that by the end of the fourteenth century Gian Galeazzo controlled, with Milan as his capital, a political state which extended to the borders of Venice and Tuscany. Gian Galeazzo employed a variety of artists at his court who practised a style known as International Gothic, then currently popular in centres throughout Europe. One of the artists was Giovanni dei Grassi, who among other works compiled the Bergamo Sketchbook which contains remarkable 116 pictures of animals. Giovanni was also involved with work on the cathedral, which was the major manifestation of Gian Galeazzo's personal ambition, as well as being inspired by the growing prosperity of the city. Planning started in 1386, but work proceeded slowly from the very beginning; the cathedral was finally completed only in the nineteenth century. Successive northern European architects were employed during the years of its conception, and the plan, a nave with double aisles, links it to the French Gothic tradition. The dim interior with its high arcades conveys the impression of a height and space in which man feels dwarfed. The elaborate decoration of the interior also ties Milan Cathedral to northern Europe and contrasts with much of the Gothic architecture in other Italian centres.

The pattern of Italian life in the thirteenth and fourteenth centuries was varied. Courts, such as those of the Angevins in Naples or the Visconti in Milan, played their part, and city-states, like Florence and Siena, were also important. Dominicans and Franciscans strongly influenced the religious mood of these years. And they all commissioned buildings and sculpture, paid artists, and provided an impetus for the creation of some of the greatest works of art of the age.

Martha McCrory

122 *below right*

GUIDORICCIO DA FOGLIANO

1328, Simone Martini, c. 1284–1344, fresco
Sala del Mappamondo, Palazzo Pubblico, Siena

The equestrian portrait of the Sienese general Guidoriccio da
Fogliano faces the artist's *Maestà* on the walls of the Sala del
Mappamondo. The victorious general is shown with two of the
towns which he captured from the Florentines, Montemassi and
Sassoforte. The towns together with the military encampments
and the barren landscape provide a neutral background for a
heraldic representation of Guidoriccio who, splendidly arrayed
in his diamond–patterned gold livery, stands as a symbol of the
recent Sienese victories.

123 *bottom right*

CANGRANDE DELLA SCALA

after 1329, stone, Castel Vecchio, Verona

This equestrian figure represents Cangrande della Scala who died
in Treviso in 1329. The Scaliger dynasty came to power at the
end of the thirteenth century and ruled Verona until the last
decades of the fourteenth. The Gothic tomb of Cangrande, which
is in the family burial ground in the churchyard of Santa Maria
Antica, is composed of a sarcophagus topped by a bier with
the statue above it. The original is now in the Castel Vecchio.

124 *above*

THE PALAZZO PUBBLICO

Siena

The Palazzo Pubblico, the seat of the city government, was the
hub of an entire city centre planned during the thirteenth
century. In type, it is typical of the town halls of Tuscany,
another example being in Florence. Work began about 1298 and
continued well into the 1300s; the tall tower, the so-called Torre
del Mangia, dates from the middle of the fourteenth century.
Decorative and colourful in the Sienese manner, the loggia on the
ground floor is built of stone, while the superstructure is brick.

THE EFFECTS OF
GOOD GOVERNMENT IN THE CITY

1338–39, fresco, Ambrogio Lorenzetti, active 1319–47
Sala dei Nove, Palazzo Pubblico, Siena

Good Government in the City is one of the frescos commissioned
from Ambrogio Lorenzetti to decorate the walls of the council
chamber of the governing committee of Siena. The remainder of
this wall shows Good Government in the Country, while the
other walls are filled with allegories of Good Government and
Tyranny and scenes of Bad Government in the City and Country.

126 *below*

SIENA CATHEDRAL

The cathedral of Siena was begun around 1250, and work went
on until the end of the fourteenth century. In 1339 an ambitious
project was conceived to make the present building the mere
transepts and choir of a vastly larger edifice, but work was
stopped by the Black Death of 1348. Some of the piers of the
projected nave were actually built, and one can be seen on the
right of the illustration. Essentially a Gothic building, Siena's
cathedral retains some Romanesque elements, such as the
roundheaded arches and the green and white stripes. Its colourful
and pictureque appearance is typical of Sienese architecture.

127 *below*

TWO ANGELS

1310–30
Lorenzo Maitani, c. 1275(?)–1330
Orvieto Cathedral

In 1310 Lorenzo Maitani was called in as Capomaestro of Orvieto Cathedral, and to him and his workshop is attributed a large part of the sculpture which decorates the four piers of the façade. The sculpture is generally considered to have been carried out in the years from 1310 to 1330, but much of it was left unfinished. This is a detail of the Creation of Eve from the story of Genesis which unfolds scene after scene on the first pier of the façade.

129 *right*

DEACON

from the tomb of Cardinal de Braye
1282 or after
Arnolfo di Cambio, active during the second half of the thirteenth century
San Domenico, Orvieto

Cardinal de Braye died in the year 1282 and was buried in the church of San Domenico in Orvieto. Arnolfo di Cambio, sculptor to popes and princes, was commissioned to create his tomb which, encrusted with coloured marbles and mosaic inlay, conforms to a type then established in Italy. Here a deacon, one of a pair, is in the act of drawing a curtain to hide from view the body of the deceased cardinal.

128 *right*

DEATH AND ASSUMPTION OF THE VIRGIN

1355–59
marble
Andrea di Cione, called Orcagna,
active 1343–68
Or San Michele, Florence

Filling the whole of the arch at the back of Orcagna's tabernacle for Or San Michele is this scene of the Death and Assumption of the Virgin, which bears the date 1359. Above, the Assumption of the Virgin is combined with the Virgin Dropping her Girdle to St Thomas. The simplicity of this event contrasts with the crowded scene below where the apostles crowd around the tomb of the Virgin, with Christ in the centre holding the soul of the Virgin, represented as a small child.

130

MARTIAL SCENE BEFORE
THE WALLS OF JERUSALEM

fourteenth century
Library of the Seminary, Padua

This illumination from the manuscript of
Burchardus Theutonicus's *Description of
the Holy Land* shows soldiers massed before
the walls of Jerusalem. Venetian in origin,
the miniature demonstrates a close link
with Byzantium through its brilliant
colours and strong stylisation. By means
of trade and diplomacy Venice was always
closely allied with the east, and her art
consistently demonstrates the importance
of these contacts with Byzantium.

131

ROOD SCREEN

1394
marble, bronze and silver
Jacobello and Pierpaolo dalle Masegne and
Jacopo di Marco Benato
St Mark's, Venice

The rood screen of St Mark's, which
separates the sanctuary from the main part
of the basilica, is signed by the brothers
Jacobello and Pierpaolo dalle Masegne and
dated 1394. It is composed of a marble
parapet bearing a row of columns which
in turn support an entablature topped by a
crucifix and a series of marble statues. The
crucifix of bronze and silver is signed by
Jacopo di Marco Benato and flanked by
statues of the Virgin and St John the
Evangelist with figures of the twelve
apostles on either side. The statues are the
work of the Brothers Masegne.

132

VIRGIN AND CHILD
ENTHRONED WITH ANGELS

1280s
Cenni di Pepe, called Cimabue,
c. 1240(?)–c. 1302(?)
152 × 88 in (385 × 223 cm)
Uffizi Gallery, Florence

The artist Cimabue is first mentioned in
Rome in 1272. The last news of him
comes from Pisa in 1302, where he is
documented as having carried out the
figure of St John for the apse mosaic in
the cathedral. Sometime between these
two dates, perhaps in the 1280s, he painted
this work for the church of Santa Trinità
in Florence.

133

TABERNACLE

1359, begun by 1355
marble and mosaic
Andrea di Cione, called Orcagna
active 1343–68
Or San Michele, Florence

The tabernacle was built to house
Bernardo Daddi's panel of the Virgin. Its
inception is usually dated to 1355, the
year in which Orcagna, who was architect
as well as painter and sculptor, became
Capomaestro (superintendant of works) of
the church. Commissioned by a lay
fraternity, the Compagnia di Or San
Michele, it is the most outstanding
sculptural complex of its time.

134 *opposite*

APSE OF SANTA CROCE

church founded 1294/95
Florence

The Franciscan church of Santa Croce
replaced an earlier church on the same site.
Its design is attributed to Arnolfo di
Cambio. Patronised by the biggest
banking families of Florence, Santa Croce
is among the most important repositories
of Italian fourteenth-century art. In the
centre the high altar is backed by the apse
containing frescos and stained glass by
Agnolo Gaddi. To the right is the small
Bardi Chapel frescoed by Giotto, while on
the left is the Tosinghi-Spinelli Chapel
which originally also had frescos by
Giotto.

135

THE ROAD TO SALVATION

1365–67
Andrea Bonaiuti da Firenze, active in the
third quarter of the fourteenth century, fresco
Cappella degli Spagnuoli, Santa Maria
Novella, Florence

This detail is from the frescos which
adorn the chapter house (later called
the Spanish Chapel) of the Dominican
friary of Santa Maria Novella in Florence
and were begun by the artist Andrea
Bonaiuti in 1365. The building and its
decoration were made possible by a
donation from the merchant Buonamico
di Lapo Guidalotti following the Black
Death. The programme of the fresco
decoration as a whole emphasises the
doctrine of the Dominican order. Here, on
the wall depicting the Road to Salvation,
the pope with his crosier and the holy
Roman emperor are shown seated before
the cathedral of Florence, complete with
its dome which had then been projected
but not yet constructed.

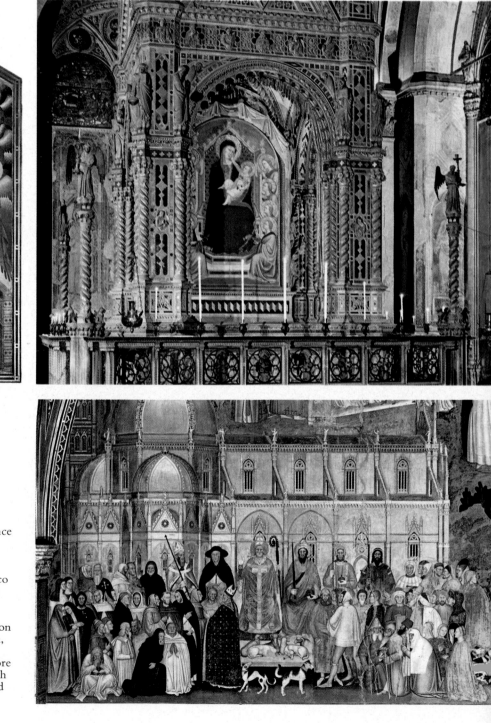

'When I was young, not only the plague, but also the evil conditions reigning in my native city caused me to leave Florence in the year of Our Lord 1400, in the company of a gifted painter in the employ of the noble duke of Pesaro. . . . My friends in the meantime wrote to me that the wardens of the church of San Giovanni were seeking masters of proven ability requesting them to submit examples of their work. In order to comply with this request and participate in the competition a host of accomplished masters journeyed thither from all parts of Italy.

'Whereupon I, too, begged permission to take farewell of our duke and of my companion . . . so I joined the artists offering their services to the master of the works of the aforementioned church. Each of us was furnished with four sheets of bronze. The wardens and officials at the head of the undertaking demanded that each artist give proof of his powers by conceiving a design for a plaque of a special subject – the Sacrifice of Isaac – to be treated by all the competitors. A year was allowed for the trial work and whoever was acclaimed the winner should be entrusted with the entire work. Without a single dissenting voice the experts as well as my fellow competitors honoured me by the presentation of the victor's palm.'

The Renaissance in Florence

That last sentence is fired by a young man's first flush of excitement as Ghiberti recalled his triumph nearly fifty years before. Personal success apart, this commission of bronze doors for the baptistery proved to be the curtain raiser on the Renaissance. The spirit of the commission exudes a new, striking confidence in the face of great material obstacles, since the war with Milan was still proceeding to Florence's disadvantage. Indeed, it is astonishing that the officers of the cloth guild (the most influential body in the city because wool was the principal Florentine industry) decided to embark on an enterprise that would eventually cost 22,000 florins – especially when one realises that it was possible to live in luxury on a mere two hundred florins a year.

Another surprising feature was that a committee of thirty-four could reach a unanimous conclusion – for Ghiberti was telling the truth. They required the scene to be enclosed within a quatrefoil so that it should be a fit companion for Andrea Pisano's door conceived seventy years before. Above all they prized fastidious craftsmanship, which probably accounted for the stipulation that the creation of the piece should take a year, as they knew that the chasing and finishing of bronze is a slow, meticulous business.

Ghiberti's craftsmanship was superb. His delicate chasing gives a stark pathos to Isaac's fearful turn as he watches the blade plunging towards his throat and makes the ram in the thicket a sacrifice of rare perfection.

Naturally Ghiberti's enthusiasm waned, and interruptions occurred: he accepted other commissions and journeyed to Rome, making casts of antique heads to adorn the roundels in the frame. The patrons impatiently drew up fresh contracts to spur him on and granted his workmen a special dispensation to be abroad after curfew to speed their progress. At last, on Easter Day 1424 the baptistery door was unveiled amid rapturous acclaim.

Meanwhile Ghiberti's only serious rival in the competition, Filippo Brunelleschi, was entrusted with a task of such magnitude that its accomplishment was a landmark in the history of European architecture – the building of the dome of Florence Cathedral. For over a century successive architects had shied away from designing a dome that would have to span $138\frac{1}{2}$ feet; they could not use a wooden centering and nobody knew what to do instead. Preposterous suggestions were made, including filling the crossing with a mountain of earth (the height from the ground to the top of the drum was 180 feet) and building the dome on top of it. We can imagine

118

142

143

136

FEDERIGO DA MONTEFELTRO AND HIS SON GUIDOBALDO

c. 1477
? Pedro Berruguete, c. 1450–1503/04
51·25 × 30·25 in (134 × 77 cm)
Palazzo Ducale, Urbino

Symbols of Federigo's two passions, war and learning, are fused here and fittingly hung in the duke's study. Though he has abandoned the emblem of power, his sceptre, to his little son, he is still clad in armour while he concentrates all his attention upon the book – thus we can believe Pius II when he said that they rode into battle together discussing the texts of Herodotus. The tiara was a gift from the shah of Persia.

137
THE TRINITY
c.1426
Masaccio 1401–28
fresco
192·5 × 124·75 in (489 × 317 cm)
Santa Maria Novella, Florence

This is the first painting in which a Renaissance architectural background and perspective was attempted, creating a sense of immutable order. The old hierarchic scale of the figures, where the largest were the most important, is now replaced by their significant positioning in space – the donor, Lorenzo Cardoni and his wife, being consigned to the outer zone. The presence of the little skeleton below gives to their prayers an especial urgency.

the relief the cathedral authorities must have felt when Brunelleschi produced a feasible model in 1417, especially as the drum had been completed *c.*1413 and Florence's neighbours had begun to snigger at her tardiness.

Work began on 1st August 1420 and by 1436 the dome had reached the stage where the lantern could be designed with confidence. Brunelleschi built the dome concentrically, tying in each course as it went. He had always loved ancient Rome and had delved among the tangled weeds for Roman sculptures, and now he saw that the answers to his questions about the dome would be provided by the vast, shaggy ruins of antiquity. He studied vaults and domes, and discovered that the famous diamond-patterned Roman 'opus reticulatum' could be translated into a herringbone system of mortaring the brickwork to absorb the strain of the inward curve of the dome. By 1432 the dome had reached a perilous stage and again he consulted the ruins, probably accompanied by Leon Battista Alberti, who later became the most influential theorist of the fifteenth century.

On his return, Brunelleschi turned his attention from the immensity of the dome to the design of a tiny, compact, centrally planned chapel commissioned by the Pazzi family. Its linear clarity reminds us that about 1415 **145** Brunelleschi invented a system of centralised perspective that revolutionised the design of pictures and sculpted reliefs.

The first painter to grasp the significance of Brunelleschi's discovery of perspective was Masaccio. He appears on the register of the guild of surgeon barbers (which included painters because of their common patron, St Luke) in 1422. In November of the same year another name occurs among the entries, that of an older artist, the Umbrian Gentile da Fabriano, who had recently arrived in Florence with a series of impressive commissions to his credit, among them frescos in the Doges' Palace in Venice which have perished. In 1423 Palla Strozzi presented Gentile's masterpiece, *The Adoration of the Magi*, to the church of Sant Trinità. It is a beguiling picture **153** and faultlessly executed in the fashionable International Gothic style.

Suddenly, only three years later, Masaccio swept aside all that Gentile and the International Gothic represented. At first sight the Florentines must have found his *Trinity* alarmingly austere, albeit compulsive, because **137** through the use of perspective they were involved psychologically in the painting in a way that no painter had attempted before. Of course, such realism would have been impossible without the enframing architectural space which Brunelleschi or Donatello probably helped him to design.

But Masaccio's fame rests on the Brancacci Chapel frescos in the Carmelites' church (the Carmine) situated in the poorest quarter of the city. Officially, Masaccio was the assistant of his fellow villager and senior, Masolino. Fortunately he was a generous, easy-going young man who seems to have accepted his inferior status without rancour. Masolino harboured no illusions about his assistant's powers and tried to modify his own style, which was closer to that of Gentile da Fabriano, imitating the chiaroscuro which made Masaccio's figures seem as solid as sculpture.

Looking at the grave, commanding group of apostles in *The Tribute* **163** *Money* it is difficult to believe that Masaccio had not visited Rome. *The Tribute Money* was painted in 1427 and the Florentine legislature had just instituted a radical, long-overdue tax reform. For years the poor had suffered the total burden of taxation while the rich escaped; now each citizen had to declare all his assets, both cash and goods, upon which he would be assessed. By imposing this voluntary self-sacrifice the ruling faction had taken a remarkable step, introducing the fairest taxation system in Europe. Among those who played a prominent role in its inception was Felice Brancacci, Masaccio's patron. It has been suggested recently that

The Tribute Money is a direct reference to the reform; obviously the measure meant much to Brancacci and even more to the poor, downtrodden parishioners of the Carmine.

Florence under Cosimo de' Medici

Until this century the Medici were always credited with this innovation in the tax system, but in fact Giovanni di Bicci de' Medici (who was head of the family) being devoid of political ambition kept quiet when his advice was sought. Instead, he concentrated upon the steady growth of his fortune which made him the richest man in Florence. However he always enjoyed the affectionate respect of the common people, and when his son Cosimo succeeded in 1429 the latter quickly seized the advantages the family reputation brought him by enlisting the support of the lesser guilds. Cosimo's rivals arrested and banished him, whereupon he removed his fortune to Venice. On his return a year later, in 1434, the populace accorded him a rapturous welcome. From that moment the city was virtually his, but he was wise enough never to become its titular head, thus avoiding the odium that his less prudent descendants incurred.

Nevertheless, unlike the older patrician banking families of the fourteenth century, such as the Peruzzi and the Bardi, the Medici were of humble origin, and their power rested on intelligence and commercial acumen. Consequently the aristocratic faction, including the Pazzi, never ceased to resent them as nouveau-riche usurpers of power. Cosimo prudently declined to flaunt his wealth, but when his grandson Lorenzo adopted the manners of a prince he stirred up venomous envy in the breasts of his opponents which exploded in the conspiracy of 1478.

According to the conventions of the day Cosimo was a pious man. One of his early acts of patronage was to purchase a tumble-down Silvestrine convent and present it to the Dominicans, commissioning the architect Michelozzo to refurbish the fabric and design a fine library. Cosimo had an especial affection for the monastery of San Marco, often staying in the guest room reserved for the patron and distinguished visitors such as the pope. Fra Angelico was among the friars of San Marco and his stamp is upon all the cells, though only a few were actually decorated by him.

It is in the decoration of the cells that Angelico made his unique contribution to Florentine art. They are saturated with the spirit of pure contemplation and are entirely different from the highly coloured aids to popular devotion that characterise the guild and family altarpieces by him and his contemporaries. Vasari tells us that Angelico never painted a crucifixion without shedding tears, and Alberti, whose intellectual alertness was formidable, admired the quality of his mind. Though Fra Angelico owes much to Masaccio's Roman 'gravitas', this spiritual and intellectual stature enabled him to invest *The Transfiguration* with a transcendental authority by means of a concentrated formal design and simple iridescent colour.

The decoration of the cells began about 1438 in a decade marked by a tremendous upsurge of artistic activity. New figures emerged and achieved fame, among them Ghiberti's erstwhile assistants, the painter Uccello and the sculptor Luca della Robbia, and Fra Filippo Lippi who transformed Masaccio's ideals into something more charming, intimate and detailed.

Although Ghiberti's second baptistery door was commissioned in 1425, the war with Milan made such catastrophic inroads into Florentine coffers that the sculptor found himself loaning money to the state instead of receiving a handsome advance on the door. Work did not begin until 1429 when the financial and political situation had eased. By 1439 the casting of the panels was complete. Long preliminary discussions took place to determine the programme for the door, for, though the artist was free to choose

138

CANTORIA
detail
1431–38
Luca della Robbia 1399/1400–82
marble
Museo dell' Opera del Duomo, Florence

Luca della Robbia, who is more familiar as the creator of tender blue and white terracotta images of the Virgin and Child, made his artistic debut with the carving of the choir gallery to go over the north sacristy door of Florence Cathedral. Brunelleschi or Michelozzo were probably responsible for the architectural framework, but the reliefs show that Luca had a finely developed sense of design and form, which was undoubtedly encouraged by the study of classical reliefs.

139

THE MEETING OF SOLOMON
AND SHEBA

1425–52
Lorenzo Ghiberti 1378–1455
gilt bronze, 31 × 31 in (79 × 79 cm)
Porta del Paradiso, the baptistery,
Florence Cathedral

Alberti mentioned Ghiberti in his dedication of the *della Pittura*, the first Renaissance treatise on painting. Indeed, Ghiberti often outstripped the painters in the flexibility of his design and lively depiction of the stories. He frequently varied the relief depth from high to the merest scratch upon the surface, giving to the scenes a fluid atmospheric quality which is enhanced by gilding. Here the effect is more static, befitting the solemnity of the occasion.

140

THE ARAGAZZI MONUMENT

1427–1437/38
Michelozzo di Bartolommeo 1396–1472
marble, Montepulciano Cathedral

The inception of the monument occurred when the artist was collaborating closely with Donatello, yet Michelozzo's interpretation of antiquity was quite distinct. As an amalgam of Christian belief and the valedictory sadness which gives to classical funeral stele their affecting emotional nobility, Michelozzo's conception has never been surpassed.

141

THE MONUMENT OF LEONARDO BRUNI

c. 1445–47
Bernardo Rossellino 1409–64
marble, Santa Croce, Florence

The design of Bruni's monument was to inspire a series of Florentine humanist tombs including that of his successor as chancellor, Carlo Marsuppini, who devised Bruni's epitaph. The colouring has disappeared from both these works, but originally a rich contrast was afforded to the red marble background by the limited use of blue pigment and gilding.

his own format, nobody would have dreamt of leaving him to devise the subject matter. Ghiberti chose a rectangular shape for the plaques and reduced their number to ten, which meant, except in one panel, compressing several episodes from a story within a single frame.

At some point the programming of the door seems to have passed from Leonardo Bruni to Ambrogio Traversari, a theologian who was responsible for the novel theory that Noah's ark was built like a pyramid and enjoyed the enviable distinction of being the only man in the papal entourage who could both read and speak Greek.

On Good Friday 1439 the union of the western and the eastern churches was proclaimed from the steps of Florence Cathedral. It was the fulfilment of a long-cherished dream and Traversari, who stares at us from the crowd in one of Ghiberti's panels, played a prominent part in the chequered negotiations. *The Meeting of Solomon and Sheba* probably symbolises this event, which caused such a stir that it was many years before the Florentines forgot it. The shopkeepers remembered several weeks of soaring profits; the elegant delighted in the eastern costumes, adopting the tall, fantastic hats; while the splendid sight of the Byzantine emperor John Paleologus on a magnificent white horse left an indelible impression on at least two artists. One of them, scarcely more than a boy, was Benozzo Gozzoli who commemorated the event twenty years later in *The Journey of the Magi* in the chapel of the Medici palace. The Medici themselves are represented not in the traditional role of humble donor but in the retinue of the Magi.

Perhaps Cosimo's most exciting moment during the Council of Florence was his meeting with the Greek philosopher Gemisthus Plethon, who expounded Plato's ideas with such passion that Cosimo resolved to set up a kind of academy dedicated to the study of Plato's works and their translation into Latin. Later Cosimo paid for the education of his physician's son, Marsilio Ficino, installing him in the Medici villa at Carreggi; thus the Platonic Academy was formed with Ficino as one of its leading members.

Cosimo's interest in ancient writing was not unique. Nearly every cultivated Florentine tried his hand at composing Latin verse. Among these was Bartolommeo Aragazzi whose sole claim to fame rests today not on his verses, which were mediocre, but on the form of his tomb which he commissioned in 1427 four years before his death. One of the first men to catch a glimpse of it was Leonardo Bruni, who was strolling below Montepulciano on a summer afternoon when he came upon some carters furiously beating their horses and cursing all poets to perdition. Then Bruni saw the first humanist monument, it was carved for Aragazzi by Michelozzo.

When Bruni himself died, his wishes for a plain tomb slab were ignored by the Signory of Florence. Bruni was a learned man proficient in Greek and Latin; as chancellor of the city he had composed a Latin history of Florence based on classical models. Bernardo Rossellino's tomb vividly recreates Bruni's funeral, which was a grand affair. Bruni was laid out in silk, crowned with laurel, and a volume of the history was slipped between his hands. As a finishing touch to the monument a precious, stylised epitaph was written by Marsuppini: 'After Leonardo departed from life, history is in mourning and eloquence is dumb and it is said that the muses, Greek and Latin alike, cannot restrain their tears.'

Another consequence of the rediscovery of antiquity was a resurgence of interest in the nude, which crystallised in the first free-standing nude sculpture since classical times, Donatello's bronze *David*. It was placed in the Medici palace courtyard where it was set up on a fine columnar base. Unhappily the base has vanished, but in 1469 the statue, still raised on high, dominated the wedding festivities of Lorenzo de'Medici.

142
THE SACRIFICE OF ISAAC

1401, Lorenzo Ghiberti 1378–1455
bronze, 18 × 16 in (45 × 40 cm)
Museo Nazionale, Florence

This is a trial relief submitted in the competition for the commission of a pair of bronze doors for the Florence Baptistery. The ease with which Ghiberti accommodated the story within the awkward quatrefoil shape shows his mastery of design. While the curving diagonal sweep of the mountainside unifies the composition, it also isolates the mystified servants waiting below from the sacrificial drama above. The style is Gothic, but Ghiberti's Isaac was inspired by a Roman carving of a captive barbarian and the relief on the altar is a typical Roman device.

143
THE DOME OF FLORENCE CATHEDRAL

begun 1420, the lantern designed 1436
Filippo Brunelleschi 1377–1446

This was the most important commission in Florence. Brunelleschi would have liked to build a classical hemispherical dome, but he was frustrated by the existing octagonal drum, and the pointed curve arose out of the need to reduce both the weight and the outward thrust to the minimum. This led to the novel construction of an inner and outer skin. In the initial stages he was assisted by Ghiberti and later by Michelozzo who carved the classical detailing on the lantern.

144

DAVID

c. 1440
Donatello, c. 1386–1466
bronze
h. 62·5 in (159 cm)
Museo Nazionale, Florence

Vasari wrote, 'This figure is so natural in its lifelikeness and
softness that to artists it seems impossible that it was not modelled
from a living body.' Yet Donatello simplified the supple body,
reducing the chest and abdomen to broad planes which increase
the tautness of the pose. It is partly inspired by the Roman
Antinous (plate **33**), but the youthful insolence of David's mien
has little to do with the flabby superiority of the antique head.

145

THE PAZZI CHAPEL

begun c. 1433
Filippo Brunelleschi 1377–1446
Santa Croce, Florence

This commission, issued in 1429, was probably inspired by the
Pazzi family's envy of the Medici, since Brunelleschi had recently
designed the similar Old Sacristy of San Lorenzo for which
Giovanni Bicci de' Medici had paid. The centralised, Greek cross
plan reflects Brunelleschi's friendship with Alberti, but the
austere linear clarity of grey 'pietra serena' mouldings,
contrasting with the white walls, is characteristic of his discreet
use of decoration. Above, terra-cotta reliefs of the Evangelists
provide a rare note of colour and may have been executed by the
architect or by Luca della Robbia and his school.

146

THE ST LUCY ALTARPIECE

c. 1440, Domenico Veneziano, active 1438–61
tempera, 82·25 × 83·75 in (205 × 213 cm)
Uffizi Gallery, Florence

This is one of the earliest examples of the
'sacra conversazione' altarpiece (a type of
representation of the Virgin and Child
with saints in which they are grouped in a
unified space and not separated as before
within individual framed panels). It was
invented by Fra Angelico whose
workshop Domenico joined when he
arrived in Florence.

147

THE MIRACLE OF THE MULE

detail, 1447, Donatello, c. 1386–1466
bronze, 22·5 × 48·5 in (57 × 123 cm)
Sant' Antonio, Padua

Unlike Ghiberti's reliefs for the Porta del
Paradiso in Florence, Donatello's scenes
for the high altar deal with single episodes
in the life of Padua's great saint. Each
miracle occurs in the centre of the plaque,
but the bystanders are simultaneously
urged forward and recoiling. No other
artist was capable of depicting this kind of
psychological turmoil until Leonardo da
Vinci painted *The Last Supper* (plate **174**).

In 1443 Donatello arrived in Padua where he spent the next ten years.
During that time a wealthy citizen, Francesco da Tergola, donated 1,500
lire to the Franciscans of the basilica of Sant' Antonio for the erection of a
high altar. Donatello evolved a daringly elaborate scheme with an impressive architectural superstructure within which the bronze figures of the
saints upon the altar were grouped about the Madonna and Child in the
manner of the 'sacra conversazione' altarpieces, which had become so **146**
popular in Florence. The figures survive but their architectural setting was
destroyed long ago. We can form an idea of its appearance, however, from
the documents and the design of Mantegna's San Zeno altarpiece and
Giovanni Bellini's *Madonna* in the Frari, Venice. These two young men **167**
were in their early twenties when Donatello came to Padua, and it is impossible to over-estimate the importance of their encounter with the great
Florentine genius.

Donatello's reliefs depicting the miracles of St. Anthony remain. **147**
Today they are rather difficult to decipher, but originally they were
heightened with silver gilt. This must have vividly accentuated the contrast
between the volatile grouping of the sceptical populace, shocked into belief
by the miracle enacted before their eyes, and the ponderous magnificence of
the Roman-inspired architecture.

The Italian courts

By mid-century, the courts of northern and central Italy were ripe for the
introduction of the new style. For many years the humanists, who were
peripatetic philologists devoted to the study of ancient texts, were welcome
at the courts, and in 1425 Vittorino da Feltre had opened a small, very exclusive school for the education of the boys and girls of the Mantuan court.

One of the first rulers to seize upon the novel situation was the un-
scrupulous tyrant of Rimini, Sigismondo Malatesta. He was an unsavoury
character who murdered three wives, corrupted his children, ruled his
people with a merciless despotism, and waged war against the church, but
his one redeeming feature was a deep love of classical learning and these
paradoxical aspects were to coalesce in his decision in about 1446 to build
the Tempio Malatestiano. With a typical disregard for the niceties of **166**
Christian morality he decided to transform the local medieval church of
San Francesco into a monument to his mistress Isotta. Alberti, the architect,
looked to the nearby Roman triumphal Arch of Augustus for inspiration in
the design of the façade; an idea which would have instantly appealed to his
intrepid warrior patron.

The boastful liar Borso d'Este, the ruler of Ferrara, was also eager to
aggrandise his court. Borso loved to dazzle his guests with lavish feasts,
dramatic performances and music, which was especially fine at Ferrara as
some of the most talented Flemish composers, including Josquin des Près,
were attracted to his court. However, few of Borso's artists remained long
in his employ because they soon found that they were paid in empty
promises. Luckily, Francesco del Cossa stayed long enough to decorate
Borso's study in the Palazzo Schifanoia. The ruler's study was always the **158**
most important room in the palace and much thought was given to the
scheme of decoration. An abstruse theme based on the signs of the zodiac
was drawn up by the court astrologers who were versed in oriental systems
of computation. Francesco tempered the seriousness with gaiety and
sharply observed details of the countryside.

There was a healthy rivalry among the courts and each vied with the
others for the artists' services. Naturally the Mantuan Gonzagas were determined not to be outdone by Borso, so in about 1473 Mantegna began to
decorate the Camera degli Sposi in the Palazzo Ducale, Mantua. Mantegna

enjoyed a special position at the court and his own involvement in the events described on the walls endows them with a rare immediacy. The series opens with Lodovico Gonzaga and his wife receiving the news that their son Francesco had been created cardinal and was about to visit them. Mantegna has classicised the architectural details, for no artist had such a relentless passion for ancient Rome, but the portraits are so vividly alive that the spectator really feels that he can overhear the message whispered in Lodovico's ear. During his stay the cardinal favoured Mantegna with a visit, and the artist prepared a huge feast in his honour. Earlier while he was taking the cure at Poretta, Francesco Gonzaga had met Mantegna, who entertained him with discourses on Roman antiquities.

Among Vittorino da Feltre's little scholars was Federigo da Montefeltro who subsequently became the ruler of Urbino. In many ways Federigo's court was unique: Vespasiano, his librarian, likened it to a monastery for meals were temperate, Latin histories were read aloud and in Lent the company listened to spiritual readings. Federigo was a sincere believer who heard mass daily, so Justus of Ghent was not indulging in conventional court flattery when he depicted his patron's hand raised in wonderment at the institution of the Eucharist, but was revealing a true aspect of his nature.

Justus of Ghent was a Fleming, and Federigo's architect was Luca Laurana, a Dalmatian, who around 1468 designed the superbly harmonious court-yard of the Palazzo Ducale. Federigo's understanding of art was profound and he liked to discuss the problems of his artists and architects with them; above all he was fascinated by problems of space, and Piero della Francesca dedicated the first treatise on perspective to him. Not surprisingly Federigo's study was decorated with elaborate intarsia perspective devices.

Not all the great masterpieces were created for the courts. Piero della Francesca's *Resurrection* was painted upon the wall of the town hall of his birthplace, Borgo San Sepolcro, where he had served as city councillor for twenty years. The spiritual reality and intellectual power of Piero's conception unified by a delicate perception of light make much Florentine art around 1460 look trite by comparison.

The great exception was Donatello, now a very old man but with his vigour unimpaired. Youthful joy has gone and all his later works are tinged with tragedy and even cruelty which is a stark feature of the *Judith*. Originally the group was a fountain in the Medici sculpture garden, and bright spurts of water gushing from the corners of the cushion would have mocked the savage horror of the gash in Holofernes's throat.

Siena

On his way from Padua to Florence, Donatello tarried in Siena. The Sienese were delighted, offering him Jacopo della Quercia's old workshop as a tempting inducement to persuade him to settle in their midst. Ten or fifteen years earlier such a thing would have been unthinkable since the Sienese would have still smarted from the recollection of the Battle of Lucca which had revived, in 1433, all the traditional hatred between the Tuscan cities. This meant that the Sienese were largely cut off from the full tide of the Renaissance, and Domenico di Bartolo's *Nurture and Marriage of the Foundlings* (1441-44) betrays the disparate artistic ambitions of the Sienese and Florentines. The perspective is faltering, and Domenico preferred to concentrate on such moving human details as the elderly foster mother receiving the swaddled orphan. In several scenes Domenico accurately portrays the provisions in the foundling hospital's charter.

It was in colour that the Sienese excelled. Their harmonies were compounded of the dark lustre of Byzantium fused with the innocent blonde tonality of the Gothic palette. Sienese paintings are generally small, and

149
THE STUDY OF
THE DUKE OF URBINO *detail*
intarsia
Palazzo Ducale, Urbino

The designs for some of the exceptionally fine examples of wooden inlay in the duke's study may have been contrived by Francesco di Giorgio, the Sienese artist who succeeded Laurana as chief architect at Urbino around 1479, or they may have been supplied by Botticelli's workshop. Their themes range from simple trompe l'oeil motifs of open doors revealing books and instruments to ambitious architectural and landscape vistas.

148

LODOVICO GONZAGA RECEIVING THE MESSENGER

detail
c. 1472–74
Andrea Mantegna 1431–1506
fresco
Camera degli Sposi, Palazzo Ducale, Mantua

The entirely secular character of the programme of the Camera degli Sposi fuses decorum, joy and learning. Mantegna's scholarly caste of mind and his intimacy with his patrons and fellow courtiers enabled him to interpret the commission with rare sympathy. He was also inventive: on the ceiling he created a mock cupola, seemingly open to the sky, from which heads peer at us. It was the first example of this kind of illusionism.

150

JUDITH AND HOLOFERNES

c. 1453–55
Donatello, c. 1386–1466
bronze, h. 93 in (236 cm)
Piazza della Signoria, Florence

This group extends the design and expressive range of free-standing statuary to a point where a number of emotional and physical states are simultaneously described: Judith is triumphant yet about to strike, while Holofernes is both slain and reeling from the blow. The forms are so lifelike that it has been suggested that wax impressions were made of actual limbs and drapery. On the expulsion of the Medici it was set up in the Palazzo Vecchio to warn tyrants of their fate.

this led to a fastidious technique and beautifully controlled line. Usually a mood of quiet devotion permeates Sienese panels, but where action occurs the scenes call forth a disquieting, refined sadism which seems to arise out of an inbred, claustrophobic society, such as that animating the dread frenzy of Matteo di Giovanni's *Massacre of the Innocents*.

Lorenzo the Magnificent

Meanwhile, the climate in Florence had changed in both rule and art. On 2nd December 1469 Lorenzo de' Medici came to power. He inherited the magnificent Medici collection, including Uccello's triptych of the Battle of San Romano which hung in his room. The three paintings represent a most chancy episode in Florentine military history in 1432 when Nicholas Tolentino and his forces were cut off by ambush. Now only one picture remains in Florence, but hung together all the surprised confusion would have built up to a superb climax of ultimate triumph. **165**

Lorenzo de' Medici was a complex character. Although he was tall and well built, he was not a handsome man and had a strange croaky voice. Because of his fine physique he excelled in the joust and was an imposing figure on horseback and loved playing football. His education had been entrusted to Marsilio Ficino who grounded him in Greek and Latin learning, so that the poets and philosophers of the academy at Carreggi were always welcome at his table, and their elevated conversation influenced the young Michelangelo whom Lorenzo took under his protection. As a patron he disappointed many, but his aesthetic judgment was absolute, and everyone consulted him about work of any importance in the city. Whereas his father delighted in gems and precious objects, Lorenzo preferred to acquire small Greek and Roman antiquities and Greek manuscripts; besides, despite the display, money was running out. There was a trace of fatalism in Lorenzo's make up and the jocund pessimism of his carnival song could have been addressed to his handsome, doomed brother Giuliano: 'How fair is youth that flies so fast! Then be happy, ye who may; what's to come is still unsure.' **22**

By 1478 Lorenzo had become entangled in a devious tussle with Sixtus IV who promptly retaliated by transferring the papal banking account from the Medici to the Pazzi bank. This whetted the Pazzi family's appetite for power as they always resented the Medici as upstarts. The plans for the notorious conspiracy crystallised swiftly: the only innocent party was the young Cardinal Riario in whose honour the high mass in Florence Cathedral was being celebrated by the archbishop of Pisa, Salviati, who was privy to the plot. As the consecration bell sounded, Francesco de' Pazzi leapt upon Giuliano de' Medici, stabbing him nineteen times. In this frenetic attack a meagre, ill-favoured man's envy of the physical beauty of his victim triumphed over any motive of political ambition: his real enemy, Lorenzo, was left to a pair of bungling amateurs. The plot was a grotesque miscalculation: the Florentines rallied to the Medici, and as the assailants were thrown from the windows of the Palazzo Vecchio the mob gleefully tore them assunder. Jacopo de' Pazzi suffered the worst indignities: having been hanged, his body was dragged from the family vault in the Pazzi Chapel and finally urchins obscenely mutilated his corpse and threw it in the Arno. **145**

Botticelli may well have witnessed these horrific events, but no hint of this latent bestiality in contemporary society mars the *Primavera* or *The Birth of Venus*. Nonetheless the purpose of these two paintings was to calm the turbulent spirits of Lorenzo di Pier Francesco de' Medici, a young cousin of Lorenzo the Magnificent, and the complex moral allegory underlying the *Primavera* would have been evolved by Marsilio Ficino who was responsible for the youth's education. **156**

Secular enthusiasms emerge more vividly in sculpture where individual pride, allied to the study of Roman portraiture, led to the popularity of the portrait bust. Also a passion for the male nude in vigorous action, reinforced by a new, more scientific curiosity about the anatomical construction of the body, encouraged the production of small bronzes, classical in theme, but with the sinews closely defined so that the act is invested with an almost **162** superhuman strength. The Labours of Hercules became a favourite subject.

A special kind of commemoration (the equestrian monument) was accorded to the heroes of the battlefield. The brilliant mercenary strategists are shown astride their horses in a pose directly inspired by the imperial statue of Marcus Aurelius but clad in the heavy, richly decorated armour of the day. The last of these to be completed in the fifteenth century **152** was Verrocchio's Colleoni Monument in Venice.

Venice

The Renaissance was slow to germinate in Venice but by the 1480s it was well established. Venice was the natural haven of Greek scholars seeking asylum after the fall of Constantinople in 1453, and some brought Greek manuscripts and portable sculptures, so that the Venetian rapidly outstripped the Florentines in the acquisition of antiquities. The Venetians were quick to recognise the importance of the newly invented printing press, and Ficino's translations of Plato and Alberti's treatise on architecture were both published there. Above all, Venice enjoyed a political and social stability denied to most other parts of Italy. It was based primarily on great wealth and supported by a sagacious diplomacy and a firm governmental order vested in the patrician oligarchy of the doges' rule. All this engendered a spirit of ready confidence which is reflected in Venetian art; the portrayal of man's wilder impulses and ambitions is entirely absent.

Civic pride prompted many of the commissions given to the official **170** state painter, Gentile Bellini, to portray the events where the joint authority of church and state were manifested in solemn processions of cherished relics. The dignified bearing of the figures reminds us that 'festina lente' (make haste slowly) was a favourite motto in the Renaissance and it was considered ill bred to scurry along the streets.

Life was colourful in Venice, sumptuous stuffs and jewels were imported from the orient and even the first Renaissance church, Santa Maria dei Miracoli, was enlivened by a pattern of coloured marble. No wonder Venetian artists quickly mastered the newly introduced oil technique which **67, 284** no one exploited to richer effect than Giovanni Bellini, and Carpaccio revelled in the opportunities it offered for the minute rendering of textures **171** and objects in the Venetian home.

Rome

Meanwhile, by 1450 Rome had begun to make her own contribution to the Renaissance, but it was the papacy of Sixtus IV (1481-84) which really established the secular power of the Vatican, so that the earlier schismatic confusion was forgotten. Sixtus was a brutal, energetic man whose practical good sense transformed the city: he improved the water supply, paved the streets and made it a safer place in which to live. He also established the Capitoline Museum, but, lacking real discernment, he discarded many of the small, precious objects amassed by Paul II. Two projects were dear to **160** his heart: the building and decoration of the Sistine Chapel and the founda- **172** tion of the Vatican Library. A fresco by Melozzo da Forlì shows Sixtus founding the library. At the centre of a distinguished circle is the kneeling scholar Platina whose devoted custody of the library transformed the Vatican court into a centre of learning.

By the end of the century Rome was under the control of the infamous

151 *right*

THE NURTURE AND MARRIAGE OF THE FOUNDLINGS

1441–44
Domenico di Bartolo, c. 1400–47
fresco
Spedale della Scala, Siena

This was the major fresco cycle carried out in Siena during the fifteenth century. It was commissioned by the rector of the hospital, Giovanni di Francesco Buzzicchelli, who was familiar with Florentine achievements and hoped that Domenico might rival them. In fact, the smiling faces with neat rows of teeth are more Gothic than Renaissance, and Domenico dwelt on vivid gesture rather than abstract intellectual principles.

152 *above*

THE COLLEONI MONUMENT

1479–1496
Andrea del Verrocchio 1435–88
bronze
Campo Santi Giovanni e Paolo, Venice

Verrocchio died before the group was completed, and it was the last-executed example from a series of fifteenth-century equestrian monuments. Much of the chasing was left to his assistants and lacks the finesse that we associate with Verrocchio, who trained as a goldsmith. The movement in the pose, however, anticipates the richer rhythms of the High Renaissance.

153 *right*

THE ADORATION OF THE MAGI

1423
Gentile da Fabriano, c. 1370–1427
tempera
Uffizi Gallery, Florence

Although Gentile's patron, Palla Strozzi, was one of the foremost champions of classical learning, he also admired the rich court art fashionable in Burgundy, and Gentile was the most gifted exponent of this style in Italy. His forms are modulated in light and the splendour of his rich hues is heightened by a judicious use of gilding. A gentle humour creeps into the grand display as the little Infant Christ sticks out his big toe for the aged king to kiss.

154 *right*

THE JOURNEY OF THE MAGI
detail
Benozzo Gozzoli, c.1421–97
fresco
Medici Chapel, Palazzo Medici-Riccardi,
Florence

Benozzo Gozzoli's earlier activities as Fra
Angelico's assistant in the Vatican and his
training as a goldsmith led Ghiberti to
employ him in the chasing of the second
door of Florence Baptistery. Benozzo was
uniquely endowed to carry out the wishes
of his gouty, immobilised patron, Pietro
de' Medici, who delighted in his collection
of gems and magnificent northern
manuscripts. Benozzo shared his interest
in Gothic detail and delicate splendour.
The Medici figure in the retinue of the
Magi: Cosimo near the centre with his son
Piero ahead of him on a white horse.

155

FEDERIGO DA MONTEFELTRO

c. 1465
Piero della Francesca, c. 1420–92
18·5 × 13 in (47 × 33 cm)
Uffizi Gallery, Florence

The representation of the duke of Urbino in the conservative profile position (which by now was only common in medals, the more intimate three-quarter position being favoured in Florence) underlines the authority of the image. The duke physically dominates his territories, superbly depicted in soft, muted tints of dun, silver and lavender. Battista Sforza, the duke's wife, was also portrayed and delightful allegorical Triumphs feature on the reverse of both paintings.

156 *left*
PRIMAVERA

c. 1475
Sandro Botticelli, c. 1445–1510
Uffizi Gallery, Florence

The languid charm of Botticelli's pictures has often led to the underestimation of the strength of his forms. The nervous tautness of the drawing, which causes the strength, invests his figures with a sophisticated abstract beauty. Fra Filippo Lippi, Pollaiuolo and Verrocchio influenced the formation of his style and, like theirs, his paintings betray an interest in both classical and Gothic art.

157
THE INSTITUTION OF THE EUCHARIST

1472
Justus of Ghent, active 1460–c. 1475
oil
113 × 122·75 in (287 × 312 cm)
Palazzo Ducale, Urbino

Vespasiano tells us that Federigo da Montefeltro 'being very knowledgeable in matters of painting, and unable to find an Italian master who could paint in oils, finally approached a Flemish painter and had him come to Urbino'. Justus had been influenced by Hugo van der Goes whose powerful design and emotionalism made a deep impression on him.

158

DUKE BORSO AND HIS COURTIERS

1458–70/78
Francesco del Cossa 1435–c.1477
fresco, Palazzo Schifanoia, Ferrara

Cossa, the principal artist engaged in the decoration of Duke Borso's study, was influenced by Piero della Francesca and Mantegna, who had worked in Ferrara. For all its complicated astrological symbolism, the room is not so much an intellectual challenge as frankly beguiling. The scheme is divided into three zones devoted to the triumphs of the divinities, such as Venus, the signs of the zodiac and activities of the months and, finally, life at the court.

159

THE RESURRECTION

c.1463
Piero della Francesca, c.1420–92
fresco, Palazzo Communale, Borgo San Sepolcro

Piero and Alberti were friends and shared a passion for classical design and minutely calculated mathematical proportions, which always formed the basis of Piero's composition. Before painting this fresco Piero had been to Rome, and the antique armour worn by the slumbering soldiers is one of the rare direct references to antiquity in his work.

160

CHRIST GIVING THE KEYS
TO ST PETER

1481
Pietro Perugino, c.1445/50–1523
fresco
c.132 × 96 in (335 × 244 cm)
Sistine Chapel, Vatican Palace, Rome

Perugino was an Umbrian artist and his
style is quite distinct from that of Florence.
After the crowded eventfulness of the
frescos by Florentines in the chapel,
Perugino's lucid space punctuated by the
symmetrical architecture is a novel respite,
although the graceful arabesques of the
figures in the middle distance prevent it
becoming too static. He was also a
felicitous colourist which was in accord
with the usually gentle mood of his work.

161

THE FALL OF THE DAMNED

1499–1505
Luca Signorelli, c.1441–1523
fresco
Chapel of Madonna di San Brizio,
Orvieto Cathedral

When Signorelli accepted this commission
part of the ceiling had already been
decorated in a very different spirit by Fra
Angelico. Thus it was on the walls that
the full conviction and ferocity of
Signorelli's vision was to be unleashed. In
its imaginative force it is second only to
Michelangelo's *Last Judgment* in the
Sistine Chapel (plate **187**).

Borgia pope, Alexander VI, and his sinister son Cesare. A huge, robust man,
Alexander had no taste for mortification, and Rome became a carnival city.
In 1493 Alexander decided to have his apartments decorated and chose an
Umbrian artist, Pinturicchio, whose vision was charmingly descriptive
rather than heroic. He was a sensitive colourist, and the deep blues, choice
gilding, rose, lilac and jade proved a delicate foil to the golden beauty of
Alexander's daughter, Lucrezia, posing as St Catherine in one of the scenes.

The climax of Alexander's reign was achieved in the spectacular pomp of
the Jubilee celebrations in 1500. But while Rome rejoiced the rest of
Europe was in the grip of a religious crisis, a dread that the end of the world
was upon them, and the Last Judgment appeared again on the walls of
churches. In Florence, Lorenzo had died and his weak, stupid heirs revolted
the people who, whipped up to repentant frenzy by the apocalyptic ser-
mons of the monk, Savonarola, expelled the Medici from Florence. Several
artists were inspired by Savonarola's preaching but none more so than
Botticelli, whose last works were passionate religious meditations. But
even as Botticelli painted these pictures the tide of fear was receding.
Michelangelo and Leonardo returned to Florence and the High Renaissance
had begun.

Maria Shirley

162

HERCULES AND ANTAEUS

c. 1475–80
Antonio Pollaiuolo 1431/32–1498
bronze
h. 17·75 in (45 cm)
Museo Nazionale, Florence

Pollaiuolo was the first Florentine to
exploit the male nude in strenuous action
in small bronze statuettes. However, unlike
Donatello's *Judith* (plate **150**), the
composition only works from a profile
position. We do not know whether this
was imposed upon him by the place it was
destined to occupy or whether it was a
limitation in Pollaiuolo's sense of design.
Lorenzo de' Medici considered him the
greatest living sculptor in the city and
may have commissioned this piece.

163

THE TRIBUTE MONEY

1427
Masaccio 1401–28
fresco
100·5 × 220·5 in (225 × 597 cm)
Brancacci Chapel, the church of the Carmine,
Florence

Masaccio's departure from the usual form
of continuous representation (in which the
story reads from left to right) focuses the
drama. Christ's words and action become
the hub of the whole event, galvanising
our attention as they would have done
that of the disciples. Every part is touched
by Masaccio's imaginative power: the
realistic modelling, the simple gestures,
and the broad sweep of the landscape.

164

THE CORONATION
OF THE VIRGIN

1441–47
Fra Filippo Lippi, c.1406–69
panel
78·75 × 113 in (200 × 287 cm)
Uffizi Gallery, Florence

Around 1440 Florentine painting became
more elaborate and ambitious. In Fra
Filippo's picture the crowded lily-bearing
angels and richly embellished throne act
as a foil to the coronation group. His
forms are fully modelled, reflecting Fra
Filippo's admiration of Masaccio, but the
details are exquisitely refined and arise
from the current passion for precious,
fastidiously wrought objects. The monk in
the foreground was probably the donor.

165

THE BATTLE OF SAN ROMANO

c.1455
Paolo Uccello 1397–1475
71·75 × 127·25 in (182 × 323 cm)
Uffizi Gallery, Florence

All Uccello's favourite themes are
crowded into this panel: perspective in
the scattered, broken lances on the
ground; the silvered ornament on the
hard, curved surfaces of cuirass, shield and
helmet; and the horses which remind us
that Uccello was so fond of animals that
he kept stuffed beasts because he was too
poor to own a pet. The formalised leaves
recall the northern tapestries which were
the prized possessions of Florentine
patrons and admired by artists.

166

THE TEMPIO MALATESTIANO

begun c.1446
Leon Battista Alberti 1404–72
Rimini

In 1452 Alberti presented his architectural
treatise to Nicholas V, and the theories he
propounded were uppermost in his mind
while he transformed this Gothic church
for Sigismondo Malatesta. Alberti spent
much time among Roman ruins and his
scholarly use of Roman forms led to a
heavier effect than Brunelleschi achieved.
The wall surface is enriched by slabs of
porphyry and red Verona marble, now
sadly faded.

167

MADONNA AND CHILD

1488
Oil
Giovanni Bellini, c.1428–1516
Santa Maria Gloriosa dei Frari, Venice

Bellini's mastery of the new oil medium
made possible the diffused light unifying
the figures and their architectural
surroundings. The medium also lends a
resonance and subtlety to his colours, which
are regarded as typically Venetian. The
music-making angels were a popular
device at this time and are partly inspired by
Donatello's altarpiece in Sant' Antonio in
Padua. Bellini, however, invests the angels
with an intimate charm which softens the
effect made by the firm classical design of
the Madonna and Child.

168 *far right*

TWO ANGELS

detail from the Portinari Altarpiece
c.1474–76
Hugo van der Goes, active 1467–82
oil
Uffizi Gallery, Florence

Owing to the Medici's commercial
activities in the north their agents
employed Flemish painters, and Rogier
van der Weyden worked for the Medici
themselves. Around 1474, or perhaps
1468, Tommaso Portinari (Lorenzo's
deputy in Bruges) commissioned this
famous altarpiece which arrived in
Florence about 1478. It made a profound
impression on local painters, but a
comparison with Botticelli's head of Flora
(plate **156**) betrays the wide gulf between
the Flemings and Florentines.

169
THE DISPUTATION
OF ST CATHERINE

c.1493–1501
Bernardino Pinturicchio 1454–1513
fresco
Appartamento Borgia, Vatican Palace, Rome

On the ceiling, which is most elaborately
decorated, are scenes from the legend of
Isis; this fusion of pagan and Christian
elements in a single scheme typifies the
late fifteenth century. Pinturicchio was a
sensitive colourist and the deep blues,
gilding, rose, lilac and jade provide a
delicate foil to the golden beauty of
Lucrezia Borgia posing as St Catherine.

170 *below*
PROCESSION OF THE TRUE
CROSS IN ST MARK'S SQUARE

1496
Gentile Bellini, c.1429–1507
oil
Accademia di Belle Arti, Venice

This is one of a series of pictures that Gentile
undertook for the Scuola di San Giovanni
Evangelista representing legends associated
with their most precious relic, the True
Cross. In 1479 Gentile had stayed in
Constantinople as painter to the Sultan
Mahomet II, and he brings out the near-
oriental splendour of St Mark's. The
original Byzantine mosaics on the façade
are still visible in this painting.

171 *below*

THE DREAM OF ST URSULA

1490–95
Vittore Carpaccio, active 1490–1526
oil
Accademia di Belle Arti, Venice

As salt in the air precluded the fresco cycles so popular in Florence, the Venetians created imposing series of oil paintings. One of the first of these was Carpaccio's St Ursula scenes, of which *The Dream* was one of the last to be executed. It reveals Carpaccio's sensitive ability to render the greenish light filtered through the tinted glass so common in Venetian houses of the period, and also his delight in textures which could vie with any Fleming's.

172 *below*

THE FOUNDATION OF THE VATICAN LIBRARY

1470–77
Melozzo da Forlì 1438–94
fresco, 144 × 120 in (366 × 315 cm)
Pinacoteca Vaticana, Vatican Museums, Rome

Melozzo portrays a distinguished circle including the stout, rather brutish-looking Sixtus. The standing cardinal is Giuliano della Rovere, later Julius II, but our attention is riveted by the finely drawn, intelligent head of the kneeling scholar, Platina. His devoted custody of the library transformed the Vatican court into a centre of learning.

'Many a time I have seen Leonardo go early in the morning to work on the platform before *The Last Supper*; and he would stay from sunrise till darkness, never laying down the brush, but continuing to paint without eating or drinking. Then three or four days would pass without his touching the work, yet each day he would spend several hours examining it and criticising it to himself. I have also seen him, when the fancy took him, leave the Corte Vecchia when he was at work on the stupendous horse of clay, and go straight to the Grazie. There, climbing on the platform, he would take the brush and give a few touches to one of the figures: and then suddenly he would leave and go elsewhere.'

Bandello's graphic description of Leonardo's impetuous methods of working transports us into the very moment of the inception of the High Renaissance. Ironically, this occurred not in Florence, but in Milan, a city where local popular taste still found the urns, ribands and candelabra of early Renaissance ornament difficult to assimilate and regarded the fussy late Gothic devices on the cathedral their chief architectural jewel.

Milan under Lodovico Sforza

About twelve years earlier, in 1482, Leonardo da Vinci had arrived in Milan bearing a rare gift from Lorenzo de' Medici to the ducal tyrant of Milan, Lodovico Sforza, known as Il Moro. The gift was an exquisitely wrought silver lyre in the shape of a horse's head, on which Leonardo performed.

Lodovico may have been beguiled by the music but his attention was truly aroused by a letter of self-recommendation that Leonardo addressed to him, in which he described all manner of strange and horrible war machines that he had invented; art is mentioned almost as an afterthought at the end: 'Also I can execute sculpture in marble, bronze or clay, and also painting. . . . Moreover I could undertake the work of the bronze horse which shall endue with immortal glory and eternal honour the auspicious memory of the prince, your father, and the illustrious house of Sforza.'

Milan suited Leonardo; he was out of sympathy with the intellectual climate of Florence dominated by poets and philosophers, for Leonardo had an omnivorous curiosity, and preferred the vigorous stimulus of the company of the doctors, mathematicians and scientists at the Sforza court. Leonardo read widely, and at the age of forty-two learnt Latin, so that he could study the writings of ancient scientific authors. In Milan he began to compile his famous notebooks, in which war machines feature prominently. The machines are of a truly malign ferocity and rendered all the more repellent because of Leonardo's capacity to convince us that the blades could rotate and cut down the enemy. Yet Leonardo was also gentle and became a vegetarian because he could not bear to harm a defenceless living creature.

However, the military instruments not only recall the contradictions in Leonardo's nature but also the dark side of the Renaissance: Lodovico Sforza was an implacable tyrant. He enjoyed immense wealth which he and his forebears deployed to promote their territorial ambitions, to secure brilliant marriages for their daughters with the royal houses of Europe and to indulge in feats of display of an unparalleled magnificence. These pageants also must have appealed to the foppish side of Leonardo, and he was much in demand designing scenes and costumes for the many masques performed at the court.

Like all cunning despots, Lodovico's ambition sometimes outran prudence. Never was this truer than when he opened his lands to Charles VIII of France during the latter's expedition in 1494 to claim the throne of Naples. Luckily, Charles was a weakling, easily side-tracked by women, and in 1495 he was forced to retreat from Italy. This was not due to any

The Painter Genius and his Patron

1500–1600

173

PERSEUS

1545–54
Benvenuto Cellini 1500–71
bronze
h. 10 ft 6 in (3 · 20 m)
Loggia dei Lanzi, Florence

When Cellini returned from Florence in 1545 he hoped for Duke Cosimo's patronage, and, after initial disappointments when he was treated by the duke with enthusiasm one moment and disdain the next, the Perseus was begun. It was a daunting task requiring all Cellini's fastidious skill in the detailing (for which his work as a goldsmith made him famous) and great technical dexterity in casting the figure. The difficulties are vividly recalled in his autobiography.

sagacity on Lodovico's part who was fool enough to boast, 'I have the pope for my chaplain, the Venetians for my treasurer, Maximilian for my condottiere general and the king of France as my messenger to come and go at my pleasure.'

Thus while Leonardo was, at Lodovico's behest, proclaiming the High Renaissance on the walls of the refectory of the Grazie, Il Moro's fateful miscalculation ushered in the political and military disasters that overshadowed Italy throughout the sixteenth century, when France, Germany and Spain competed for mastery of the peninsula.

175

SANTA MARIA DELLE GRAZIE
c.1487–c.1497
Donato Bramante 1444–1514
Milan

Bramante made no concessions to the late Gothic style of the nave, and his additions at the apse end and crossing are entirely Renaissance in spirit. Nothing could illustrate as vividly the change which had come about than his arched curves of the dome and vaulting. The wheel windows on the architrave are, in fact, painted, recalling that Bramante graduated to architecture from painting in which he was noted for his skilful use of perspective.

175 At the same time Bramante's completion of the adjacent church of Santa Maria delle Grazie was under way; it consisted of a vast, domed crossing with apsed transepts and choir which sounded a new note in Milanese architecture. Bramante and Leonardo were friends, and the numerous drawings of centrally planned churches in Leonardo's notebooks testify to their mutual enthusiastic study of Alberti's doctrines enshrined in the newly published *De Re Aedificatoria*.

Meanwhile the ineffectual Charles VIII had been succeeded by Louis XII who cast greedy eyes on the Milanese duchy. Lodovico's proud boast rang hollow when the French concluded an alliance with Venice and the Vatican which left the Sforza dangerously isolated. On 6th October 1499 the French struck and entered Milan; Leonardo fled to Florence and Bramante sought refuge in Rome, where he remained for the rest of his life.

In returning to his native city, Leonardo had not chosen a haven of social stability. At the turn of the century the Florentine government was singularly inept (a result of the system of electing a new council every two months) and militarily impotent. Thus, when Cesare Borgia crossed the Tuscan borders in 1501 the whole land was terrified but could do nothing to resist him. Eventually Pietro Soderini was elected gonfalonier for life, on the pattern of the Venetian doges. An able administrator, Soderini was a stickler for procedural detail and just if not imaginative. Fortunately for him, Pope Alexander died and his successor Julius II was determined to curb Cesare Borgia's rapacious territorial greed.

199 This lull encouraged Soderini to issue three great state commissions: the frescoing of the council hall with battle scenes by Leonardo and Michelangelo and the latter's *David*. It is ironic that *David*, the epitome of heroism, should have arisen in a milieu that enjoyed a brief, false prosperity and timidly quaked before the threat of every foe. News of this masterpiece reached the Vatican, and in 1505 Julius summoned Michelangelo to Rome.

Julius II

172 Every aspect of Julius's reign was marked by his intrepid, impatient character. As Cardinal Giuliano della Rovere he had urged the Italian expedition on Charles VIII in an attempt to embarrass his old enemy Alexander VI, and, on his elevation to the papacy, he immediately entered the field at the head of his troops and reclaimed the papal states from Cesare Borgia. In his desire to secure the church's temporal power, he entered into a series of alliances, hastily concluded and as swiftly broken. Equally, he kept a vigilant eye on the members of the curia, preventing a French bid for domination and outwitting the Spaniards who had supported the wily machinations of the Borgias. His role as a patron was similarly imaginative, bold and unpredictable. Quite how unpredictable Michelangelo was soon to discover.

On assuming office Julius consulted Bramante about the fabric of old St Peter's, which had caused concern for half a century. With characteristic daring he decided to pull down the most hallowed structure in Christendom and erect a new, even grander cathedral based upon a Greek cross plan.

THE LAST SUPPER *detail*

1495–97
Leonardo da Vinci 1452–1519
fresco
Santa Maria delle Grazie, Milan

Leonardo's passion for experiment induced him to try out quick-drying agents and oil in this fresco which led to its early deterioration. Yet, even in its ruinous state, we can see how he infused this popular episode for refectory decoration with a new cohesion of design which allowed the most exciting contrast between the calm authority of Christ and the turbulent perplexity of the apostles.

176
MOSES

begun 1506/13
Michelangelo Buonarroti 1475–1564
marble
92·5 in (235 cm)
San Pietro in Vincoli, Rome

When Condivi, Michelangelo's devoted assistant and biographer, wrote of the Moses, 'His face is full of vitality and spirit, apt to arouse both love and terror', he might well have been describing Julius II. If the work was begun in 1513, as seems likely from its style, then Michelangelo's recollections of his testy old patron would have been purged by Julius's recent death and the idealised conception real both in a personal and stylistic sense.

Bramante, who had already given proof of his inventiveness in the little Tempietto, was entrusted with the task.

It was a most unpopular move, but nothing could baulk Julius. The devout felt deprived of a shrine which they deeply venerated and the faithful as a whole resented the cost. Julius could not see the force of their objections since he was frugal to the point of meanness in his personal life, and to him the project could only redound to the glory of the church, about which he cared passionately. At last, a deep hole was dug, it became waterlogged and the surrounding soil loosened. On 18th April 1506 Julius, bearing a large stone, clambered down into the hole shouting angrily to the crowd to keep back lest the whole thing collapse and bury him. Thus the foundation stone was laid, and Julius's emergence alive was taken as an auspicious sign of divine approval of the enterprise.

No sooner had Bramante's plans taken shape than Julius was seized by another audacious idea; he commanded Michelangelo to devise a truly mighty monument to him to be erected in the new cathedral. The quarrels that ensued over the tomb are well known, and indeed they continued long after Julius's death so that the final structure was but a pale shadow of the two men's grandiose dream. However, one awe-inspiring figure remains to give us a sense of the original scale of both the project and the character of the patron, the idealised portrait of Julius as Moses.

Once Julius had approved one of Michelangelo's designs for the tomb, the sculptor set out for the quarries at Carrara to select the marble. On his return he was dispirited, it rained incessantly, the marbles were held up on the road and, worse still, Julius's ardour had cooled inexplicably. The artist was in a quandary and without money for his lodgings or his assistants.

Julius was capricious by nature, and no doubt he realised that he would never live to see St Peter's sufficiently advanced to house his tomb. Furthermore, in 1506, he decided to have the Sistine Chapel ceiling decorated. When it was first mentioned to Michelangelo he demurred, offering all sorts of excuses, but eventually in 1508 Julius got his way and work on the ceiling began. Neurotically jealous of Bramante and Raphael (who had just arrived in the city), Michelangelo locked himself in the chapel, admitting no one save the boy who ground his colours and Julius, whom he could not very well keep out. The old pope was terrified that he might die before the ceiling was finished and impatiently climbed up the scaffolding to berate Michelangelo for being so slow. But Julius was unfair; the ceiling is virtually the creation of a single mind and hand and it is a miracle that Michelangelo completed it in a mere four years. Of course, Julius was right to commission it, for it released gifts of pictorial expression in Michelangelo that the artist himself scarcely suspected.

Many of the older painters, including Perugino, hoped in vain for papal commissions. When Julius, tired of being daily reminded of his hated Borgia predecessor, moved into another suite of rooms in the Vatican he chose Raphael, Perugino's pupil, who had never before attempted a large fresco cycle, to decorate his apartments. No one was better endowed to interpret the learned, forceful subjects concerned with the proof of divinity through the activities of reason and miraculous intervention. Julius himself figures in one scene, *The Mass of Bolsena,* as a resolute defender of the faith. This is not strange, for like all his contemporaries Julius did not spurn supernatural manifestations and pondered omens and consulted the stars.

Leo X

Leo X's accession in 1513 changed the Vatican overnight. When he was raised to the cardinalate at the tender age of thirteen his father, Lorenzo de' Medici, gave him sanguine advice: 'A man of your kind should use silk and

177

THE BIRTH OF THE VIRGIN

1514
Andrea del Sarto 1486–1531
fresco
Santissima Annunziata, Florence

While Michelangelo, Raphael and
Leonardo were absent from the city,
Andrea del Sarto became the leading
artist in Florence. This work shows
Andrea's debt to Leonardo in the soft
modelling, which enhances the easy
movements and ample volumes of his
figures while increasing the illusion of
depth; likewise Michelangelo inspired his
fine draughtsmanship; but the delicate
colour is entirely his own.

178

LEO X WITH CARDINALS
LUDOVICO DE' ROSSI AND
GIULIANO DE' MEDICI

1518–19
Raphael 1483–1520
oil, 61 × 45 in (154 × 114 cm)
Palazzo Pitti, Florence

Raphael was a remarkable portraitist.
Although he was inspired in his youth by
the first glimpse of Leonardo's *Mona Lisa*,
he outstripped the latter in the intimacy of
his psychological insight, which here
involves the interplay of three distinct
personalities. The 'natural' grouping was
unified by an encroaching chiaroscuro
which added richness to the colour and
substance of the forms, especially to the
flabby bulk of the self-indulgent pope.

jewellery with discretion. Rather have some exquisite antiques and beautiful books.' Leo loved luxury and did not heed him. Raphael shows him characteristically seated before a splendid illuminated tome, with a magnifying glass in his well-manicured hand. Unlike Julius, Leo's grasp of literature was profound. The finest poets and scholars were attracted to his court, including his old tutor Bibbiena, Pietro Bembo and Baldassare Castiglione, whose book was the model for civilised conduct; all were Raphael's friends. **17**

Leo encouraged a sumptuous way of life in Roman society, but even he was astonished at the reckless splendour when the banker, Agostino Chigi, entertained him to dinner at the Villa Farnesina. The beautiful villa was built on the outskirts of Rome between 1509–11 and was never intended to be lived in; Raphael and the architect Peruzzi collaborated, evolving an ensemble of rare distinction. **18**

All the works of the time have one thing in common: a nobility of scale fostered by a closer, more sophisticated scrutiny of classical remains. In 1516 Leo appointed Raphael overseer of the Roman antiquities and ordered him to draw up an archaeological report on their condition. As a result Raphael excavated the Golden House of Nero which was the prototype for his Villa Madama, where the artist dreamt of entertaining his guests with dramatic performances staged in the gardens and viewed from the amphitheatre terraced in the hillside above. But Raphael died before it was completed, worn out by the excessive commissions given to him by his patrons.

A year later, in 1521, Leo himself died. Having spent to the hilt, he had emptied the Vatican coffers and there was not even sufficient money to buy new candles for his funeral. Even worse, he bequeathed his successor a hideous legacy of political and religious confusion, for Luther had defied the pontiff five years before and the Reformation had begun. In Rome the High Renaissance was over and a new less-rational ethos and style, called Mannerism, was to take its place.

Florence and Clement VII

Meanwhile, in August 1512, a detachment of Spanish troops descended on Tuscany, plundering and murdering as they went; the panic-stricken Florentines hastily paid a huge ransom for their safety. Inadequate, guileless Soderini fled in terror. His steadfast refusal to betray his French allies earned him no credit and Machiavelli's cynical epitaph on his old master summed up everyone's sentiments: 'Pluto snorted: silly soul, hell is no place for you; your place is in the limbo of babies.' Thus the brief republic perished; time was ripe for the reinstatement of the Medici.

Ostensibly, Leo's nephew Lorenzo now governed the city, but his youth made him a mere papal pawn. In 1515 Leo paid a triumphal visit to his native city. It was preceded by feverish activity and even the churches became temporary workshops for the construction of ornate floats. The climax of the decorations was achieved by the sculptor Sansovino, who devised a superb trompe l'oeil façade on board for the cathedral. This audacious piece of ephemera has long since vanished, but echoes of the design are to be found in one of Andrea del Sarto's Scalzo frescos.

Young Lorenzo died in 1519 and was succeeded by the pope's right-hand man, Cardinal Giulio de' Medici, who was the illegitimate son of Leo's murdered uncle, Giuliano, and destined to become Clement VII. In 1520 he commissioned Michelangelo to build the family mausoleum. At first a **203** massive catafalque was to stand in the centre, but eventually the only Medici to be prominently commemorated were Leo's likeable, scholarly brother Giuliano, whose delicate physique was ill-suited to the Roman armour recalling his elevation to the captaincy of the church, and Lorenzo, a more viciously ambitious man whose desire for a dukedom bankrupted

179
THE TEMPIETTO

begun 1502
Donato Bramante 1444–1506
San Pietro in Montorio, Rome

A misinterpretation of early texts led to the belief that St Peter was martyred on the site where Ferdinand and Isabella of Spain caused Bramante to erect the Tempietto. Its round shape was common to Early Christian martyria, but the actual form was culled from such Roman remains as the Temple of Vesta (plate **34**) or the Temple of the Sibyl at Tivoli, although he replaced the ornate Corinthian by the severe Tuscan Doric order. The lantern, with its alien motifs, was added later.

180
THE SALA DELLE PROSPETTIVE

c. 1511
Baldassare Peruzzi 1481–1536
Villa Farnesina, Rome

When, in 1509, the Sienese banker Agostino Chigi chose his compatriot, Peruzzi, to build the first 'villa suburbana', the architect was also required to decorate part of the interior. This celebrated piece of illusionism momentarily deceives the visitor, who imagines that he is looking at actual views of Rome. Peruzzi revived the antique theatre and his stage sets probably inspired this novel scheme.

THE STAIRS IN THE VESTIBULE

designed 1558/59
Michelangelo Buonarroti 1475–1564
Biblioteca Laurenziana, Florence

Almost twenty-five years after his departure from Florence, Michelangelo sent Vasari a model for the staircase, which was built by Vasari and Ammanati. Its spirit is quite alien to that of the reading room. Though the central flight was for dignitaries and the side for their servants, perhaps the curved and angular shapes symbolised the hazardous pursuit of knowledge and the irresistible spread of the learning acquired in the room above.

182 *above*

THE READING ROOM

begun 1524
Michelangelo Buonarroti 1475–1564
Biblioteca Laurenziana, Florence

Difficult projects appealed to Michelangelo. He scorned a convenient site in the market place and elected to build the library above the clerics' quarters. As a result the pilasters, which are usually merely ornamental, mask the wall buttresses which were necessitated by the great weight of the books housed in the reading room. Furthermore his sense of volume led to the creation here of the first room in which the design of the walls, ceiling and floor form a totality.

183

CASKET

1530–32
Valerio Belli 1465–1546
rock crystal mounted in silver gilt and enamelled
each panel 5·75 × 5·5 in (15 × 14·5 cm)
Museo degli Argenti, Florence

As Vasari noted that Belli 'had such undoubtable skill that no one would equal him or turn out more works than he', it is surprising that the casket occupied him for two years. But he wished to reward Clement VII, who had shown him much encouragement, with a piece of exquisite refinement. In 1535, however, the pope parted with it to Francis I on the occasion· of the marriage of his son, the future Henry II, to Catherine de' Medici.

184
THE MEDICI VASE

1583, Bernardo Buontalenti 1536–1608
lapis lazuli, Museo degli Argenti, Florence

In the sixteenth century the Medici commissioned the finest craftsmen to fashion objects from semi-precious stones such as onyx, lapis lazuli and chalcedony. These were unlike the simple Roman vessels mounted by contemporary goldsmiths which were collected in the fifteenth century; instead the pieces were embellished by intricate carvings of motifs such as classical masks. This vase was intended for the Studiolo (plate **195**) and is a fine example of Buontalenti's style.

185 *left*
VASE WITH A FIGURE OF HERCULES

1581
Michele Mazzafirri, c. 1530–97
jasper
h. 13·5 in (34 cm)
Museo degli Argenti, Florence

The execution of this sophisticated piece for the grand duke Francesco de' Medici was brought to perfection by the common practice of employing experts in various allied crafts. Mazzafirri almost certainly made the little gold Hercules and supplied the design, but the carving of the jasper and the mounting of the pearls in gold was most likely carried out in Milan by the famous Saracchi, who also worked for the houses of Savoy and Bavaria.

THE SCHOOL OF ATHENS

1510–11
Raphael 1483–1520
fresco
Stanza della Segnatura, Vatican Palace, Rome

The architecture is so close to Bramante's ideas for St Peter's that it may have been drawn by him: it is entirely Roman and quite un-Athenian. Beneath the lofty spaces the figures move freely, analogous to the range of the human spirit bounded solely by reason. Raphael's style is fresh, owing much to fragments of antique painting, but the colour is his own and exceptionally delicate in the opposition of warm and cool tints.

THE TEMPTATION AND EXPULSION OF ADAM AND EVE

1508–12
Michelangelo Buonarroti 1475–1564
fresco
Sistine Chapel, Vatican Palace, Rome

Michelangelo's first task in the Sistine Chapel was to transform the dull barrel vault by inventing a trompe l'oeil architectural framework, thus varying the spatial depth by an alternating rhythm of expansion and contraction. This scene shows how sensitively he adjusted the design, so that the yielding mood of the Temptation leads inevitably to the fear of the Expulsion.

the Vatican. Thus two of their most effete sons symbolise Medicean power.

182   Another project dear to Clement's heart was the building of the Lauren-
tian Library. Not only had the building to be secure and fireproof, but
Clement required that the room should reflect the nobility of learning. No
wonder that Michelangelo was so exhausted by 1534 that his friends feared
for his life. Besides, he was disgusted by the latest Medici tyranny and in
September he abruptly left for Rome, never to return to Florence.

The Rome he settled in was a very different place from the city he had
left some twenty years before. A terrible event overshadowed Clement's
reign and Romans still trembled at the recollection of it seven years later.
On the night of 6th May 1527 a rabble of forty thousand starving, unpaid
imperial troops from Catholic Spain and Protestant Germany poured into
Rome and sacked it. For four days they pillaged, burned, raped and dese-
crated the churches; so great was the horror that women put out their eyes
rather than witness it. No one escaped and the pope was taken prisoner. By
the end of June, famine and plague scourged citizens and soldiery alike, and
no commander had the courage to impose discipline on his mutinous mob.
Not till November was Clement released, the army paid and some sem-
blance of order restored. Both Catholics and Protestants regarded the sack
188   as a divine judgment on the Holy City. It was left to Michelangelo to give
the dark moment of judgment visible form.

Artists fared no better than anyone else in this holocaust; some like
Peruzzi and Cellini were imprisoned. Of the others, the elegant Parmigi-
anino (who only recently had been hailed as another Raphael) survived
half-crazed striking terror in the hearts of children by his wild appearance,
and in his pictures, once noted for their graceful forms, the poses of the
figures took on a disconcerting hallucinatory jerkiness. Rosso dug up corpses
in the night and practised diabolic rites, but he and his fellow Florentine,
206   Pontormo, had reacted immediately to the early rumblings of spiritual crisis
and their paintings showed none of the idealised confidence that typified
the High Renaissance. The fortunate escaped to Venice.

Venice
Venice's territories were wide flung: she commanded the Adriatic and her
defences against the Turk extended to Dalmatia and Crete, in the north
her interests included Bergamo, and to the west, the city of Verona. True,
Maximilian I, the German emperor, made incursions into her northern
lands, Genoa was her trading rival, Islam represented a constant threat and
Vasco da Gama's discovery of a sea route to India disturbed her commercial
security. French ambitions in Lombardy needed careful watching too, and
in Julius's time relations with the Vatican were often uncertain and stormy,
but all these factors were mere irritants compared to the catastrophe which
engulfed central Italy in the 1520s. The system of government remained un-
challenged, the religious communities were rich, and until the middle of
the century the patrician merchants still enjoyed a scarcely diminished
prosperity. Equally, the Venetian attitude to doctrinal strife was more
tolerant than elsewhere, even German Lutherans were welcome in the city,
and Venetian Renaissance culture was enriched by the proximity of small
cultivated courts on the Venetian mainland.

Among these courts was that of the ex-queen of Cyprus Caterina
Cornaro at Asolo where Pietro Bembo composed his love poems *Gli
Asolani*. Not surprisingly the desire to recreate a kind of buccolic golden age
made Virgil's *Eclogues* and the *Georgics* favourite reading, in preference to
the heroic strains of the *Aeneid*. The pictorial interpretation of this dream
210   fell to Giorgione; he was young, handsome, amorous and a welcome guest
at parties because of his skill as a lutenist and beautiful singing voice. Alas,

188
THE LAST JUDGMENT
1534–41
Michelangelo Buonarroti 1475–1564
40 × 45 ft (10·25 × 13·71 m)
Sistine Chapel, Vatican Palace, Rome

When the painting was unveiled Pope
Paul III was so carried away that he was
heard to mutter, 'Lord, charge me not
with my sins when Thou shalt come on
the Day of Judgment.' It is the most
complete expression of Michelangelo's
'terribilità', and the self-portrait in the skin
held out by St Bartholomew betrays a
spiritual desolation bordering on despair
which marked his later years.

189
PIETRO ARETINO
1545, Titian 1485/89–1575
oil, 42·5 × 29·75 in (108 × 75 cm)
Palazzo Pitti, Florence

Aretino, as his name suggests, was Tuscan by birth. This portrait was dispatched to Duke Cosimo I in Florence. It is one of Titian's greatest essays in portraiture; the composition is simple but vigorous and his feeling for sumptuous texture is gratified in the bold, fluent accents which bring out the lustrous sheen of the silken collar. These, however, are merely a setting for the superbly alert head which betrays all the contrary aspects of his friend's character.

190
POPE PAUL III
WITH HIS NEPHEWS
1545–46
Titian, c. 1485/89–1575
oil
83 × 68·75 in (210 × 174 cm)
Museo Nazionale, Naples

By the time that Titian executed this family group the pope had cause to rue his youthful excesses and suspect the motives of his nephews. Titian captured the false Ottavio, his obsequious bow emphasised by the great looped up curtain behind, and the old man's baleful, suspicious glare. The painting was never finished.

he was carried off by the plague in 1510, but not before he had revolutionised Venetian painting with the idealised sensuality and gentle landscapes whose poetry Titian was to translate into a more assertive realism.

When Titian painted *The Assumption* it was so revolutionary that the Franciscans of the Frari momentarily recoiled from such overt physical immediacy, but they changed their minds, and when it was unveiled in 1518, even Sanudo, the state chronicler, was so impressed by Titian's prowess that he mentioned it in his records. The altarpiece was executed only a few years earlier than Pontormo's *Resurrection*; nothing could afford 20(a sharper contrast with the prevailing mood in Florence.

During the next decade Titian neglected his obligations as official state painter and was more active in the service of the rulers at Ferrara, Mantua and Urbino. Many of these works have been dispersed: Alfonso d'Este, anxious to be in Charles V's good books, gave several of the finest canvases to the emperor; and the Gonzagas sold their collection in the seventeenth century; but the works for the ruler of Urbino, Francesco Maria della Rovere, passed to Florence. The recumbent *Venus of Urbino* is a superb 20(example of those qualities of sensuous truth, fine design and colour that Titian's patrons admired.

There were a number of talented portraitists in Venice including Lotto, 211 whose friendship with the northern reformers encouraged the revelation of hidden depths of psychological unease. But in looking at Titian's portrait of his friend Aretino we can concur with Sansovino's exclamation: 'What 18(rich man would not like to have his portrait painted by Titian?'

Pietro Aretino was a skilful man of letters whose scurrilous, defamatory verses often made him feared. He was also the first art critic in the modern sense of the term, and used this position to his advantage, flattering and bullying artists by turn until they found it politic to give him their paintings; thus he amassed one of the finest collections in Venice. Michelangelo, who failed to succumb to his entreaties, was cruelly libelled by him. Yet it must be admitted that he had an intelligent sensitive eye, and in one of his letters to Titian, vividly describing the Venetian scene below his window, we can see what drew the two men together.

Sometimes, of course, Aretino's friendship could work to the artist's advantage. The unfortunate Sansovino discovered this when a pier in St Mark's Library split during a severe frost and it required the combined 20. efforts of Titian, the ambassador of Charles V and Aretino to secure his release from prison. The Venetian authorities had charged the architect with negligence, but their summary treatment can be explained by the fact that it was a commission that they were anxious to see completed. About fifty years earlier the famous Greek theologian, Bessarion, had died and left his celebrated collection of books to the state, and its failure to provide suitable accommodation for the bequest became a source of embarrassment.

The Counter-Reformation in Rome

Titian's arrival in 1545 in Rome was a prelude to an even more important event in his life. Charles V, who had met the painter in 1532, invited him to come to the court at Augsburg; thus began a long friendship between the Hapsburg emperor and Titian. It reminds us of the dramatic changes that had occurred in the artist's social prestige: Leonardo, Dürer and Titian enjoyed the friendship of kings, and Michelangelo was treated as an equal by the succession of popes who employed him, including Paul III whom Titian depicted with his two egregious nephews. It is one of the 19(most devastatingly truthful groups ever painted and was never completed.

Despite his nepotism, Paul III was quick to recognise the urgent need for reform in the church, and on 13th December 1543 the Council of Trent was convened; it was to meet intermittently for the next twenty years. During that time doctrines were defined, rules for clerical conduct laid down, and not even music and art escaped its strictures. Indeed, it provided the inspiration for the erection of Palladio's Venetian church, San Giorgio

93 Maggiore, where the construction was determined by the requirements for the performance of Palestrina's masses, which were regarded as the most perfect musical setting of the liturgy.

91 The major edifice of the Counter-Reformation was St Peter's. Although begun thirty years before, very little had happened; money had run out. During Leo's reign the traffic in indulgences had reached scandalous proportions, especially in Germany where the greed of the archbishop of Mainz found a ready instrument in the Dominican Tetzel, who arrived in Wittenberg (where Luther was a professor at the university) in search of money; Tetzel's visit had been the catalyst that set the Reformation in motion. From that moment it was useless to look for support from the Germans, and even at home the faithful were disillusioned; after the sack of Rome they had no heart for such grandiose schemes as rebuilding St Peter's.

Now, with the renewed spiritual zeal of the Counter-Reformation, building began afresh, though at first with no success; San Gallo's plan was incompetent and the contractors artfully inflated the costs. Michelangelo was so incensed that he produced a design showing how the expense could be drastically reduced. He was consequently very unpopular with the contractors, but in 1546 Paul III appointed him overseer of St Peter's.

Michelangelo was a man of the most profound spiritual conviction who counted among his intimate friends the most austere supporters of the Counter-Reformation: the devout widow Vittoria Colonna, the Englishman Cardinal Pole and St Ignatius Loyola, the founder of the Jesuits. To Michelangelo the building of St Peter's was a sacred act and he refused all payment; labouring incessantly, he daily inspected the site to consult the

191 workmen and to make modifications. The dome presented an intractable problem and unhappily he never saw it carried out, for when he died in 1564 the structure had only risen to the drum; it was left to his successor, Giacomo della Porta, to interpret his ideas.

When Paul died in 1549, his successor Julius III was overwhelmed by the magnitude of his spiritual and political responsibilities: he was beset by French and Spanish pressure; the success of the Protestant campaigns in the Tyrol led to a suspension of the Council of Trent; and most horrifying of all, the Turks, flushed by their triumphs in southern Italy and the Hungarian plains, boasted that they would soon be in Rome. Julius's solution was to build himself an exquisite retreat on the outskirts of the city. There he delighted in the gardens which were excitingly laid out on different levels. Vasari, who had met the pope on the way to the electoral conclave and had high hopes for his preferment in the new reign, was employed as a kind of advisory overseer but soon left in a fit of pique. The labours were divided between Vignola who was mainly responsible for the villa itself,

192 and Ammanati who designed the elegant, dramatic nymphaeum, inspired by Hadrian's Villa outside Tivoli. Not that the two architects were left in peace to carry out their ideas; Julius was frequently on the scene, together with Michelangelo, proffering advice and suggesting alterations. In some ways the Villa Giulia was the culmination of Raphael's earlier experiments in the Villa Madama and the novelties devised by his brilliant pupil, Giulio Romano, in the layout of the Palazzo del Tè at Mantua.

Palladio and the Venetian mainland

On the Venetian mainland around 1555, the conception of a villa under-

194 went a remarkable change. Except in rare cases, such as the Villa Rotonda,

191
ST PETER'S FROM THE EAST
1546–90
Michelangelo Buonarroti 1475–1564
Rome

Maderno added the nave in deference to liturgical needs and Bernini transformed the interior, so that the scale of Michelangelo's achievement is most truly visible in the exterior of the choir and transept. The dome caused him such concern that he wrote to Vasari asking for information on Brunelleschi's methods. Della Porta had to abandon Michelangelo's hemisphere and introduced a more acute curve.

192
THE NYMPHAEUM
1550–55
Giacomo da Vignola 1507–73
and Bartolomeo Ammanati 1511–92
Villa Giulia, Rome

By the mid-century Italian garden design became more ambitious, taking advantage of water engineering, natural changes of level and sometimes resorting to massive excavations to create a surprise effect. The nymphaeum became the most popular device and that in the Villa Giulia is one of the loveliest examples. Graceful architectural and sculptural forms are combined with a skilled exploitation of the natural characteristics of the site.

it was no longer constructed purely as a place for cultivated dalliance. The Rotonda was exceptional because it was built for a retired monsignor who liked giving parties. Palladio defended its unusual design, writing: "Because it enjoys the most lovely views on all sides, some screened, others more distant, and others reaching the horizon, loggias were made on each face.'

The other villas that Palladio created arose out of a fusion of climate, terrain and economic necessity. They were the practical, elegant dwellings of a new race of gentleman farmers. At last, the Venetians felt the pinch; the slow caravans from the east were superseded by speedy, foreign maritime routes. Even the distant English threatened her supremacy in the Mediterranean and the concentrated power of the great European monarchies was inimical to the prosperous survival of the old city-states.

In an effort to stave off disaster, the Venetian patricians turned their attention to the ill-cultivated malarial swamps of the hinterland. Rather than rely on others to conduct their new industry, farming, they left their palaces in Venice to live in the villas Palladio designed for them. They were

193
SAN GIORGIO MAGGIORE
begun 1565
Andrea Palladio 1518–80
Venice

The splendid stone façade masks the humbler brick of the main body of the church. The treatment of the façade is typical of all Palladio's Venetian churches with its raised pedimented central bay and more modest, lower order articulating the flanking wings. The latter, because of the girth of the columns in the centre section, appear to be slightly recessed.

194
THE VILLA ROTONDA
1550–51
Andrea Palladio 1518–80
Vicenza

Palladio's wanderings among the Roman ruins led him to the strange conclusion that the temple portico descended from ancient domestic building practice, so it became for him the most desirable kind of frontage. This particular villa also had a strong appeal for English architects in the eighteenth century and Burlington's Chiswick House and Campbell's Mereworth Castle were partly inspired by it.

195

THE STUDIOLO OF FRANCESCO DE' MEDICI

1570–73
Giorgio Vasari 1511–74 and assistants
Palazzo Vecchio, Florence

Although the decoration was entrusted to Vasari, he was enfeebled by age, and much of the conception and painting of the learned allegories of the Four Elements was left to a team of twenty assistants whose style favoured the elegant colour and drawing of the late sixteenth century. The room was intended for the grand duke's antiquities and precious objects.

THE CAPITOL
begun 1546
Michelangelo Buonarroti 1475–1564
Rome

Michelangelo's transformation of the Capitoline Square was his
greatest secular commission. The Palazzo Senatorio and the Palazzo
dei Conservatori already existed, but he dramatically altered them,
the latter being refaced so that the Giant order makes its first
appearance in Rennaissance domestic architecture. The unity was
completed by the erection of the functionless Palazzo Nuovo.

a remarkable group of men, epitomised by Daniele Barbaro, an urbane, well-read collector of works of art, who also prided himself on his grasp of water engineering and agricultural innovations. Daniele had been a diplomat and was richer than most of his kind, so that his villa at Maser, decorated by Vittoria's sculptures without and by Veronese's frescos within, was more splendid than usual. It was the result of a happy collaboration between artist and patron, for Daniele Barbaro had accompanied Palladio to Rome in 1554 and two years later Palladio illustrated his patron's edition of Vitruvius. The villa at Maser was one of the few to be actually erected according to the scale of the original conception. Alas, we know how sadly reduced most of them were because Palladio published the drawings with the original dimensions in his *I Quattro Libri dell' Architettura*.

An extraordinarily large number of treatises on aesthetics began to appear in the latter half of the sixteenth century. They stemmed from the newly formed academies, and although Palladio's volume is notable for its practicality, his first patron, the nobleman Trissino, invited his protégé to become a member of the Accademia Olimpica which he founded in Vicenza in 1555. This was the first academy, and differed from its successors in being a gathering of men famed in many branches of learning, including mathematics. However, when Vasari delivered the opening oration at the Accademia del Disegno in Florence in 1562, it was clear that his concern lay solely in the promulgation of canons of artistic perfection.

Florence and Rome

In many ways the academy impeded real imaginative invention, but it reflected the autocratic tyranny prevailing in Florence. To maintain his

201 hold, the grand duke Cosimo I instituted a vastly inflated bureaucracy. Vasari designed the Uffizi especially to house this army of civil servants, and the regimented appearance of the exterior reflects its deadening purpose.

For some time Cosimo had grown dissatisfied with his ancestral residence, the Palazzo Medici. A hundred years before, Cosimo de' Medici had turned down Brunelleschi's plan for the palace as being unseemly and vainglorious and had chosen Michelozzo's more modest design instead; now with an arrogant disregard for civic traditions Duke Cosimo decided to move into

117 the old centre of Florentine liberty, the Palazzo Vecchio. Vasari, assisted by a huge retinue of assistants, was called in to transform it into palatial

202 apartments. Bronzino designed magnificent tapestries and one of the most

195 superbly refined schemes of decoration was evolved for the Studiolo of

10 Francesco de' Medici. Cosimo and his son were generous patrons, en-

200 couraging the genius of Benvenuto Cellini, Giovanni da Bologna and several others.

From about 1520, painters, sculptors and architects displayed an obsessive liking for sharply receding vistas. The most significant and exciting expression of space in the sixteenth century appears in Michelangelo's plan for

196 the Capitoline Square. In 1536, when Charles V had paid a triumphal visit to the city, the Romans felt ashamed that the Capitol, the old 'caput mundi' of antiquity and still the centre of their civic administration, was reduced to such a squalid mud heap that it was inaccessible to the emperor. Michelangelo miraculously transformed it, exploiting its trapezoid axes and placing the illustrious statue of Marcus Aurelius (still believed to be Constantine) in the centre from which radiates a star-patterned pavement.

It is indeed fitting that this superb entity should have been created in Rome; for the history and art of the sixteenth century in Italy was rooted in and radiated from Rome, inspired by antiquity and the political and spiritual tribulations of the Vatican.

Maria Shirley

197

THE APOTHEOSIS OF VENICE

c. 1580
Paolo Veronese, c. 1528–88
oil
Doges' Palace, Venice

Veronese was uniquely endowed to undertake the decoration of the Doges' Palace, for his command of foreshortening and illusionism gave to such sumptuous allegories as this a credibility and pomp necessary to the praise of the state. Yet because of his light pigments, azure, coral, pearl and gold, his conceptions do not overpower the spectator. Although he was born in Verona, his colour and the play of light on marble and stuffs was essentially Venetian.

198

THE FALL OF THE GIANTS

c. 1533
Giulio Romano, c. 1492–1546
fresco
Palazzo del Tè, Mantua

The palace was, in fact, the first 'villa suburbana' to be built in north-east Italy and was merely a summer retreat for the duke's guests to repair to and admire his horses, his gardens and the sophisticated decorations within. These betray the lowering of moral tone which characterised the later Gonzagas; many of the scenes are salacious and even this famous room shocks by the claustrophobic effect engendered by Giulio Romano's cunning perspective and exaggerated forms.

199

DAVID

1501–04, Michelangelo Buonarroti 1475–1564
marble, h. 171 in (434 cm), Galleria dell' Accademia, Florence

In fifteenth-century Florence sculptors were daunted by the sheer
size of this block of marble. Agostino di Duccio gave up after
gouging out the gap between the legs. Later they regarded the stone
greedily. Finally Soderini awarded it to Michelangelo who alone
could create a masterpiece from its awkward proportions. He was
inspired by the antique Horse Tamers on the Quirinale, but infused
David with such life that Soderini regarded him as the greatest
genius in all Italy.

200

THE RAPE OF THE SABINES

c. 1579–83, Giovanni da Bologna 1529–1608
marble, 13 ft 4·5 in (4·10 m), Loggia dei Lanzi, Florence

Giovanni's aesthetic, rather than literary, preoccupations are dis-
closed in a letter to the duke of Parma. Describing the bronze
which contained the germ of the idea for the marble group, he
said: 'The aforesaid figures can be interpreted as the rape of Helen,
or even as that of Proserpine, or as the rape of one of the Sabine
women. The subject was chosen to give scope to the knowledge
and study of art.'

201

COSIMO I DE' MEDICI

1545–47, Benvenuto Cellini 1500–71
bronze, h. 43·25 in (110 cm), Museo Nazionale, Florence . .

Cellini lavished his finest workmanship on this bust (as indeed he reminded Cosimo in 1548, and the payment was still outstanding in 1570!). Originally the armour was heightened with parcel gilt and the eyes enamelled. That bolting, nervous stare affords a vivid insight into the tyrant of Florence whose expression is both callous and weak. The turn of the head is typical of mid-century court portraiture and is redolent of the precarious despotism exercised by rulers throughout Europe.

202 *below left*

JOSEPH AND POTIPHAR'S WIFE

1546–49, tapestry, Palazzo Vecchio, Florence

This splendid set of Florentine tapestries devoted to the Old Testament story of Joseph may have been designed in Bronzino's workshop. He was court painter to Duke Cosimo and was also responsible for the decoration of the chapel of his consort Eleonora of Toledo in the palace. The scenes are characterised by the same excited activity and refined idealisation, especially in the drawing of the heads.

203 *below right*

DAWN

from the tomb of Lorenzo de' Medici
1520–34, Michelangelo Buonarroti 1475–1564
marble, New Sacristy, San Lorenzo, Florence

Even as late as 1562, Cosimo I tried to get Michelangelo to write to him specifying how he wished the sculptures in the chapel to be set out, for when Michelangelo left Florence the famous allegories were still lying, uncompleted on the floor. The figures of Giuliano and Lorenzo, however, are most elaborately wrought, and offer a poignant contrast to the urgent force, still partially imprisoned in the rough block, of the allegorical figures resting on the lid of the sarcophagus below.

204

THE LIBRARY OF ST MARK'S

begun 1536
Jacopo Sansovino 1486–1570
Venice

A dramatic change had taken place in Italian architecture;
Bramante's severity gave way to an effect of accumulated richness.
In the upper zone not only are columns attached to piers, but
colonnettes flank the arches leading the eye to the deeply recessed
windows. The keystones become masks, the spandrels are infilled
with reliefs and the frieze animated by one of the most beloved
Renaissance motifs, putti holding swags of fruit.

205 *bottom*

THE TEATRO OLIMPICO

1579–80
Andrea Palladio 1518–80, Vicenza

As early as 1561 Palladio devised the setting for the performance
given before the members of the Accademia Olimpica of his patron
Trissino's tragedy, *Sofonisba*. In 1579 they all clubbed together to
erect a permanent theatre and, naturally, the commission went to
Palladio. Like all Renaissance theatres it is made entirely of wood.
Palladio took great pains to make his theatre as authentically Roman
as possible and pored over the most obscure passages in Vitruvius.

206 *right*

THE RESURRECTION

1522–25
Jacopo Pontormo 1494–1556
fresco
The Certosa, Val d'Ema

Pontormo's style was a far cry from that
of his master, Andrea del Sarto, for he
was one of the earliest exponents of
Mannerism. He counted among his most
treasured possessions a copy of Dürer's
woodcuts of the Passion. The knotty
joints may stem from the rugosities so
beloved of German artists, but the strange
dream-like mood, the abstract patterning
of the huddled shapes of the guards and
the stiff, weightless body of the Risen
Christ are Pontormo's alone.

207 *bottom left*

THE GUIDARELLI EFFIGY *detail*

1525
Tullio Lombardo, c. 1455–1532
marble, Museo Civico, Ravenna

Pomponius Gauricus's exorbitant claim that Tullio was 'the greatest of all sculptors that any age had seen' can be put down to friendship. However, the learned Paduan humanist could have found much to admire genuinely in his work, especially Tullio's beautifully controlled classical forms inspired by the antique sculptures he kept in his studio. The Lombardo family was largely responsible for the typical Renaissance form of Venetian monuments.

208 *bottom right*

THE ASCENSION

1520–23
Antonio Correggio 1489/94–1534
fresco, San Giovanni Evangelista, Parma

Correggio almost certainly visited Rome in his youth and this coupled with the influence of Mantegna explains his obsessive fascination for forms seen from below in extreme foreshortening. His figures float free on clouds and are bathed in a radiant golden haze. He was the first to perceive that Leonardo's soft modelling could be extended to create an all-embracing atmospheric effect.

209 *right*

THE VENUS OF URBINO

c. 1538
Titian, c. 1485/89–1575
oil
47·25 × 65 in (120 × 165 cm)
Uffizi Gallery, Florence

When Giorgione died, Titian completed his *Sleeping Venus*. This inspired Titian to paint a Venus series of his own, although his goddess is wide awake. This example was painted at a moment of golden equilibrium in Titian's style when touch, colour and contour was rich but distinct. Shortly afterwards his pigments became more sombre, the handling looser and the outlines of the forms blurred by shadow.

210 *above*

THE TEMPEST

c. 1505, Giorgione 1475/77–1510, oil
Accademia di Belle Arti, Venice

It is vain to seek a precise literary meaning in this picture, for X-ray has revealed that Giorgione improvised, changing the sex and position of the figures. This is perhaps the first 'free' invention of the Renaissance. Thus the mystery is conjured from purely visual sources: the averted gaze, the distance separating the soldier and gipsy and, above all, the lightning playing over the little town of Castelfranco, Giorgione's birthplace.

211

A YOUNG MAN IN HIS STUDY *detail*

c. 1524, Lorenzo Lotto, c. 1480–1556, oil
Accademia di Belle Arti, Venice

Unlike Titian's, Lotto's sitters often display a nervosity of temperament bordering on the neurotic. Here the pallid young man's tense features suggest that the fine distinctions of intellectual activity cause him pain. The sharp direction of his pose, the paper in his hand and the general arrangement of the room set up a number of contrary axes in the design which emphasize the restlessness of the characterisation.

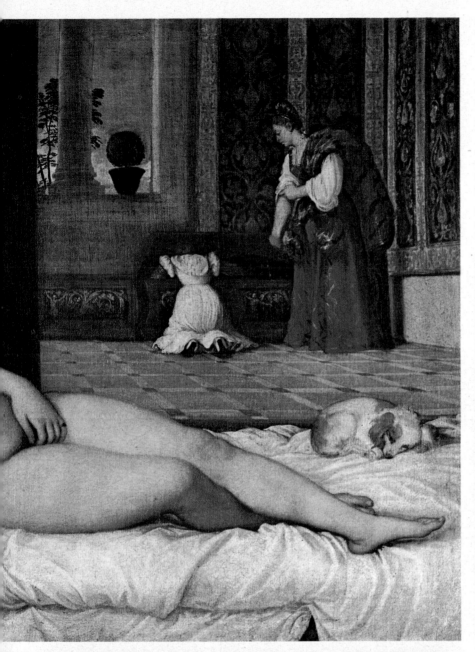

212 *below*

THE ASSUMPTION
OF THE VIRGIN

1518
Titian, c. 1485/89–1575
oil, 22 ft 8 in × 11 ft 10 in (6·90 × 3·60m)
Santa Maria Gloriosa dei Frari, Venice

Around 1500 the Venetian sculptor Tullio
Lombardo executed a relief of *The
Assumption* for the Barbarigo tomb. Titian
obviously knew this work and the
parallels are striking – the same shallow
space, like a 'tableau vivant', and similar
gestures silhouetted against the sky.
Whereas, however, each figure exists in
isolation in Tullio's relief, Titian unifies the
group so that all the apostles are gripped by
identical astonishment and grief.

213 *left*

THE NATIVITY *detail*

1576–81
Jacopo Tintoretto 1518–91
oil
17 ft 11 in × 14 ft 5 in (5·45 × 4·38 m)
Scuola di San Rocco, Venice

Titian's most serious rival in Venice never
aspired to the commissions from foreign
monarchs and, apart from his work for
the state, Tintoretto's most famous work
was undertaken for the Scuola di San Rocco
(1564–88). *The Nativity* is typical of his
unusual powers of composition; the Holy
Family is elevated to the loft, while the
shepherds for all their yearning gestures
still seem bounded by the earthy realities
of the cattle. A suffused starlight bathes
the scene.

In the Counter-Reformation climate of the late sixteenth century Italy underwent many changes. But it was not until the threat of Protestantism had been overcome and the great Catholic reformers, St Ignatius Loyola, St Philip Neri, St Charles Borromeo and St Teresa, were all dead that the spirit of the era began to be reflected in contemporary art and to gather momentum with ensuing generations. Harsh and gloomy Spanish influence was replaced by a rapprochement with France. A feeling of relief ensued and with it a new joie de vivre. This was mingled with exultant piety which called upon the faithful to rejoice and participate in elaborate and saintly visions and to admire and emulate the heroic deeds of biblical heroes and heroines, such as David and Judith. Scenes of repentance were also popular: St Mary Magdalene was a favourite subject. Yet discipline was relaxed and the atmosphere ripe for new artistic manifestations which would carry into effect theories already established but scarcely implemented: clarity and intelligibility in execution combined with emotional stimulus to piety.

Rome

Rome, rich and international, had already emerged as the formative influence in the arts for all Italy. Its patronage was concentrated chiefly in the hands of the papal families and their adherents. The importance of the city-states and feudal courts had declined accordingly.

Two great painters reached the climax of their oeuvre in the last decade of the sixteenth century. Neither of them was Roman but both found their opportunities in that city; and each in a very different fashion made a complete break with the current late Mannerist output. The ideas and intentions of the Lombard Michelangelo Merisi, called Caravaggio, were at variance with academic theorists, past and present. He never attempted the fashionable and decorative medium of fresco, dispensed with any form of preparation and painted whatever lay in his mind's eye directly upon the canvas. This habit, together with his revolutionary use of light to crystallise the forms and rivet the attention of the spectator, gave his work a hitherto-unknown immediacy and poignancy. The impact was further increased by violence of gesture and a realism in the treatment of religious subjects which paradoxically shocked the populace and the lower clergy, but attracted rich liberals like Cardinal del Monte, the Marchese Giustiniani and Cardinal Scipione Borghese. Caravaggio's influence in Rome was short-lived but it had repercussions, especially at Naples and in the Netherlands. Even in Rome his talented followers Vouet and Valentin were Frenchmen.

The other great man was Annibale Carracci, flourishing member of a famous studio at Bologna. He imbibed learned theories and contrived to cater for the taste of an exclusive upper class. Paradoxically, he himself always remained a man of the people and laid far firmer foundations for true contemporary genre painting than Caravaggio. But this was a side line. He won European fame with his fresco decoration of the Palazzo Farnese in Rome for Cardinal Odoardo Farnese. There he depicted Love ennobled by the Gods of Antiquity in mythological scenes from Ovid and other classical sources. Over a thousand preparatory drawings were made, and he re-established the compositional methods used by Raphael. Indeed many saw in his work a return to the High Renaissance. In fact, the brilliant and dazzling vault established the direction of the artistic trends of the next two centuries: the study of classical antiquity and the decorative exuberance of the Baroque.

Under Paul V and Gregory XV, with their nephews and retinues, patronage gathered momentum. The most important event of Paul's reign was the building of a nave for St Peter's, required by new religious circumstances but not in Michelangelo's centrally planned structure. The task was

214
THE ECSTASY OF ST TERESA
detail
1645–52
Gianlorenzo Bernini 1598–1680
Santa Maria della Vittoria, Rome

The Cornaro Chapel, designed by Bernini for the Venetian cardinal, Federigo Cornaro, is one of the most perfect of Baroque works. The scene seems both real and visionary, for Bernini with the use of colour, light and illusionism conveys to the spectator with great force the ecstasy of St Teresa as the angel pierces her heart with the arrow of divine love. Although it fulfilled Bernini's purpose so convincingly, only the central group of St Teresa and the angel are by his own hand.

215
APOLLO AND DAPHNE
1622–25, Gianlorenzo Bernini 1598–1680
marble, life size
Galleria Borghese, Rome

Made for Cardinal Scipione Borghese, this work brings to an end the phase in Bernini's career before Urban VIII ascended the throne. The original cartouche of the subsequently enlarged pedestal is inscribed with lines improvised by Urban when as a cardinal he came to inspect the group.

216
THE TRIUMPH OF DIVINE
PROVIDENCE
detail
1633–39
Pietro Berrettini da Cortona 1596–1669
fresco
Palazzo Barberini, Rome

This vault of the Gran Salone represents in allegorical terms the apotheosis of the papacy in the reign of Urban VIII. Cortona, a protégé of the Barberini, came to complete maturity with this commission and produced the most perfect High Baroque vault in Rome. Enshrined in a laurel wreath held by the theological Virtues are the heraldic Barberini bees.

given to Carlo Maderno, the architect of the new Baroque Santa Susanna. His solution was not altogether successful, although he went to great pains to reproduce Michelangelesque motifs.

Meanwhile Carracci's pupils attained maturity. All were employed in Rome on famous projects. Domenichino, Lanfranco, Reni, Albani, each developed his own manner. Reni had a classical style infused with a certain sweetness which was essentially seventeenth century; while Domenichino, especially in his St Cecilia frescos in San Luigi dei Francesi, drew closer to Raphael than Annibale Carracci had ever done. Albani, too, sought inspiration at the fountainhead, but he had a light-hearted grace which looked forward rather than back; and Lanfranco indicated his heritage as a citizen of Parma by translating Correggio into fully fledged Baroque. A younger artist whose admiration for Ludovico Carracci helped to form his style, Guercino da Cento, brought to Rome a more violent, powerful and 'tenebroso' (low-key) version of the Baroque.

The cardinals Maffeo Barberini and Scipione Borghese launched the genius of the century, Gianlorenzo Bernini. His *David* and *Apollo and* 21 *Daphne* displayed, besides astonishing technical virtuosity and echoes of Hellenism, a new sense of dramatic moment and involvement of the spectator in the creation of a work of art.

The Counter-Reformation had brought forth several new influential religious orders. The most outstanding were Philip Neri's Oratorians and Ignatius Loyola's Jesuits. In spite of differences both combined a juxtaposition of worldliness and mysticism characteristic of the age. Along with the older orders, they were conspicuous patrons of the arts. In the opening decade of the seventeenth century the young Rubens completed three pictures for the choir of the Oratorians' new church, Santa Maria in Vallicella. In Sant' Andrea della Valle the Theatines employed Domenichino and Lanfranco in bitter rivalry. Domenichino painted the pendentives and the vault of the choir while Lanfranco executed the Correggesque, illusionistic dome – the first High Baroque dome – which was finished in 1627.

Maffeo Barberini, who was Pope Urban VIII 1623-44, with considerable justification saw himself as a new Julius II, but there were Counter-Reformation overtones in the splendour of his court. He was a poet in his own right and at the centre of intellectual life. His nephews, especially Cardinal Francesco and Cardinal Antonio Barberini, shared his taste for art and learning. The secretary of the former, Cassiano dal Pozzo, continued the trend for archaeological research and the study of antiquity. He was the personal friend of both Poussin and Duquesnoy. Besides Poussin and Claude, the Barberini encouraged a new generation of Italian artists. The renovation and decoration of their palace at Quattro Fontane, bought from Alessandro Sforza, gave them ample scope. Pietro da Cortona painted the famous vault of the Gran Salone with Divine Providence glorifying the reign of 21 Urban VIII, which marks a turning point in the history of Baroque painting. Spectacular illusions composed of swirling figures moving into infinite depth constitute the elaborate allegory. This contrasts with Andrea Sacchi's *Divine Wisdom* in an adjoining room, which eschews exaggerated illusionism and with few figures maintains an ordered, classical equilibrium. The architect was at first Carlo Maderno, but at his death in 1629 Bernini took over and assumed the direction of all Urban's artistic projects.

These were too numerous to discuss in detail but we may mention Urban's own tomb, with which Bernini set the Baroque pattern for funeral monuments for more than a century; the Baldacchino, the triumphant canopy over the tomb of St Peter for which the Pantheon was despoiled of its bronze ornaments; the decoration of Bramante's piers at the crossing of

St Peter's, for which Bernini himself sculpted St Longinus, while a team of sculptors carried out the rest of the work under his orders. Altarpieces were commissioned for the new chapels. One of them, the *Martyrdom of St Erasmus*, Poussin's only public commission in Rome, was a compromise with the fashionable Baroque style. Its failure to please, in spite of the approbation of Bernini, disposed Poussin, a Frenchman, to follow his bent for small easel pictures painted for private patrons. After a brief interlude of Venetian inspiration, his style grew ever closer to the antique.

Many churches were renovated or built in the religious enthusiasm of the Counter-Reformation. Cortona's Santa Martina e San Luca, financed for the Academy of St Luke by Cardinal Francesco Barberini, established his skill as a Baroque architect. Even more striking was San Carlo alle Quattro Fontane, built by Bernini's greatest rival, the Lombard Francesco Borromini. Applying geometric principles possibly deriving from northern Gothic practice, he created a style which eschewed polychrome marble and relied for effect purely on mathematical unity and the interplay of curves.

Borromini's masterpiece, Sant' Ivo della Sapienza, (ironically, he owed the commission to Bernini) is a star hexagon in ground plan formed by the intersection of two equilateral triangles. The originality of this shape is offset by the use of bizarre late antique motifs apparently derived from Baalbek. His oratory of St Philip Neri is justly famous for the subtle use of curves in the construction of its façade. It was built for Padre Virgilio Spada of the Oratorians who designated him official architect of the congregation. For Vigilio's brother Borromini renovated the Palazzo Spada.

Although learned and aristocratic taste dominated the arts, there were painters, mostly Flemish in nationality, chief of whom was Pieter van Laer, who chose to depict the street life of Rome with great realism and naturalistic verve. In spite of the opposition of the theorists who condemned the choice of 'mean subjects', the work of Van Laer and his Italian follower, Michele Cerquozzi, was snapped up by rich collectors and soon commanded high prices which set these *bambocciate*, as they were called, out of the reach of the common man. The middle-class collector, the lower clergy, the lawyer or doctor had to make do with hack copies of famous pictures or with the work of artists who were out of fashion.

With the accession of the Pamphili Innocent X in 1644 came the disgrace of the whole Barberini family and an almost complete reversal of patronage. Both Bernini's rivals were swept into favour: Borromini and the classicising Bolognese sculptor Alessandro Algardi. Paradoxically, it fell to the latter to initiate the High Baroque relief with his *Leo I and Attila* in St Peter's. The great achievement of Innocent X was the perfection of the Piazza Navona where Borromini was employed in various capacities, while Cortona painted the most elegant of his frescos in the gallery of the Palazzo Pamphili and Bernini was approached to design the Fountain of the Four Rivers. Bernini at this period found time for private commissions. The chapel in Santa Maria della Vittoria representing the Ecstasy of St Teresa, which he built for the Venetian Cardinal Federigo Cornaro, is a perfect example of the complete Baroque entity of the arts of sculpture, painting and architecture united to offer the beholder a mystical experience.

Meanwhile Claude, from Lorraine, reached full maturity in the 1640s and continued to paint the country around Rome. His classical landscapes, very different in atmosphere and construction from Poussin's, were none the less perfect of their kind.

The Sienese pope, Alexander VII (1655–67), reinstated Bernini, who was put in control of his grandiose artistic programme. The most important event of the reign was the construction of the piazza of St Peter's. Here

217

POPE INNOCENT X

1650, Diego Rodriguez de Silva Velasquez 1599–1660
oil on canvas, 41 × 40.25 in (104 × 102 cm)
Galleria Doria-Pamphili, Rome

This portrait was painted by Velasquez during his second visit to Italy when he was commissioned to buy paintings and antique sculpture for Philip IV of Spain. It is not known who arranged for the pope to sit to Velasquez, but at all events it was an artistic challenge since Innocent X was both an ugly man and an excellent connoisseur. The result was a resounding success with the pope and the Roman world: Innocent recommended that Philip IV should ennoble Velasquez and many copies were made.

218

THE ENCOUNTER OF LEO I AND ATTILA

1646–53, Alessandro Algardi 1595–1654
marble, high relief, c. 25 ft (760 cm)
St Peter's, Rome

Under Innocent X Algardi temporarily replaced Bernini in papal favour. His 'modello' for this great altarpiece was ready in time for the Holy Year of 1650. The event depicted constituted a symbol of the miraculous salvation of the church from terrible danger. The inspiration for the composition was Raphael. However, in size and in the use of the graduated figures to produce an illusion of depth the classicising Algardi paradoxically created the High Baroque relief, a form which became enormously popular in ensuing years.

219

THE FACADE AND PIAZZA OF ST PETER'S

1607–67, piazza begun 1656
Carlo Maderno 1556–1629 and
Gianlorenzo Bernini 1598–1680
Rome

Carlo Maderno built the nave and façade in trying circumstances. The nave inevitably eclipsed Michelangelo's dome; and the façade was too wide for its height because of a papal decision, afterwards rescinded as impracticable, to erect lateral towers. When (under Alexander VII) Bernini came to design his famous piazza he had to rely on optical illusion to remedy these defects. His final solution of an ingenious and free-standing colonnade surmounted by statues was revolutionary in conception and provided the requisite grandeur and dignity for the all-embracing arms of the church.

220

CONSTANTINE

1654–70
Gianlorenzo Bernini 1598–1680
marble statue with stucco drapery
The Scala Regia, St Peter's, Rome

In 1654 Innocent X commissioned a statue of Constantine for the interior of St Peter's, but under Alexander VII the scheme was changed. The statue forms the point of focus from the portico of St Peter's and the new Scala Regia. The execution was essentially Bernini's own in spite of the scale of the work, and the drapery was designed to enhance its dynamic quality and make the pose convincing. The monument incurred savage criticism, but it became the model for all Baroque equestrian monuments.

221 *far right*

THE RIVER GANGES

1648–51
rock, travertine and marble
Piazza Navona, Rome

The Fountain of the Four Rivers supporting an Egyptian obelisk surmounted by the Pamphili dove, symbol of eternity, is more a monument harnessing the elements than a fountain. It was designed to emphasise the centre of the long Piazza Navona and to harmonise with Borromini's Santa Agnese. Bernini himself touched up the lion, horse and palm tree and left the execution of the Four Rivers to assistants.

Bernini had to devise a plan that would show off the façade of St Peter's to **219** advantage and diminish its breadth to the eye. An arcade was envisaged until Bernini hit upon the brilliant notion of a colonnade with an Ionic entablature resting upon massive, sculptural Tuscan columns four abreast, curving round an oval piazza to enclose the multitude awaiting the pope's blessing. The inspiration was Hellenistic. Bernini's achievements at this time were multifarious: there was the Vatican Scala Regia where he turned to advantage a narrow and awkward site by a skilful use of trompe l'oeil perspective; the equestrian statue of Constantine which became the model **220** for all Baroque equestrian statues; finally the Cathedra Petri. This resplen- **220** dent enshrinement of the ancient wooden stool of St Peter represents not only the apotheosis of the papacy but also of Bernini's art. Alexander's successor, Clement IX, who had been a poet and playwright in the Barberini circle and shared their enthusiasm for artistic enterprise, carried on much that had been initiated by Alexander. In addition he commissioned from Bernini the graceful angels for Ponte Sant' Angelo.

The Barberini influence was also perpetuated by Urban VIII's nephew,

Cardinal Antonio, who brought into prominence Sacchi's pupil, Carlo Maratta. His academic late Baroque style harmonised with the classic-idealist doctrine of Giovanni Bellori and was to dominate the Roman world of art for several generations. At the same time a more isolated figure made his mark in Rome: the poet and painter Salvator Rosa, who shunned the usual patrons of the epoch. Although he aspired to succeed in history painting, it was his romantic landscapes which caught the public imagination and in the eighteenth century were regarded as more sublime than the serene beauty of Claude.

After the death of Clement IX in 1669 papal patronage declined rapidly, partly because the prodigious extravagance of Urban VIII was still making itself felt, but chiefly owing to the rise of France as an economic and artistic power in Europe. However, Clement X and his family, the Altieri, employed Maratta and the aged Bernini, and private patrons such as Grand Constable Colonna and Cardinal Camillo Massimi (who had been Poussin's friend in his old age) kept Claude and other artists busy. The presence of ex-Queen Christina of Sweden brought a new vivacious personality to patronage. Though she did not distribute many commissions, she did found the Accademia Reale and assiduously cultivated Bellori, the mouthpiece of the classical cause whose *Idea*, read to the Academy of St Luke in 1664, was the most influential discourse on artistic theory of the century.

It was the Jesuits who gave most scope to late Baroque fresco decoration. G. B. Gaulli, called Baciccio, Bernini's protégé who was inspired by his **33** master's late style, painted on the vault of the nave of the Gesù an ethereal illusion of divine illumination. Padre Andrea Pozzo in Sant'Ignazio painted a complex architectural illusion with figures floating up into the clouds. Both were works which in their buoyancy and atmospheric lightness of touch ushered in the eighteenth century.

Mantua

The ascendancy of Rome in the seventeenth century must not blind us to the fact that there were other centres of patronage in Italy. In Mantua the ancient privileges of the city-state were slow to die: Duke Vincenzo I Gonzaga and his Medici wife Eleonora were remarkably active. They maintained a preference for Flemish art and in 1600 engaged the young Rubens as their court painter. Rubens's astonishing intellect and visual memory assimilated the art of his great Italian predecessors as no other northern artist had ever done. Before he left Italy in 1608 he had evolved a more advanced Baroque style than any of his Italian contemporaries.

Soon after Cardinal Ferdinando Gonzaga's accession as duke in 1613, his Roman protégé Domenico Feti, an artist of singular originality, was working to his command in Mantua. Feti produced inspired religious pieces, interesting genre pictures and portraits of outstanding quality. Ferdinando was also much addicted to the school of Bologna and employed several of its leading members: Reni, Albani and Guercino.

However, the fundamental weakness and degeneracy of the court came to a head with Vincenzo II who in 1627 sold the cream of the great Gonzaga collection to Charles I of England. War and strife and the succession of the Nevers-Rethel branch of the family put an end to patronage for a time. During the second half of the century, however, Carlo II showed discrimination in entertaining at his court the Genoese painter, Giovanni Benedetto Castiglione, whose picturesque and evocative treatment of classical subjects heralded a new era.

Florence

The artistic supremacy of Florence was a thing of the past. Although the city had become a provincial backwater, the Medici still reigned and were

222

THE CATHEDRA PETRI

1657–66
Gianlorenzo Bernini 1598–1680
St Peter's, Rome

The Cathedra Petri marks the climax of Bernini's career and of the full Baroque style. It was first conceived on a more modest scale and enlarged as the conception took shape. A complex unity and chromatic impression is achieved by the use of materials as diverse as marble, gilt bronze and stucco, bathed in golden light. They form a tribute to the church of dynamic intensity. A team of assistants worked to Bernini's orders, but he himself supervised every detail.

the principal patrons. Cosimo II (1609–21) had enough perception to attract Filippo Napoletano and to pension the Frenchman Jacques Callot. Callot's etchings illustrated fêtes and recorded scenes for the Medici theatre. His delicate but satirical vein later formed the inspiration for Stefano della Bella, who was less well appreciated at the Medici court than his predecessor and took his sensitive art abroad.

234   The Fleming Justus Sustermans became the court portrait painter in the 1620s, but the most important artistic event of the reign of Ferdinand II was the commission given to Pietro da Cortona. He had come to Florence in 1637 in the train of Cardinal Giulio Sacchetti and frescoed the Sala della
228   Stufa and other rooms in the Palazzo Pitti eventually finished by Ciro Ferri. Unfortunately these dazzling Baroque masterpieces of paint and stucco begat few followers in Florence. Instead, local painters such as Furini, Lorenzo Lippi, Dolci and Martinelli did a brisk business among the nobility and merchant classes. Some of the latter, for instance Agostino Galli and the Brothers Del Rosso, were more adventurous than the aristocracy in their choice of artists.

The greatest fresco cycle painted in Florence during the reign of Cosimo
229   III (1670–1723) was by the Neapolitan Luca Giordano, who worked in the palace recently taken over from the Medici by the Riccardi. Native talent in sculpture was more conspicuous. Prominent was Giovanni Foggini who had been Ferrata's pupil in Rome and who was the all-powerful court sculptor in Florence. He is perhaps most famous now for his reliefs in the chapel in the Carmine commissioned, along with frescos by Giordano, by the noble Florentine family of Corsini in the 1680s.

The maritime cities

The rival cities of Venice and Genoa were only lesser powers in the seventeenth century. In Genoa the rich mercantile aristocracy and the religious orders continued to be the principal patrons of the arts on whom the local schools flourished, but the most important painters such as Strozzi, Gaulli and Castiglione worked extensively elsewhere. On the other hand, famous foreigners such as Rubens, Van Dyck and the French sculptor Pierre Puget were attracted from abroad. Filippo Parodi, assimilating foreign influences, emerged as a precursor of Rococo sculpture.

In Venice, although Feti, Strozzi and Giordano worked there, painting suffered an interregnum between the sixteenth and eighteenth centuries and architecture was the leading form of art in the city. The state as a patron had declined, but after the plague of 1630 an official competition, which was won by Baldassare Longhena, was held for the design of Santa
224   Maria della Salute. While retaining some Palladian elements, its scenographic exuberance temporarily broke with the strong Palladian tradition. He also built the staircase hall for the monastery of San Giorgio Maggiore, which was not only scenic but also far in advance of its time.

Other than the religious orders the principal patrons were the nobility who, isolated and provincial as they were, chose to glorify their families with resplendent palaces on the Grand Canal. Such was Longhena's Palazzo Pesaro built for Doge Giovanni Pesaro's nephew, Leonardo. Bequests for church building were not uncommon. The most spectacular of these was Santa Maria del Giglio by Giuseppe Sardi, the façade of which celebrates the exploits of Antonio Barbaro and his forbears.

Naples and Sicily

Naples introduced foreign influences into Italy, notably that of Spain which had controlled southern Italy since the mid-sixteenth century. Intellectual life surprisingly persisted under Spanish domination with such figures as Giuseppe Valletta, but the viceregal court and nobility remained

223
SANT' ANDREA AL QUIRINALE
interior
1658–70
Gianlorenzo Bernini 1598–1680
Rome

By far the most perfect of Bernini's churches, Sant' Andrea was commissioned by Cardinal Camillo Pamphili for the novices of the Jesuit order. Its originality lies in its oval plan with a transverse axis closed by pilasters and at the same time longer than the main axis which opens into a chapel. All lines of the severe architecture converge on the figure of St Andrew soaring up to heaven on a cloud. Subtle colour and lighting enhance the effect.

224
SANTA MARIA DELLA SALUTE
1631–87
Baldassare Longhena 1598–1682
Venice

After the deliverance from the plague of 1630 the republic of Venice decided to erect a church in gratitude. The competition which was accordingly held was won by Longhena and resulted in his masterpiece which dominates the entrance of the Grand Canal. His novel, centrally planned design combined elements of the late antique, the Palladian tradition and the north Italian Bramantesque style. It was above all scenographic. This Venetian Baroque, so different from the Roman, came into its own as an inspiration to many European architects working during the following century.

reactionary and unenlightened and the religious orders were, perhaps, still the most important patrons. There was no well-defined artistic position except a close provincialism which bred hostility to 'foreign' artists such as Domenichino and Lanfranco or even to Finelli, the Roman-trained sculptor who was by birth a Neapolitan. The followers of Caravaggio (known as Caravaggisti), Giovanni Battista Caracciolo and Jusepe de Ribera and his school, held the day. An exception to the narrow viceregal outlook was the Count de Monterey, who had been ambassador to Rome and welcomed Velasquez in 1630.

A remarkable patron in Naples in the seventeenth century was a rich Antwerp merchant named Gaspar Roomer who lived for many years in Italy. Although he had a taste for his native Flemings and obtained a late work by Rubens, he shared with the Spaniards a liking for the grotesque in Ribera and for the Caravaggisti Valentin and Massimo Stanzione.

Meanwhile two artists of international distinction emerged: Mattia Preti and Luca Giordano. Although both left interesting work in Neapolitan churches, they were greatly in demand outside the kingdom. Giordano's complex style laid the foundation of eighteenth-century developments.

In Sicily, apart from the religious orders who employed the brilliant
244 stuccoist and sculptor Serpotta, only Don Antonio Ruffo stands out as a patron. Of ancient, noble family, seldom stirring beyond his own domain, his singular collection included paintings by Rembrandt, and he sought eagerly after early, 'robust' Guercinos.

Turin

All members of the house of Savoy in the seventeenth century were enthusiastic patrons of the arts and a means whereby French and Austrian influences entered Italy. In particular they were especially active as builders
225 and promoters of the theatre. The scenery for the court representations was designed at first by leading architects of the day such as Amadeo di Castellamonte and the engraver Giovenale Boetto. But in 1689 the Venetian Brothers Mauro came to Turin to be followed shortly afterwards by the famous Ferdinando Galli Bibiena.

In the early years of the era Charles Emmanuel I and Victor Amadeus I were in touch with Rome and Bologna through Cardinal Maurizio, who commissioned pictures from Albani, Guercino and many other famous artists, and through Abate Tesauro at the court of Turin, who was in correspondence with Cassiano dal Pozzo. Nevertheless, all members of the family showed a distinct preference for Caravaggisti.

The house of Savoy, more than any other dynasty in Italy, was interested in town planning. They enlarged Turin after the French fashion and rebuilt the Palazzo Reale with Amadeo di Castellamonte as architect. Among others, the Brothers Dufours, Charles Claude Dauphin and Jan Miel were engaged to decorate the interior; Miel's hunting series at the Venaria was particularly acclaimed. Daniel Seyter of Vienna undertook the decoration of the gallery of the Palazzo Reale after refusals by Maratta and Ciro Ferri. The result in paint and stucco was Cortonesque but heavier and darker.

In 1666 the arrival of the learned and much-travelled Theatine Guarino Guarini summoned by Charles Emmanuel II transformed the architectural scene. He put into practice new mathematical theories derived from Desargues's *Projective Geometry* of 1639. His work in Turin, especially the
226 church of San Lorenzo and the Cappella della Santissima Sindone with their diaphanous domes, is justly famous. Influenced by Borromini and Pozzo, harking back to Buontalenti, borrowing ideas even from the Hispano-Moresque, he evolved a style which was to sweep into Austria and the north.

Frances Vivian

225
GARDEN SCENE
FOR THE OPERA LISIMACO
1681
Giovanni Tommaso Borgonio, ? 1627/28–91
pen and wash drawing
17 × 22·75 in (43 × 58 cm)
Biblioteca Nazionale, Turin

The opera *Lisimaco*, composed by Christopher Ivanovich, canon of St Mark's, and elaborated by the Florentine Giovanni Pagliardi, was first performed in Venice in 1673. It was put on in Turin for the carnival of 1681. Borgonio was secretary to both Charles Emmanuel II and Victor Amadeus II and made a speciality of recording the court theatrical performances in a style which is both vivid and elegant.

226

SAN LORENZO

interior of the dome, 1668–87
Guarino Guarini 1624–83
Turin

This Theatine church was built chiefly
between 1668 and 1679, but not fully
completed until 1687. Guarini's diaphanous
domes were not Roman in origin, nor
even Hispano-Moresque. He alone
eliminated wall surface between the ribs
and perched high structures on their
points of intersection. He used here a
combination of new, advanced geometry
and the methods of medieval Gothic
architecture. In contrast the system of
lighting from above is distinctly Baroque.
It is a case of modern mathematical
mysticism: a suggestion of infinity by
means of architectural devices.

227

SAN CARLO ALLE QUATTRO FONTANE

interior of the dome, 1638–41
Francesco Borromini 1599–1667
Rome

This comparatively small church is a perfect
example of Borromini's art and is
fundamental to the development of
Roman High Baroque architecture. The
plan is based on a diamond pattern
formed by two equilateral triangles with
a common base along the axis of the
building. The unusual honeycomb coffers
have prototypes in the late antique. They
conceal windows which produce a
uniform and brilliant light.

228 *above far right*

THE SALA DI VENERE

1641–42
Pietro Berrettini da Cortona 1596–1669
fresco, Palazzo Pitti, Florence

The enlargement of the Palazzo Pitti by
Cosimo II de' Medici inspired his heir,
Ferdinand II, to plan new decorative
schemes. Pietro da Cortona's frescos in the
small Sala della Stufa of 1637 brought the
Roman High Baroque to Tuscany. Their
success engendered a commission to
decorate a further series of rooms. Francesco
Rondinelli devised the theme of an
astro-mythological representation of the
virtues necessary to a ruling prince of the
house of Medici. In the centre Pallas seizes
Adolescence from the arms of Venus.

229 *bottom far right*

JANUS AND THE FATES

detail
1682–83, Luca Giordano 1632–1705
fresco, Palazzo Medici-Riccardi, Florence

Michelozzo's Medici palace was acquired in
1659 by Raffaello Riccardi who built a
great gallery to house his collections. His
son, the Marchese Francesco, commissioned
Luca Giordano to fresco the vault. The
programme is an elaborate allegory of
human life interwoven with representations
of the dynasty of the Medici. The
inspiration was Cortona's Sala della Stufa
and the approach to classicism is elegiac in
mood, foreshadowing the eighteenth
century.

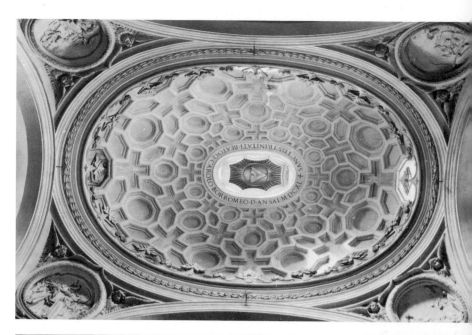

230 *left*

CARDINAL BENTIVOGLIO

1623
Anthony van Dyck 1599–1641
oil on canvas
76·75 × 58 in (195 × 147 cm)
Palazzo Pitti, Florence

This portrait dates from Van Dyck's
visit to Italy and was probably painted
in Rome in 1623. It already shows the
artist's tremendous sensibility as a portrait
painter, and the sitter, Cardinal
Bentivoglio, was a worthy subject. He had
been in the confidence of many popes
since Clement VIII and was created
cardinal by Gregory XV in 1621. He was
also a prominent man of letters and patron.

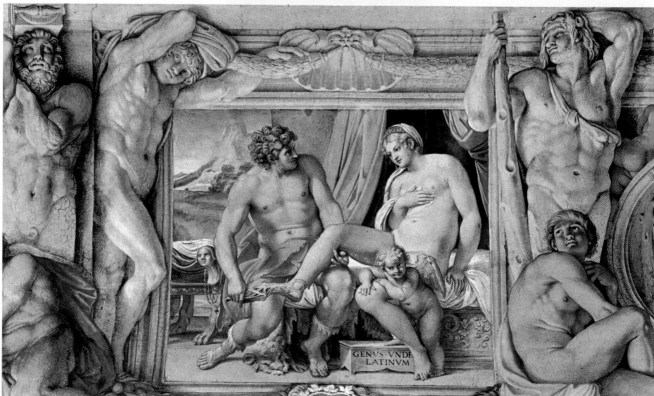

231 *above*

VENUS AND ANCHISES

c. 1598
Annibale Carracci 1560–1609
Palazzo Farnese, Rome

The underlying theme of the decoration
of the Palazzo Farnese, commissioned from
Annibale Carracci by Cardinal Odoardo
Farnese in 1597, is the power of love to
exalt and transfigure the human soul.
The revelation of the spiritual through the
medium of the sensual is a typical Baroque
concept. This scene, Venus (the goddess)
yielding to Anchises (the mortal), forms
part of the elaborate frieze of the ceiling.
The whole complex decoration of the
vault interlocked with architecture
supported by audaciously forceful
illusionistic figures was devised by
Annibale himself.

232

ST MATTHEW AND THE ANGEL

c. 1600–01
Michelangelo Merisi, called Caravaggio 1573–1610
oil on canvas
116 × 76 in (295 × 195 cm)
Contarelli Chapel, San Luigi de' Francesi, Rome

The commission to decorate the chapel with an altarpiece and two lateral pictures was probably secured for Caravaggio in 1597–98 by his most important early patron, Cardinal Francesco del Monte. The first altarpiece failed to please, was rejected and bought by the Marchese Vincenzo Giustiniani, who also put up the money for this, the second one, which is still there. Here Caravaggio depicts the angel in conventional fashion, but the use of light is revolutionary.

233

TRIUMPH OF THE NAME OF JESUS

detail of the vault of the nave, 1676–79
Giovanni Battista Gaulli, called Baciccio 1639–1709
The Gesù, Rome

The severe interior of the Gesù was completed in 1584, but this elaborate decoration was commissioned from Gaulli in 1672 by the Jesuit order under Padre Oliva. The inspiration ultimately derives from Correggio's dome in the cathedral at Parma, but the influence of Bernini's late style makes itself more strongly felt. The dynamic masses of figures are integrated with the architecture and seem to hover over our heads as tangible celestial beings, while the vault appears to open to allow the heavens to enter the church.

234 *far left*

THE EVILS OF WAR

c. 1637–38, Peter Paul Rubens 1577–1640
oil on canvas, 81 × 123 in (206 × 342 cm), Palazzo Pitti, Florence

In February 1638 this picture was sent by Rubens from the Netherlands to his Antwerp compatriot Justus Sustermans in Florence. It was probably intended for the latter's Medici patron, Ferdinand II. Rubens excelled at allegory and he described this one in detail himself: Mars is being restrained by Venus, but enticed by the Furies to bring destruction on humanity; he tramples art and learning underfoot.

By the eighteenth century Europe had become conscious of the Italian artistic heritage. Ennobling and moral qualities were discerned in connoisseurship, especially after the publication of the third earl of Shaftesbury's *Characteristics* in 1711, and an appreciation of art became the hallmark of a gentleman. Paradoxically, although contemporary Italian supremacy in the arts was now seriously challenged by France, there was a greater influx of foreign patrons into Italy than ever before. Meanwhile the dawn of Romanticism coloured and subtly transformed the current attitude to classical antiquity.

Venice

Although her political and economic power was perceptibly on the wane, Venice unaccountably experienced so great an upsurge of creative art as to outshine Rome in achievement. The old pattern of society was maintained. The nobility continued their traditional role; they sought to stress past grandeur, and for this purpose they found ideal expression in the grand manner of Giambattista Tiepolo. The excellence of his fresco cycles can bear comparison with anything which preceded them and were the last great manifestation of Italian art. His first essay in this medium, in which the dazzling lightness of his palette, the effortless rapidity of his brushstroke and the fertility of his invention combined to astonish the beholder, was carried out in the archbishop's palace at Udine. Twenty years later, in about 1745, Tiepolo painted in the Palazzo Labia in Venice his frescos of Antony and Cleopatra, which to modern eyes are perhaps the most perfect of all his works. The marriage of Ludovico Rezzonico and Faustina Savorgnan which Tiepolo depicted on the ceiling of the Palazzo Rezzonico echoes the glories of the Wurzburg Residenz. The decor of Venetian palaces was completed by elaborate, Baroque, sculptural furniture, for instance Andrea Brustolon's famous pieces executed for Pietro Venier di San Vio. But it was in a lighter key and more idyllic mood that Tiepolo and his son Domenico undertook in 1757 the frescos in Count Valmarana's villa near Vicenza. Giambattista's poetic interpretation of Homer draws the beholder into an enchanting mythological world while Domenico's genre scenes evoke the atmosphere of Mozart's *Figaro*.

Meanwhile a very different artist, Pietro Longhi, painted small intimate easel pictures of the everyday life of the Venetian upper classes. He eschewed satire or irony (which would have displeased his clientele) and he was no draughtsman, but his art had a subtle flattery that made it very popular.

The architecture which the nobility and the religious orders commissioned seldom followed the Rococo rhythms fashionable in so much of Europe. Instead, as in England, it recaptured Palladian inspiration and anticipated the Neo-classic style. In San Simeone Piccolo, Giovanni Scalfarotto blended Palladio with antiquity and Byzantium, while Francesco Cabianca adorned the church with Rococo sculpture. Andrea Tirali's Palazzo Manfrin is almost twentieth century in its severity, and Giorgio Massari's Gesuati (built for the Dominicans) harks back to the sixteenth century, although it is gorgeously decorated by Tiepolo and the sculptor Gian Maria Morlaiter and has altarpieces by Sebastiano Ricci and Piazzetta. This contrast of severe architecture with exuberant pictorial decoration was a particularly Venetian phenomenon dating back to the collaboration of Palladio and Veronese at Maser.

The rise of the *vedutisti* (painters of *vedute*: views) is perhaps the best known Venetian manifestation of the eighteenth century. This type of painting originated with the Roman *bamboccianti* (painters of scenes of low life) and was carried on successfully by the Dutchman Gaspar van Wittel. His visit to Venice in about 1695 produced a series of topographical views

235

AN ANGEL
detail from the Sacrifice of Isaac
c. 1726
Giovanni Battista Tiepolo 1696–1770
fresco
Palazzo Arcivescovile, Udine

For Dionisio Dolfin Tiepolo painted his first important fresco cycle outside Venice. In the archbishop's palace he decorated the gallery, stairs and the Sala Rossa. The treatment is dazzling in tonality and theatrical in content: the effect is of the Renaissance recreated in terms of eighteenth-century opera.

236

THE BANQUET OF ANTONY
AND CLEOPATRA
c. 1745–50
Giovanni Battista Tiepolo 1696–1770
fresco
Palazzo Labia, Venice

Painted for the noble Labia family, these frescos represent the culmination of Tiepolo's preoccupation with the story of Antony and Cleopatra – a subject not previously popular with painters. Girolamo Mengozzi-Colonna painted the stupendous trompe l'oeil architecture which embraces the whole room and frames on one main wall this scene of the banquet, derived from Pliny, but by no means authentic in costume. Again Tiepolo is primarily concerned with dramatic effect.

of both charm and accuracy. He was followed by Luca Carlevaris of Udine. The latter both etched and painted Venice with great assiduity. His pictures frequently represented a special occasion such as a regatta or the ceremonial entry of an ambassador. Foreigners like Lord Manchester were the principal clients for the *vedute* which were to reach their apotheosis with Canaletto. Manchester was an enthusiast for all Venetian painting, and it was his secretary, Christian Cole, who encouraged Rosalba Carriera to take up pastels. Her portraits with their graceful, Rococo charm took Europe by storm. Her brother-in-law, Gian Antonio Pellegrini, together with Marco Ricci, accompanied Manchester to England in 1708, and all Pellegrini's best work was done outside Venice in northern Europe.

Probably the most influential patron in Venice was an Englishman named Joseph Smith, whose long period of activity stretched from about 1700–70. A merchant banker of dubious character and British consul from 1744–60, he got into financial difficulties at this period and retrieved his fortune by selling a large part of his collection to George III in 1762. He is most famous for his connection with Canaletto whom he employed constantly from about 1728 until the artist's death in 1768. Although Canaletto had begun as a painter of stage scenery, after a visit to Rome he returned to Venice and soon captured the market with his *capricci* (imaginary views) and *vedute*. His early works were large atmospheric canvases peopled by figures typical of Venetian life. His commissions became so numerous that he had to make use of studio assistants. The finished product became rather mechanical, although he altered topographical details for the sake of aesthetic effect more frequently than is realised. Smith had a business understanding with him, introduced him to many itinerant Englishmen with a view to commissions and encouraged him to visit England. Very few Canalettos remained in Venice and many found their way to Britain.

Francesco Zuccarelli, the Tuscan whom Venice adopted, painted his finest series of pastoral landscapes for Smith. The cult of Rousseau had made Zuccarelli popular all over Europe, and he may have persuaded Richard Wilson to take up landscape painting. Smith also promoted the fortunes of the uncle and nephew Sebastiano and Marco Ricci, the former producing history and religious paintings and the latter Smith's favourite *capricci* in both oil and tempera. These *capricci* and the evocative landscapes of the Venetian mainland and of Belluno were to have a considerable influence on the development of Italian landscape painting.

Smith's neglect of Tiepolo can only be accounted for by the latter's curious failure to make any impression on English taste. Nevertheless, he did have a set of Tiepolo's etchings. His collection of drawings and etchings was one of the most varied in the world and furnished Venetian artists with easy access to Dutch and Flemish works. This northern influence, especially that of Rembrandt, also made itself felt through numerous paintings which were on view at the English merchant's house to all who chose to study them. But Smith's patronage went further. He had a passionate interest in Palladian architecture: his position was closer to that of Leoni than that of Lord Burlington, albeit influenced by later Paduan developments sponsored by his great friend, Giovanni Poleni, FRS. With the help of the architect and engraver, Antonio Visentini, Smith carried out an architectural programme not only in stone in the case of his palazzo and villa on the mainland, but also in pictorial and graphic form.

Smith's other great contribution lay in the world of books. In the early 1730s when Venetian printing and book illustration led the world, Smith set up a press under Pasquali, a young corrector of the Stamperia Pecori, which was to rival the publishing houses of Albrizzi and Zatta. The

Pasquali bookshop became the meeting place for intellectuals in Venice. The firm published Muratori and Mme du Châtelet and brought out a translation of Ephraim Chamber's *Cyclopaedia* several years before the idea of an encyclopedia took root and caused such a stir in France. Smith imported books from all over Europe and with Pasquali easily got the better of the haphazard censorship. Novelli and, on one occasion, Piazzetta, who was pre-eminent as an illustrator, were engaged; but the artist who designed the firm's printer's mark, all the tailpieces for both special and everyday editions and rendered exquisite vignettes, was Antonio Visentini, the architect whose illustrations were remarkable for their Rococo delicacy.

There were, of course, many other artists and patrons. Anton Maria Zanetti the Elder collected much the same things as Smith, so that his friendship with the English merchant was obscured by rivalry, although Zanetti had the advantage of being a practising draughtsman and engraver himself. Francesco Algarotti, a personal friend of Tiepolo, was conspicuous for obtaining German patronage for Venetian painters. He wrote in favour of the rising fashion for Neo-classicism which both Zanetti and Poleni promoted by their publications. But Algarotti was too much a Venetian not to preserve that balance between classicism and flamboyant decorative art which persisted throughout the period in question.

Almost last to remain on the scene was the enigmatic figure of Francesco Guardi. It is difficult to disentangle his work from that of his brother, Gian Antonio Guardi, who died in 1760 and never painted *vedute* so far as we know. Gian Antonio was probably responsible for the lovely organ panels of Tobias in the church of the Angelo Raffaele. Although related by marriage to Tiepolo, neither Guardi received great commissions or widespread appreciation for many years. Francesco found that English patrons increased after the death of Canaletto, and he was especially sought after by the resident John Strange in the 1770s and 1780s. Experts still dispute the date when Francesco abandoned figure painting to become a *vedutista*, but he is said to have studied with Canaletto and certainly took inspiration from Marco Ricci. He was in many ways the most Rococo of all Venetian painters and the 'incorrect' drawing which displeased his contemporaries enhance his *vedute* today. He painted in addition many *capricci* and included not only Venice but also the lagoon in his repertory. His pale tonality made full use of the softest blue-greens in a dreamlike atmosphere of sea and sky, sometimes only punctuated by a ruined tower or the sail of a boat. It was an ethereal beauty that lived on almost until the break-up of the republic in 1797. Meanwhile Domenico Tiepolo's ironic scenes of bourgeois life made little headway in a society which, until it was engulfed by the cataclysm caused by Napoleon's invasion, did not yield to new trends.

Rome

In the first half of the eighteenth century, the papacy was still vigorous in promoting the arts. Various famous projects were set in motion: the Spanish Steps by De Sanctis, the competition for the façade of the Lateran won by Alessandro Galilei, the Trevi Fountain by Nicola Salvi, the Capitoline museums founded and the interior of the Pantheon brought up to date. The Florentine Benedetto Luti succeeded Maratta as first painter but carried his style into a minor key. The seat of the most enlightened patronage was the papal chancery where the Venetian Cardinal Pietro Ottoboni was vice-chancellor for many years until 1740. Music, drama, painting and architecture flourished. Trevisani was summoned from Venice, Gaulli became more academic under the Ottoboni influence and Sebastiano Conca came from Naples and remained to acquire great fame and paint in a delicate and lively Rococo manner, akin in spirit to the work of the sculptors Filippo della

238

237
THE MORNING TOILET
c. 1745
Pietro Falda, called Longhi 1702–85
oil on canvas
23·5 × 19·25 in (60 × 49 cm)
Accademia di Belle Arti, Venice

This painting, typical of the work of Pietro Longhi, shows an intimate scene from the life of the Venetian nobility (who liked to see themselves represented in this manner). The picture probably dates from the 1740s when Longhi first established himself as a genre painter and has the freshness of handling and vivacity of the pair at Windsor dated 1744 which belonged to Consul Smith. There is an uncertainty in the placing of the table which reflects Longhi's limitations but does not detract from the overall effect.

Valle and Pietro Bracci, who were also active at this time. And the great Sicilian architect Filippo Juvarra designed sets for the Ottoboni theatre which astonished Rome.

Another factor in Roman artistic life in the eighteenth century was the French Academy, which had been increasing in importance since its foundation in 1666. This influence tended from the outset towards reason, restraint and the study of antiquity in reaction to the Baroque. Some French sculptors worked extensively in Rome, such as Pierre Legros the Younger, Pierre Etienne Monnot and a generation later, 'Michelangelo' Slodtz. All, however, remained to some extent under the Roman spell of Bernini and his followers until in 1767 Jean Antoine Houdon broke entirely with the prevailing tradition with his statue of St Bruno in Santa Maria degli Angeli.

At mid-century the tide of Neo-classicism set in strongly, hastened by the

238

THE SPANISH STEPS

1723—25
Francesco de Sanctis 1693—1740
Rome

This major work of the Roman Rococo is comparable in scale to the great Baroque achievements of the previous century. It embodies a comprehensive vision which unites the whole area from Trinità dei Monti to the Tiber. The scheme harks back to the town-planning enterprises of Sixtus V which focused on long avenues and distant viewpoints.

239

CAPRICCIO WITH THE STATUE OF MARCUS AURELIUS

c. 1740—50
Giovanni Paolo Panini 1692—1765
oil on canvas
72 × 60·25 in (185 × 153 cm)
Galleria Nazionale d'Arte Antica,
Palazzo Corsini, Rome

This is a mature work by Panini, one of a pair. It is not known for whom they were painted, but they must rank among his finest productions, free from dependence on former masters and imbued with poetic inspiration characteristic of the eighteenth-century attitude to antiquity. Panini had a host of followers and imitators, the most important of whom was Hubert Robert.

discovery of Herculaneum and Pompeii in the 1730s and 1740s. This was a European rather than an Italian manifestation, with England and France in the lead, especially in appreciation of Greek art. In 1743 Piranesi's *Prima Parte di Architetture e Prospettive* appeared, followed in 1756 by the *Antichità Romane*. These etchings were not only archaeological but also scenographic and romantic in conception. The famous *Carceri* (scenes of prisons) are said to have grown out of designs for an opera set and were certainly indebted to Juvarra. After Bottari, Piranesi's principal patrons were the Venetian Clement XIII, enthusiast for everything to do with the arts, and his nephew, Cardinal Rezzonico. For them Piranesi designed interiors and remodelled Santa Maria del Priorato. *Della Magnificenza ed Architettura dei Romani* was dedicated by him to Clement XIII in 1761.

It was also Clement XIII who appointed Johann Joachim Winckelmann director general of antiquities. Winckelmann, a German scholar, was the archpriest of classical doctrine and went further than Bellori had done in his praise of noble simplicity. His emphasis on Greek as opposed to Roman studies was more appreciated in England and France than in Italy, although the controversy raged throughout Europe for several decades. His patron, Cardinal Alessandro Albani, put him in charge of his famous library at the

Palazzo del Drago and entrusted to his care Cassiano dal Pozzo's *Museum Chartaceum*, until it was sold in 1762 to James Adam for George III. The Villa Albani was built in the 1750s as an Imperial 'villa suburbana' lavishly adorned with antique marbles. Here, in 1761, Anton Raphael Mengs, a German artist of mediocre talent who inspired vast admiration at the time, painted his famous *Parnassus* which was hailed as a return to Raphael and pre-Christian murals.

241   Throughout the century more and more foreigners on the Grand Tour congregated in Rome. The painters Gian Paolo Panini and Pompeo Batoni satisfied their requirements, the former with precise, bold and elegant views of Rome and ruins and the latter with sophisticated portraits in classical settings. It had become de rigueur for foreign artists to study in Rome, and besides the sculptors we have mentioned, the famous French painters
249   Claude Joseph Vernet, Hubert Robert and Fragonard spent many years in Italy and drew inspiration from the eternal city. Englishmen such as Reynolds, Joseph Wilton, Thomas Banks, William Chambers and Robert Adam were profoundly influenced by their studies abroad. Some, for
240   instance Gavin Hamilton, painter, archaeologist and pioneer of Neo-classicism, settled in Rome and acted as guides and dealers.

Turin

The house of Savoy continued its vigorous patronage. Victor Amadeus II was king of Sicily for a brief five years (1713-18) until he took over the Sardinian title. In 1714 he imported Juvarra to Turin to remain there until 1735. Juvarra became the artistic dictator of the court at Turin. He manipulated with ease the principles and developments of the last three hundred years of Italian architecture besides adopting new ideas from Austria. He built whole streets, churches and royal residences: the Superga, grandest
246   and most Roman of mountain sanctuaries; the Palazzo Madama; and above
255   all, Stupinigi, the inspired, scenographic hunting lodge. He employed artists from many nations: his friends the Ricci, Crosato and the Valeriani from Venice; C. A. van Loo who combined French and Roman training; Trevisani and Imperiali came from Rome; and Claude Beaumont from

240

THE RAPE OF HELEN

1784
Gavin Hamilton 1723–98
oil on canvas
Museo di Roma, Palazzo Braschi, Rome

This picture was part of a decorative scheme designed by Gavin Hamilton of Lanarkshire at the request of the Marchese Marcantonio Borghese. The architect Antonio Asprucci was in charge of the modernising process of the seventeenth-century Palazzina Borghese which took place *c.* 1775–90, but Hamilton was allowed a free hand in his part of the decoration. The theme from the Iliad was a favourite one with the learned Scots archaeologist, who had been a pioneer in the Neo-classical movement. The result excited universal admiration.

241

THE FALL OF SIMON MAGUS

1755
Pompeo Batoni 1708–87
oil on canvas
Santa Maria degli Angeli, Rome

This is a masterpiece by Batoni in his full maturity. It combines the lucidity of his work of the 1730s with more solemn and emotive romantic energy. It also clearly manifests that Batoni's Neo-classicism was only of the surface kind. He combined the best Roman tradition from the Renaissance to the eighteenth century. The altarpiece was commissioned for St Peter's and was exhibited there for Easter 1755, but it failed to please and the commission was transferred to Mengs.

145

Trevisani's studio was given office at the court and brought something of the grace of François Lemoyne to his frescos. Pictures were obtained from Solimena at Naples and his pupils; Corrado Giaquinto and later Francesco de Mura did some of their best work at Turin. The sculptors were Francesco Ladatte, trained in France; Pierre Legros; Juvarra's own nephew Simone Martinez; the stuccoist Giuseppe Muttoni and many others. All complied with Juvarra's overall direction, and the result was a highly imaginative and elegant form of Rococo. In his interiors Juvarra controlled the design of furniture, 'boiseries' and silver. Following his manner the cabinet makers

248 Luigi Pinotto and Pietro Piffetti, aided by Ladatte, produced superb pieces.

242 But the royal tapestry works were chiefly the concern of Beaumont and did not come fully into being until after Juvarra's departure.

Outside the court a local architect, Bernardo Vittone, worked for the clergy and small communities. Unlike Juvarra, he was influenced by Guarini, and the chapel (financed by a rich banker) which he built at Vallinotto for agricultural labourers was not rustic but a sophisticated Rococo.

When Juvarra left for Spain there was no immediate change in style at the court of Charles Emmanuel III. The Sicilian architect's followers carried on his manner. It was only in the next generation that the Neo-classic style began to penetrate with the stage sets of the Galliari. Meanwhile the Roman-trained sculptors Ignazio and Filippo Collino introduced a more rigorous dependence on the antique which prevailed towards the end of the century.

Florence

Florence in the eighteenth century settled still further into provincialism with an excessively dull local school of painters. The chief exception was Alessandro Gherardini, who acquired a Venetian palette from Giordano and Ricci. The most active patron before the extinction of the Medici was Grand Prince Ferdinand, son of Cosimo III, who favoured Venetian art and whose intellectual circle was frequented by the Bibiena and Scarlatti. But Ferdinand's chief contribution was his patronage of Sebastiano Ricci

250 whom he summoned to Florence in 1704. He introduced Ricci to the Brothers Marucelli who responded by commissioning the famous frescos in the Palazzo Marucelli. For Ferdinand himself, Sebastiano painted among other things a small room in the Palazzo Pitti which in its pale tonality, Ovidian lightness, asymmetry and delicacy foreshadows the French as well as the Venetian Rococo. Ferdinand's other most notable protégé, the Bolognese artist Giuseppe Maria Crespi, was very different. He came intermittently to Florence in 1708-09 and produced for his employer 'tenebroso' genre scenes such as the intimate and touching *The Painter's Family*, which gives us a foretaste of the work of his great Venetian pupil, G. B. Piazzetta.

The best of Foggini's pupils in Tuscany was Giovanni Baratta, but the most interesting sculptor in the early eighteenth century was Massimo Soldani, who led the Florentine tradition of working in bronze to a new Rococo perfection, especially in the composition of his reliefs.

The last of the Medici, Gian Gastone, reigned from 1723 to the annexation of Florence by Austria in 1737. With the advent of Francis of Lorraine and the Austrian regency the minor arts continued to flourish. The import-

243 ant Doccia porcelain factory was founded in 1737 by the Marchese Ginori who employed the sculptor Gaspero Bruschi with great success. Otherwise, it must be admitted that in the days of the grand duke Leopold the interest both of the residents and of the constant stream of visitors to Florence was concentrated on the glories of the past in the great gallery of the Uffizi. The collections of the Medici family, which the public had been able to visit under the late dukes, were preserved intact for the state of Tuscany by the Austrians. The gallery was considered the finest in Europe and no gentle-

242
CAESAR UNDER
THE WALLS OF ALEXANDRIA
1750
Claudio Francesco Beaumont 1694–1776
and Francesco Demignot, active 1730
tapestry, wool and silk
183 × 118 in (465 × 300 cm)
Palazzo Reale, Turin

The tapestry series, *Storia di Cesare*, from the royal factory at Turin was carried out in 1741–50. Based on sketches by Beaumont, the cartoons were made by various minor artists under his direction and the weavers were Antonio Dini and Francesco Demignot. *Caesar under the Walls of Alexandria* was the last of this series destined for the tiring room of Charles Emmanuel III. Felice Manassero was the painter and Demignot the weaver.

243

VASE WITH MEDALLIONS

c. 1737
Gaspero Bruschi, active 1737–80
porcelain
Palazzo Reale di Capodimonte, Naples

This Doccia factory vase was probably made in honour of Francis of Lorraine, husband of Maria Teresa of Austria. It has an urn-shaped body surmounted by a lid in the shape of an imperial crown. The body is divided into eight bands each containing four medallions representing duchesses of the house of Lorraine. Great elegance is shown in the modelling and the colour. The pale apple green with deep purple, blue and touches of gold is characteristic of the early years of the factory.

244

THE MARTYRDOM OF
ST LAWRENCE

1703
Giacomo Serpotta 1656–1732
stucco
San Lorenzo, Palermo

This work constitutes part of the decoration of the Oratory of San Lorenzo commissioned from Serpotta by the Compagnia di San Lorenzo and carried out *c.* 1699–1707. Brilliantly scenographic in a graceful and elegant style that is at once Hellenistic in inspiration and Rococo in effect, this representation of the martyrdom of St Lawrence is based on an engraving by Gerard Audran after a painting by Eustache le Sueur – an academic Frenchman whose works Serpotta can never have seen.

man who visited Italy dared admit that he had not been there at least once.

Naples

Spanish domination was succeeded by Austrian at the outset of the eighteenth century, but it made very little difference to the trend of patronage or to the buoyancy of an intermittently persecuted intellectual life. The leading painter Francesco Solimena, heir to Luca Giordano, absorbed a complex mixture of Spanish as well as Italian influences, until he evolved a powerful and decorative late Baroque style. He was constantly employed by the religious orders on such fresco cycles as the chapel of San Carlomanno at Montecassino, and his most famous works in Neapolitan churches are probably those in San Paolo Maggiore and the Gesù Nuovo. **251** He was also much in demand by the secular authorities since his reputation extended throughout Europe; the viceroys acquired pictures from him intended for Vienna. Meanwhile aristocratic taste in palaces and elaborate fêtes favoured the Rococo of Solimena's pupil Ferdinand Sanfelice.

With the advent of the Bourbon Charles III (1734-59) a new era of enlightened despotism began. A tapestry factory was started in San Carlo delle Mortelle. A porcelain factory was set up at the instance of the young **253** Saxon queen Maria Amalia. Above all, building was undertaken on an unprecedented scale. The theatre of San Carlo appeared almost overnight, the palace at Capodimonte developed and the Villa Portici was built to house the Farnese treasures. As part of the refurbishing of the Palazzo **22** Reale, the elderly Solimena painted an allegory of matrimonial felicity, since destroyed. His pupil Giuseppe Bonito eventually held the office of court painter, and Solimena's style was perpetuated in a lighter, Rococo form by several artists from his studio.

The climax of the reign was reached in 1752 when the first stone was laid of the magnificent palace at Caserta which was intended to outshine **247** Versailles. It was designed by Luigi Vanvitelli (son of Gaspar van Wittel) by that time a famous architect. In a sense Caserta is the swan song of the Italian late Baroque. The scale is immense, the effect theatrical and the plan logical in the extreme. But the classical elements incorporated were more akin to the French seventeenth century than to the Neo-classic style. A vast area of formal gardens was laid out in the French fashion, and numerous fountains, surpassing in grandeur anything else of the kind in Italy, were envisaged by Luigi. They were carried out by his son Carlo on a slightly **281** reduced scale with picturesque groups of classicising Rococo sculpture.

In spite of the foundation in 1755 of the Accademia Ercolanese or the furore over the discovery of Paestum and the activities of foreign antiquaries like Sir William Hamilton, Neo-classicism as practised by the architect Mario Gioffredo was slow to break through the prevailing frivolous taste in Naples. Sicily, on the whole, was equally resistant. In the early part of the eighteenth century Serpotta continued his graceful stucco **244** decoration for the religious orders. After the earthquake of 1693 a flowering of weird and extravagant Baroque occurred. Catania was rebuilt by G. B. Vaccarini, a Sicilian architect from Cardinal Ottoboni's circle at Rome; while at Modica and Ragusa, Rosario Gagliardi erected great churches of astonishing vitality and originality, curiously akin in spirit to the Austrian Baroque. In the neighbourhood of Palermo the nobility built palaces, striving to express feudal dignity in Baroque terms. In 1769 Don Salvator Branciforti, Prince of Butera, transformed his ancestral town of Bagheria in a manner which could only have been achieved by the will and imagination of a single individual. Such treatment could not survive the advent of a more democratic age.

Frances Vivian

245

PALAZZO DI STUPINIGI

1729–34
Filippo Juvarra 1678–1736
near Turin

This enormous hunting lodge was
commissioned from Juvarra in 1729 by
Victor Amadeus II. Juvarra wavered in his
original design between the French and
Italian types of country house. He finally
chose the latter with a star-shaped plan
and radiating wings, which was afterwards
adopted in Austria and even copied in
France. But Stupinigi is on a huge scale in
a class of its own. Much was added by
other architects to Juvarra's structure but
probably to his design.

246 *bottom left*

STAIRCASE

1720
Filippo Juvarra 1678–1736
Palazzo Madama, Turin

This palace screens a medieval castle and
was built for the widow of Charles
Emmanuel II, Maria of Savoy-Nemours.
It contains one of the grandest staircases in
Italy which stretches the whole width of
the present façade. The ornament consists
of a curious fusion of almost Neo-classic
motifs juxtaposed with exuberant
Borrominesque detail. The inspiration of
Longhena and of Austrian prototypes is
also evident.

247 *bottom right*

THE GRAND STAIRCASE

begun 1752
Luigi Vanvitelli 1700–73
Palazzo Reale di Caserta

Caserta was perhaps the last late Baroque
palace to be erected in Italy as well as the
largest. Vanvitelli's classicism looks back
more to Versailles (and the Louvre) than
forward into the Neo-classic age.
Commissioned by Charles III of Bourbon,
the building lapsed for several years on his
return to Spain in 1759. It was completed
by Luigi's son, Carlo Vanvitelli, in the
subsequent reign. From an octagonal
vestibule in the centre of the palace rises
Italy's grandest and most theatrical stair.

248

STEPS AND TABLE WITH MATCHING CUPBOARD AND MIRROR

1731–33, Pietro Piffetti, c. 1700–77
marquetry with inlays of ivory and
mother-of-pearl, and ormolu mounts
141·75 × 59·75 in (360 × 152 cm)
Palazzo Reale, Turin

This is one set of a pair of similar pieces ordered by Charles Emmanuel III for the dressing room of Queen Polissena Cristina. The ormolu mounts are by Francesco Ladatte and Paolo Venasca. Superb craftsmanship was necessary to produce such furniture, although to more sophisticated French eyes it might have appeared overladen.

249 *top right*

CAPRICCIO ON THE THEME OF THE MAISON CARREE AT NIMES

Hubert Robert 1733–1808
oil on canvas
16·5 × 12·5 in (42 × 32 cm)
Galleria Nazionale d'Arte Antica,
Palazzo Barberini, Rome

Hubert Robert, protégé of the powerful family of Stainville, spent eleven formative years in Rome (1754–65). He was much influenced not only by his surroundings but also by Panini. This picture shows in addition a strong affinity with Fragonard. Robert's oeuvre is difficult to date because he tended to repeat motifs, but this work possibly belongs to the 1770s.

250 *bottom right*

VENUS TAKING LEAVE OF ADONIS

1706–07, Sebastiano Ricci 1659–1734
fresco, Palazzo Pitti, Florence

This fresco covers the ceiling of a small, intimate room on the ground floor of the Palazzo Pitti. It was decorated with scenes from Ovid's *Metamorphoses* by the Venetian painter Sebastiano Ricci, for Grand Prince Ferdinand de' Medici. In keeping with the prince's character, Sebastiano eschewed heavy drama and ushered in the new century with a lightness of composition, tonality and spirit. The costumes were inspired by Veronese and the sleek greyhound, later Tiepolo's favourite animal, appears.

251 right

251 right

HELIODORUS CHASED FROM THE TEMPLE

1725
Francesco Solimena 1657–1747
fresco
Gesù Nuovo, Naples

This mature work embodies all Solimena's past experience and is a good example of the academic late Baroque, inspired by sixteenth-century models from Raphael to the Venetians. Some contemporaries accused it of being too static and not sufficiently expressive. It is signed and dated 1725, but the preliminary oil sketch, originally bought by an English collector and now in the Louvre, was executed a year or two earlier.

252 above

CHARIOT OF PHAETON WITH ALLEGORIES OF THE FOUR CONTINENTS

c. 1753
Giovanni-Battista Crosato 1697–1756
fresco, Palazzo Rezzonico, Venice

This ceiling is the focal point of the trompe l'oeil decoration by Pietro Visconti of the great ballroom at Palazzo Rezzonico. It reflects the work which Crosato had recently completed at Stupinigi and marks the culmination of his career. Although resplendent both in execution and composition, it falls short of Tiepolo's virtuosity. In this ballroom on 7th June 1764 Procurator Ludovico Rezzonico received the duke of York, brother of George III.

253 right

CHINOISERIE FIGURES

detail of the Porcelain Room
1757–59
porcelain
Palazzo Reale di Capodimonte, Naples

Among the projects carried out for Queen Maria Amalia of Saxony by the Capodimonte porcelain factory was the decoration of a whole room. The room, originally in the Palazzo di Portica and now installed in the Palazzo di Capodimonte, is entirely adorned with porcelain figures, flowers and swags in the currently popular Chinese style.

254 *below*

CAPRICCIO WITH A COLONNADE

1763, Antonio Canal, called Canaletto 1697–1768
50 × 36 in (127 × 91 cm)
Accademia di Belle Arti, Venice

This was the picture presented by Canaletto to the Venetian
Academy after his election on 11th September 1763. It is his last
signed and dated painting. The Venetian Academy was founded
in 1756 as a centre for instruction for artists, but Canaletto's
membership was resisted on the grounds that view painting was
not a serious branch of art. However, after Pittoni became
president a vacancy occurred in September 1763, and Canaletto
was elected with a complimentary notice.

255

THE GRAN SALONE

c. 1731
Filippo Juvarra 1678–1736 and assistants
Palazzo di Stupinigi, near Turin

It is disputed when the Gran Salone of
Stupinigi was completed, but the Venetian
brothers Giuseppe and Domenico
Valeriani were commissioned to decorate
it on 10th February 1731. Under Juvarra's
orders they carried out frescos depicting
mythological scenes of Diana which were
probably ready for the inaugural royal
hunting party in November of that year.
Every detail was supervised by Juvarra
himself and the overall effect is both
grandiose and theatrical.

For Italy, the nineteenth century was of great importance politically and socially, but not artistically. By 1900, she had been transformed from a disparate collection of independent states into a united political entity, engaged (particularly in the north) in changing rapidly and fundamentally from an agricultural to an industrial community. Throughout the nineteenth century Italian art floundered in a provincial mire as if weighed down by Italy's long and brilliant artistic history. An atmosphere of change did not really affect her art until the beginning of the twentieth century when she once more began to make an original contribution to European culture.

Since the second half of the seventeenth century, Italy had begun to relinquish her cultural leadership of Europe to France. However, throughout the eighteenth and for much of the nineteenth century she remained an inspiration to artists from all over Europe, who now came, not so much for commissions as they had in the seventeenth century, but to study the remains of her classical past. Rome and its glorious ruins became in the second half of the eighteenth century the centre of the Neo-classical movement, which continued well into the nineteenth century.

The Neo-classical movement

Although it was mainly foreign artists who were involved with Neo-classicism, Italy did produce one major exponent of the style: Antonio
58 Canova. Canova was directly influenced by one of the central figures of the Neo-classical movement, the Scottish archaeologist and painter Gavin
40 Hamilton, who was working in Rome when Canova arrived there shortly after 1779. Much of Canova's work was devoted to portraits, and he based many of these on actual classical patterns, clothing contemporary figures in the trappings of antiquity. A very good example of this is the statue of Napoleon as 'imperator' of which there is a reduced bronze version in the courtyard of the Brera Gallery in Milan. Canova was a great admirer of
59 Napoleon; he sculpted several figures of him as well as of members of his
58 family. In his portrait of Napoleon's sister, Pauline Borghese, the sitter is portrayed as Venus, dressed in classical draperies and reclining on a sofa.

A very similar kind of elegance can be seen in the marble reliefs on the
70 walls of the Sala di Marte in the royal palace at Caserta near Naples, decorated by Antonio di Simone in 1807. Inspiration here was obviously derived from the graceful linear qualities of Greek marble reliefs; Simone's reliefs add lightness to the proportions of this large room, counter-balanced at the same time by the contrasting fluted pilasters in between. In its rare combination of richness and lightness, this interior is a fine example of empire decoration. The royal palace itself had been designed half a century earlier
47 by Luigi Vanvitelli, and like so many of the projects of the Napoleonic era, the interior was not to be finished until much later; in this case by Gaetano Genovese in 1839-45.

Much more severe in feeling, and therefore stylistically closer to the work of a leader of the Neo-classical movement in architecture like Claude-
58 Nicholas Ledoux, is the new wing of the Vatican Museums in Rome. This bold interior executed for the pope by Raffaelle Stern in 1817-21 consists of two long galleries with barrel-vaulted coffered ceilings, divided by a domed area in the centre. Niches with plain round arches are let into the walls at regular intervals. These frames provide a simple and uncluttered background for the sculptures, which are then allowed to create the main points of interest and variety for the eye as one looks along the gallery.

The Machiaioli and Rosso

Because of the close connection between the ideas of the Neo-classical movement and the philosophy behind the teaching in art academies, which came into existence in many of the cities of Europe in the eighteenth century,

256
UNIQUE FORMS
OF CONTINUITY IN SPACE
1913
Umberto Boccioni 1882–1916
bronze
43.5 in (110.5 cm)
Galleria d'Arte Moderna, Milan

Boccioni's move in 1907 from Rome to Milan was a significant denial of the traditional Italian artistic centre in favour of the dynamism and European outlook of Italy's largest industrial city. There Boccioni and his Futurist colleagues attempted to capture in art the motion of twentieth-century life. *Unique Forms of Continuity in Space* is one of the clearest illustrations of his belief that sculpture should consist of actively open rather than passively closed forms.

257
IMPRESSION
OF A BOULEVARD
1892
Medardo Rosso 1858–1928
wax
Galleria Nazionale d' Arte Moderna, Rome

For twenty years between 1890 and 1910 Medardo Rosso enjoyed European fame and was even said to have aroused the envy of Rodin. In Paris he absorbed the ideas of the Impressionists, yet it was his search for freedom from his Italian background that propelled him in their direction. Like many of the Italian artists who were to follow him, he felt that the strength of his native tradition was a handicap to valid contemporary expression. His attempts to capture the impression of ordinary experiences were a revolt against the formalisation of fashionable academic sculpture and his experiments with the portrayal of light prepared the way for the Futurists.

258
PAULINE BORGHESE AS VENUS
1805
Antonio Canova 1757–1822
marble
70 × 81 in (160 × 205 cm)
Galleria Borghese, Rome

Gavin Hamilton's advice to the young Canova about an early work was 'to unite with this so exact and beautiful imitation of nature the fine taste and "beau ideal" of the ancients.' Canova acted on this and produced a style that swept across Europe. He was in constant demand by princes of both church and state in Italy and abroad and was already well established when he agreed to do a sculpture of the sister of Napoleon, wife of Camillo Borghese.

Rome remained a centre for artistic pilgrimage throughout the nineteenth century. Unfortunately, the artists who came tended to leave little behind in the way of work or influence, even when they remained as long as eighteen years, as did Ingres, who was there from 1806–24. One exception to this seems to have been Corot, who visited Italy several times and whose painting at least prepared the way for the 'Machiaioli', a group of painters who began working together in Florence in the early 1860s. Some of these artists had taken part in the wars of the Italian Risorgimento in 1859–60 and 1866 in the hope of gaining greater freedom for their country and their art. The fact that Rome was at the centre of the academic tradition made it considerably more difficult for Italian artists to foster or hold new attitudes, and must certainly have contributed to the general stagnation of Italian art in the nineteenth century. The linking by the Machiaioli of art and politics was a pattern followed by Italian artists in the twentieth century.

The Machiaioli painted pictures of everyday scenes in which they aimed to represent the phenomenon of light as objectively as possible. In a similar way to Corot, they attempted to incorporate light into the tonal variations in their colour, but, in fact, unlike Corot, the mood in their paintings is one of wistfulness and isolation. For instance, the figures in a painting like *Rotonda di Palmieri* of 1866 by Giovanni Fattori, the leader of the group, seem to have no relationship, either with one another or with their surroundings. Even in *The Visit* by Silvestro Lega, in which the figures are seen greeting one another, the atmosphere is cool, distant and unreal, while in Corot's landscapes the figures are positively related to their surroundings.

The work of the Machiaioli represents the most original development in nineteenth-century Italian painting, but much nearer in attitude and technique to the discoveries being made at this time in France by the Impressionists is the late nineteenth-century sculpture of Medardo Rosso. The Impressionists were not only interested in the phenomenon of light itself, but in the way form is dissolved by light, and this was precisely what Rosso tried to explore, working mainly in the malleable materials of plaster and wax. Rosso produced his most original work between the years 1890–1906. The finest collection of these unique sculptures is now in the Galleria d'Arte Moderna in Rome. In his *Impression of a Boulevard* of 1892, the 25

features of the woman's face are softened and reduced, as it were, almost to a shadow so that they appear to alter and change as we look at them. By creating this kind of surface, Rosso denied not only the classical and academic ideal of a highly finished and technically perfect figure, but also the other traditional concept that sculpture should be able to be looked at in the round. A few years later, in 1896, he carried these ideas still further in the *Portrait of Madame Noblet* where the features on one side of the face are obliterated as if the light were falling from the left and only leaving the right eye and the right side of the nose and mouth visible. The figure emerges from the formless plaster as if being revealed, by magic, before our very eyes.

Apart from Rosso, Italy produced no other artists of real merit in the later part of the nineteenth century, and the architecture of this period tended simply to reflect the styles that were prevalent in Europe at the time: Neo-Renaissance, Neo-Gothic, Neo-Baroque and Art Nouveau. Although Italy's contribution to Art Nouveau was in no way original, its fairly widespread acceptance was an indication that she was at last awakening to the experiments being made elsewhere in Europe. In 1895 the first Biennale held in Venice introduced Italians to the French Symbolists. Then in 1902 an international exhibition of decorative arts in Turin made a profound impression with the Art Nouveau work being done in that field. It was for this exhibition in Turin and for another at Udine that the most impressive Italian Art Nouveau buildings were commissioned. Raimondo d'Aronco's pavilions are fantastic examples of exhibition architecture.

Part of the reason for the poverty of Italy's art at this time must be that during the latter part of the nineteenth century she was undergoing the most profound political and social changes. Unification of the country had taken place finally in 1870, and since then Italy's industrial revolution had forged ahead rapidly. The achievement of political unity was greatly aided by the spirit of nationalism which had been developed under the leadership and idealism of Mazzini and Garibaldi, but it became a reality with the diplomatic manoeuverings of Count Cavour. It was nationalism which was one of the motivating forces behind Futurism, the movement which brought Italian art into the twentieth century. The artistic task was felt to be a national task. Indeed as the First World War threatened, the Futurists identified themselves with the state and used their pictures as propaganda.

The Futurists

In the manifesto of 1909, which was written by their leader the poet F. T. Marinetti, the Futurists declared battle against inertia, indifference and intellectual passivity. It reveals the artists' awareness of the arrival of a modern age of technology and the urgent necessity to reject altogether a heritage which had retarded artistic growth. It also has an aggressive spirit which was unpleasantly prophetic of Italy's Fascist future. Although Futurism was contemporary with Cubism in France, it was essentially a reflection of Italy's changed situation.

The five main Futurist painters, Giacomo Balla, Gino Severini, Carlo Carrà, Umberto Boccioni and Luigi Russolo, subsequently published their own technical manifesto, in which they set down their ideas about how painting in particular should express the Futurist attitude. Their main point was that they should try to express the dynamism of the modern era with images that captured the effect of movement and change. Because of this new preoccupation and awareness of the energy of modern life they were all very interested in Impressionism and its still more scientific development in Divisionism, which gave the effect of a world which was never still. Later on, however, Futurist painting developed away from the Impressionist technique to become a style more dependent on planes of colour which,

259
THE VICTOR EMMANUEL
MONUMENT
1885–1911
Giuseppe Sacconi 1854–1905
marble
Rome

Dominating an ancient site in Rome is this immense Graeco-Italic monument to Victor Emmanuel II, the first king of united Italy. It was the outcome of an architectural competition held in 1884 and won by Sacconi against 293 rivals. Although built well before the period of Fascist megalomania, it is obviously intended to proclaim the grandeur of Rome and the glory of the Italian state.

260
CARDINAL
Giacomo Manzù, born 1908
bronze
Museo Internazionale d'Arte Moderna, Venice
Fifteenth-century Italian sculpture and the
work of Donatello and Medardo Rosso
strongly influenced Manzù as a young man,
and his handling of religious imagery still
bears the traces. Among his restricted range
of subjects, studies of cardinals are frequent.
They stand or sit in meditation with a
timeless grace.

through their interaction on the beholder's eye, break up the surface of the object and create a dynamism of their own.

It was probably Boccioni who came closest to an embodiment of the idea of dynamism, particularly in his sculpture. In his *Manifesto of Futurist Sculpture* of April 1912, he talks about the absolute and complete abolition of definite lines and closed sculpture; the figure is opened up yet enclosed by its environment. In his sculpture *Unique Forms of Continuity in Space* Boccioni expressed this idea very clearly. The striding form moves firmly out into the space around it. The outlines do not describe nor detract from the sensation of physical activity, and yet, at the same time, the flowing surfaces give a feeling of the passage of air. In other words, one is made conscious simultaneously of the figure, its movement and its environment.

Besides theories about poetry, painting and sculpture, Futurism also produced ideas on architecture. Antonio Sant' Elia, an architect from Como, joined the Futurists in 1914. He published a manifesto in July of that year in which he suggested that, rather than drawing their inspiration from nature, architects should embrace the world of mechanics, of which architecture should be the most beautiful expression, the most complete synthesis, the most efficacious artistic integration. Although he never actually managed to build anything because of his premature death in 1916, hundreds of his drawings still exist (many of them are now in the Museo Civico in Como) showing how he saw his city of the future, with soaring skyscrapers, external elevators and split-level streets.

During the years before and just after the First World War Florence became a centre for the study of the history of art. The American Bernard Berenson and the Englishman H.P. Horne were instrumental in encouraging the collection of Italian works of art of the thirteenth and fourteenth centuries and the Renaissance. At Horne's death in 1916 his collection was preserved in his fifteenth-century palace which is now a museum.

Fascist influences

A second, if brief, radical revision of Italian art occurred with the 'metaphysical' work of De Chirico and Carlo Carrà. For several years they painted dreamlike, disconnected landscapes which were a precedent for the European Surrealist movement. However, their rejection of their earlier metaphysical principles and of experiment in general coincided with the desire of Fascist leaders for an art form which could be widely comprehended. Fascism encouraged the 'Novecento Italiano' movement that had developed almost immediately after the First World War. It advocated a return to the classical values of Italy's great past. Architecture was also affected. In the late 1930s, when he came under German influence, Mussolini commissioned Neo-Roman buildings like La Padulla's Palace of Italian Civilisation in Rome from Marcello Piacentini.

However, in the early years of Fascism, architecture escaped from the retrogressive movement. Mussolini encouraged modern experimentation in architecture in an attempt to make Fascism seem progressive and youthful. The desire to be up to date did not mean that good architecture necessarily resulted. Indeed most Fascist architecture is only superficially modern, but Giuseppe Terragni who was himself a Fascist and a member of the Novecento Italiano was able to create a series of designs of genuine originality. The Casa del Fascio is essentially a plain cube whose exterior is articulated only by the square frames in front of the windows which create a striking contrast between light and shade all the way along the façade. In its sculptural feeling this building conforms to the desires of the Novecento Italiano to revive the plastic values of the classical tradition in architecture, but essentially its effect is one of interesting modernity.

Postwar architecture

Fascist tolerance of experimentation in architecture meant that after the Second World War Italy immediately took a leading and exciting part in modern building, particularly in industrial and public architecture. Italian architects have been fortunate in the willingness of several large industrial firms to commission unusual and adventurous premises. A good example of this is the Palazzo Olivetti in Milan by Gian Antonio Bernasconi and others in 1954. The lightness of this building and its elegance are characteristic of much Italian design of the period. Similarly graceful is the Termini station in Rome of 1951 by Eugenio Montuori and others, with the roof of its entrance hall shaped like a wave on the sea, moving out from the plain linear façade of the railway station proper behind.

But, older than either Terragni, Bernasconi or Montuori is the remarkable architect and engineer, Pier Luigi Nervi, who remains to this day one of the most original artistic figures Italy has produced. His work is governed by the desire to combine a technical mastery of his material with aesthetic beauty. He works almost exclusively in reinforced concrete and it is through his experiments with the structural possibilities of this fabric that he has created some of his most original buildings. The roof of the exhibition hall in Turin of 1948-49 and the huge mushroom-like shape of the Palazzetto dello Sport in Rome of 1956-57 must be among the most exciting architecture of the twentieth century.

Much of Nervi's inspiration comes from his understanding of organic structures in nature. The Pirelli skyscraper in Milan on which he worked with Gio Ponti relies for its strength on the structural principles of a tree, for its four main supports grow ever more slender towards the top. This remarkable building, with its hexagonal shape and sides curved like a ship's bows, has come to dominate the whole area around it. It is a symbol of a forward-thinking attitude worthy of the best ideals of the Italian Futurists and indeed of the twentieth century.

Italian artists in European movements

Although Italy has produced no major movements in painting and sculpture since Futurism, there have been a number of artists of individual interest and significance, such as Lucio Fontana, Alberto Burri and Giuseppe Capogrossi. Better known are Amedeo Modigliani, Giacomo Manzù and Marino Marini who have been concerned in differing ways with revitalising their classical tradition. Modigliani thoroughly absorbed the work of the Italian old masters but spent most of his working life in Paris, where he came into contact with the Fauves and the Cubists and all that was going on in the art world during this exciting era.

The sculpture of Giacomo Manzù and Marino Marini is characterised by a similar combination of classicism and individuality. In his ecclesiastical figures Manzù creates an almost hieratic image, similar in feeling to some early Renaissance sculpture. Marini's particular fascination is the theme of the horse and rider, an inspiration originally derived from the equestrian monuments of the Roman empire and the Italian Renaissance. His concern is the exploitation of the relationship between the forms of man and horse. Modigliani, Marini and Manzù all have an individual vision of a traditional form of subject matter.

The Italian-Swiss Giacometti was another sculptor well known in Europe. From about 1930-35 he exhibited with the artists of the Parisian Surrealist group, during which time many of his sculptures consisted of selections of evocative objects mounted on plinths, for example *Project for a Piazza*. He then decided that it would be helpful to resume modelling from nature, and after the Second World War, in the tall thin figures with which

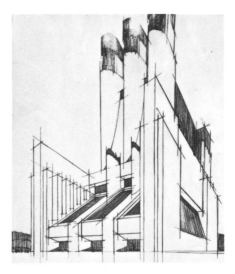

261

SKYSCRAPER

c. 1914
Antonio Sant' Elia 1880–1916
ink
Museo Civico, Como

Along with his fellow Futurists, Sant' Elia's work was directed towards revivifying Italy. Inspired by the romantic aspects of the industrial cities in the United States, he worked out detailed plans for a city of the future, complete with towering buildings, external elevators and multi-level roads. Although only one of his designs was actually built and that was posthumous, Italy was shaken and the problem of building for modern life was looked at afresh.

262

THE PALAZZO DELLO SPORT

1960
Luigi Nervi, born 1891
Rome

The two sports arenas necessary for the Olympic games held in Rome in 1960 were built by the Italian engineer Nervi as works of unequalled elegance. The inverted dish dome of the Palazzo dello Sport floats above the whole stadium like a luminous web which recalls Guarini's dome for San Lorenzo in Turin (plate **226**). It is made, however, of essentially twentieth-century materials: lightly reinforced prefabricated concrete elements.

157

he is normally associated, he concentrated on trying to capture what he called likeness. Looking at a sculpture like *The Lion Woman* of 1946-47 which is typical of his work, one has the feeling that one is seeing a presence rather than a representation of a human being.

Attitudes to modern art

Although artists like De Chirico and Giacometti have been connected with European movements, the attitude of the Italians to modern foreign works of art has been very conservative. To some extent this must have been due to the nationalistic and reactionary attitude of the Fascist régime between the wars, but even so, the improvement since 1945 does not appear to have been very rapid. For the most part the museums of modern art are full of Italian works of the nineteenth and twentieth centuries, rather than those of foreign artists associated with the major artistic trends of the time.

Private collectors have shown a similar lack of interest, although several far-sighted connoisseurs have formed fine collections of twentieth-century Italian and European painting and sculpture. Among the most notable are 271, 273 the Mattioli and Jesi collections in Milan. The rich, industrial north is also the recipient of some patronage of the arts by industrial firms.

The first city, however, to show any interest in contemporary art was Venice, which has held its International Biennale of Modern Art regularly since 1895, although no Impressionists or Post-Impressionists were shown there until 1905. Venice's permanent Museo Internazionale d'Arte Moderna is less nationalistically inclined than those of other cities, possessing as it does minor works by such major artists as Whistler and Matisse. In particular, it 272 has a superb painting by Pierre Bonnard, *Nude before a Mirror*.

Apart from its position as a centre for modern art, Venice also possesses one of the finest private collections of twentieth-century painting and 263, 264 sculpture in Europe, that of Peggy Guggenheim in the Palazzo Venier dei Leoni on the Grand Canal, which is open to the public three times a week.

It is one of the few collections in Europe with a systematic historical basis. Basing her purchases on lists drawn up by the art historian Sir Herbert Read, the painter Marcel Duchamp and Petra Van Doesburg, widow of the De Stijl artist, not simply on her own taste, she built up her collection between 1942 and 1947. Most of the important painters of the century are 274, 275 represented: Picasso, Kandinsky, Klee; several De Stijl artists and Mondrian; early Cubist works by Duchamp, Robert Delauney and Metzinger. The particular strength of the collection, however, is its very complete representation of Surrealist art. A wide range of examples of the work of the Surrealist artists Max Ernst, Yves Tanguy, André Masson, Giacometti, Mirò, Paul Delvaux and Magritte are included.

The presence of Peggy Guggenheim's collection in Italy and its exhibition in 1948 in the Biennale did much to introduce modern art to young Italian painters who had been cut off from it during the years of Fascism. Knowledge of modern art has since been furthered by the Galleria Nazionale d'Arte Moderna in Rome. During the last twenty years it has acquired many works by European artists of the nineteenth and twentieth centuries including paintings by the French Impressionists as well as by Modigliani, Kandinsky, Klee, Pollock and Tobey. It has also become the most important collection of modern Italian art in existence.

Italy's greatest artistic achievements during the twentieth century have therefore been in architecture, and, although public museums and galleries have not always kept abreast of developments elsewhere in the west, acquiring mainly works by Italian artists, the interest of private collectors has caused an ever-increasing number of foreign works to enter the country.

Mary Acton

263
BOXERS
1935
Alexander Archipenko 1887–1964
terra-cotta
h. 31 in (79 cm)
Peggy Guggenheim collection, Venice
Certain similarities to Archipenko's work can be seen in some of the sculpture of Futurists, despite the principles of Cubism to which Archipenko adhered being so very different. However in this piece, which is a slightly enlarged version of one done in 1913, the object is an excuse for the representation of the concept of movement in space. Boccioni's sculpture could be described in similar terms.

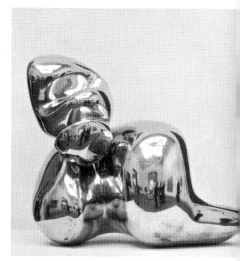

264
SHELL AND HEAD
1933
Jean Arp, born 1887
bronze
h. 8 in (20 cm)
Peggy Guggenheim collection, Venice
This was the first piece of sculpture bought by Peggy Guggenheim who was taken by Marcel Duchamp to the foundry in Paris where it was being cast. She recalled that as soon as she had handled it she wanted to own it. Seven works by Arp in this collection play a part in representing Surrealist art, its most important feature.

265
THE VISIT
1868, oil on canvas
Silvestro Lega, 1826–95
12 × 24 in (31 × 60 cm)
Galleria d' Arte Moderna, Rome

The mild atmospheric realism of the
Machiaioli of the later 1860s did not
transform contemporary vision as the
Impressionists had done in France. But
Lega's ability to distil the essence of a
mood recalls their subjects, if no more.

266 *bottom left*
DANCER = SEA
1913
Gino Severini, born 1883
oil on canvas
39·75 × 31·75 in (100 × 80·5 cm)
Peggy Guggenheim collection, Venice

Dancers and the opportunities they offered
for depicting movement were a favourite
theme of Severini's during his Futurist
period. He saw and declared in paint a
similarity between the movement of a
dancer and the dancing of the sea. In this
painting the moving and flowing planes
create a sensation equivalent to both the
constant ebb and flow of water and the
undulating rhythm of the dance.

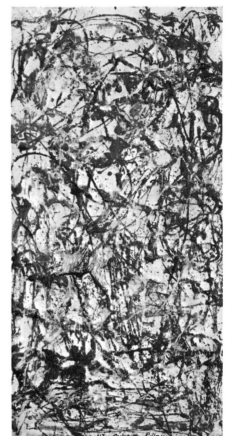

267 *above*
ENCHANTED FOREST
1947
Jackson Pollock 1912–56
oil on canvas
84 × 44·5 in (219 × 113 cm)
Peggy Guggenheim collection, Venice

The development in New York in the
1940s of an entirely new type of painting,
Abstract Expressionism, was closely
associated with Peggy Guggenheim's
gallery there. One of the stars of the
gallery was Jackson Pollock, who was
introduced to the American and European
public very largely through Miss
Guggenheim's efforts. Jackson Pollock's
method of painting, which he claimed
enabled him to become thoroughly
involved in creation, has become a legend.
This work was mainly achieved by
splashing or dripping paint onto a damp
canvas and allowing it to run.

268

THE NEW WING
OF THE VATICAN MUSEUMS

1817–22
Raffaelle Stern 1774–1820
Rome

Pope Pius VII continued the work of his
predecessors in expanding and
reorganising the Vatican Museums. The
Braccia Nuova, the New Wing, of the
Museo Chiaramonti was built to house
some of the major pieces of the collection
including the Augustus of Primaporta.
The eminent suitability of its Neo-classical
decor, designed by Canova, for displaying
Roman sculpture is an all-too-rare
example of successful nineteenth-century
building.

269

NAPOLEON

1803
Antonio Canova 1757–1822
marble
Galleria d'Arte Moderna, Rome

Canova's European fame led him to make
two journeys to Paris to do portraits of
Napoleon and his family. On his arrival
for his first visit in 1802 he was greeted
with great honour and stayed at Saint
Cloud with Napoleon and Josephine. In
1810 he was ordered to come again and
this time Napoleon tried hard, but
unsuccessfully, to persuade Canova to
stay. Napoleon's admiration for Canova
was reciprocated: Canova's many portraits
of Napoleon show him as an idealised,
somewhat gentle, hero.

THE SALA DI MARTE

begun 1807
Palazzo Reale di Caserta

The Bourbon dynasty brought over a
century of wealth and expansion to
Naples. In 1757 Charles III started to
build a palace to rival Versailles in size
and situation, and almost a hundred years
later parts of the interior were still being
magnificently decorated. The Sala di
Marte was begun in 1807 under the
French influence of Napoleon's brother
and was continued after the Bourbon
restoration. The large relief panels
represent the heroic virtues, while the
smaller ones show scenes from the *Iliad*.

271
NUDE
Amedeo Modigliani 1884–1920
Gianni Mattioli foundation, Milan

Naples, Florence, Venice and Rome have been called Modigliani's true masters. It was not, however, until he turned his back on this national heritage that he was able to develop as an artist. Paris was at the time capital of the arts, and it was there that Modigliani painted his many characteristic nudes and portraits. Only in the last few months of his life was he sufficiently independent as a painter to wish to return to Italy and to the great achievements of her past, so stultifying for any artist at the beginning of the century.

272 *bottom left*
NUDE BEFORE A MIRROR
1933, Pierre Bonnard 1867–1947
oil, 59·75 × 40·25 in (151·7 × 102 cm)
Galleria Internazionale
d'Arte Moderna, Venice

The year after its completion this painting was exhibited at the Biennale at Venice, and it is now among the few twentieth-century non-Italian works in the Galleria Internazionale d'Arte Moderna. All Bonnard's paintings are characterised by an intense love of what he was painting. Recording a shifting pattern of light and colour which corresponded to the idea rather than to the actuality of what he saw, he achieved a personal poetry and vision.

273
BUST
Marino Marini, born 1901
plaster
Jesi collection, Milan

Marini is widely recognised as the leading Italian sculptor since Boccioni and Rosso. Unlike them, however, he has not reacted against the Italian artistic past but has assimilated and made use of it. In his work traditional and modern expressions meet. His portraits and his famous Horse and Rider series express his foreboding in always vigorous and sometimes violent forms.

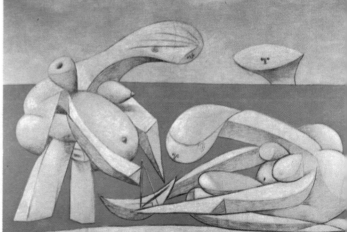

274 *bottom left*
BATHERS

1937
Pablo Picasso, born 1881
oil, pastel and crayon on canvas
50·5 × 76·75 in (128 × 195 cm)
Peggy Guggenheim collection, Venice

The representation of Surrealist art in this collection would not be complete without works by Picasso done during his Surrealist period. The subject of this painting is light hearted and clearly associated with the outside world, yet it has been disorientated and bears some resemblance to his earlier terrifying bone-like figures. It is this combination of the happy and the frightening that gives the work its disquieting power.

275
UPWARD

1929
Wassily Kandinsky 1866–1944
oil on millboard
27·5 × 19·25 in (70 × 49 cm)
Peggy Guggenheim collection, Venice

The various works by Kandinsky in Peggy Guggenheim's collection trace his development towards abstraction. In this work he is well on the way, although he uses individualistic shapes rather than the strictly impersonal squares and rectangles of pure abstraction. Kandinsky was at this time happily teaching at the Bauhaus, and the suggestion of a face in the work is reminiscent of the light-hearted approach of Paul Klee, a colleague of his there.

276 *above*
THE DISQUIETING MUSES

1916/17
Giorgio de Chirico, born 1888
oil on canvas
38·25 × 26 in (66 × 97 cm)
Gianni Mattioli foundation, Milan

The Mattioli collection ranks high among privately formed collections of twentieth-century Italian art on account of both the quality and the historical importance of the works in it. It is indicative of the standard of works that this De Chirico may well be the greatest painting of his career. The haunting sculptured mannequins and the strange objects of their dream world are set against a fairly exact representation of the Castello Estense at Ferrara. This balance between fantasy and reality illustrates the ambivalent metaphysical nature of De Chirico's early art.

Museums and Monuments

AGRIGENTO, Sicily
1 **Ruins of Acragas**   Greek, subsequently Roman. Many ruins including: Temple of Concord, Temples of Hera, Olympian Zeus, Hercules.

AMALFI, Campania
2 **Cathedral**   w front and approach steps built 1204 in Lombard-Norman style. Campanile (1276): lower storeys Romanesque, upper Saracenic. Bronze doors made before 1066 in Constantinople by Simeon of Syria. Cloisters: 13th c with interlacing arches of strong Moslem influence, contain museum with architectural exhibits.

ANCONA, Marches
3 **Cathedral**   11th–13th c, important example of the fusion of Hellenistic and Romanesque architecture. Interior: Greek cross with central dome.

AOSTA, Piedmont
4 **Sant'Orso**   8th c crypt; Romanesque campanile; Gothic nave; 16th c choir stalls. 12th c cloisters with interesting capitals.
5 **Arch of Augustus**   Triumphal arch erected 23 BC.

AQUILA, Abruzzi
6 **San Bernardino**   Built 1454–72, façade by Cola dell'Amatrice (1527). Interior: imposing central nave with Baroque woodwork.

AQUILEIA, Friuli-Venezia Giulia
7 **Basilica**   Romanesque built by Poppo (1021–61) with Gothic and Renaissance additions on 4th c constructions. Notable mosaic from 4th c basilica and other remains.

AREZZO, Tuscany
8 **San Francesco**   Gothic, started in 1322. Frescos of the legend of the Cross by Piero della Francesca executed 1452–66.

ASCOLI PICENO, Marches
9 **Palazzo del Popolo**   13th c; remodelled during the Renaissance. Houses the archaeological and Roman collections of the municipal museum.
10 **Pinacoteca**   Paintings including Titian, *St Francis.*

ASSISI, Umbria
11 **Cathedral of San Rufino**   Romanesque, begun 1140, consecrated 1228. Interior 1571.
12 **Basilica of San Francesco**   Consists of two superimposed churches built between 1228–53. Lower Church: frescos including Simone Martini, *Life of St Martin,* 1326; Cimabue, *Virgin, Angels and St Francis* and on vault above high altar *Triumph of St Francis,* 14th c. Upper Church: frescos by Cimabue and his school and possibly by Giotto, *Life of St Francis,* 1296–1304.
13 **Santa Chiara**   Gothic, by Da Campello (1260). Interior: 14th c frescos.
14 **Santa Maria sopra Minerva**   Formerly 1st c Temple of Minerva, Corinthian hexastyle pronaos still exists.
15 **Rocca Maggiore**   Fortress erected in 1367.

BARI, Apulia
16 **Basilica of San Nicola**   The first major Norman church in Apulia. Episcopal throne of white marble.
17 **Pinacoteca Provinciale**   Works by Veronese, G. Bellini, Tintoretto.

BASSANO, Veneto
18 **Museo Civico**   Paintings including works by Bassano. Remondiniana collection of engravings.

BENEVENTO, Campania
19 **Arch of Trajan**   Built AD 114; richest memorial of the period. Bas-reliefs depicting the life of Trajan.

BERGAMO, Lombardy
20 **Santa Maria Maggiore**   Started 1137 in Romanesque style. Porch by Giovanni da Campione (1353). Interior: late 16th c Florentine tapestries and marquetry chancel stalls.
21 **Cappella Colleoni**   Built by Amadeo in 1476. Interior: tomb of Colleoni and daughter and ceiling by Tiepolo (1733).
22 **Accademia Carrara**   Picture gallery containing an important collection of paintings: Lotto, G. Bellini, Botticelli, Pisanello, Mantegna, Raphael and Fra Angelico; including Botticelli, *Giuliano de' Medici,* Raphael, *St Sebastian.*

BITONTO, Apulia
23 **Cathedral**   Important Romanesque building,

constructed 1175–1200. Richly decorated central portal, rose window and gallery; pulpit by Maestro Nicola.

BOLOGNA, Emilia-Romagna
24 **San Petronio**   Begun 1390 in Gothic style to the designs of Antonio di Vicenzo, construction continued until 1659. Centre portal has sculptured decorations designed by Jacopo della Quercia. Interior: very fine proportions and decorations.
25 **Museo Civico**   Etruscan and Greek antiquities, and medieval exhibits.
26 **Pinacoteca**   Major collection of paintings, mostly Italian: Raphael, *St Cecilia in Ecstasy*; Della Francesca, *Malatesta in Prayer*; Monaco, Nicola Pisano, Costa, Romano, Reni, Vasari, Perugino, the Carracci.

BOLSENA, Latium
27 **Santa Cristina**   Renaissance façade (1494); terra-cottas by Della Robbia.

BRACCIANO, Latium
28 **Castello Orsini**   Well-preserved building of 15th c. Apartments decorated by F. Zuccari contain good furniture.

BRESCIA, Lombardy
29 **Duomo Nuovo**   Built early 17th c; dome by L. Cagnola (1825). Interior: nave and 2 aisles, 15th c chancel, 9th c crypt.
30 **Rotonda (Duomo Vecchio)**   Romanesque, 12th c with circular ground plan.
31 **Loggia**   Early Renaissance, built 1492–1574 after design by J. Sansovino.
32 **Museo Civico Età Romana**   Incorporates remains of Roman temple 74 BC, Greek and Roman exhibits. 1st c Winged Victory, 2nd c mosaics. Also **Museo Civico Età Christiana.**

CAGLIARI, Sardinia
33 **Cathedral**   Rebuilt in 13th c, extensive Baroque alterations 1669–1702. Interior: pair of pulpits made by Guglielmo 1162. Museum containing works of art from the treasury; triptych by Gerard David.
34 **Basilica of San Saturnino**   One of the earliest Christian basilicas in Italy.
35 **Amphitheatre**   Most remarkable Roman building in Sardinia.
36 **Museo Archeologico Nazionale**   Prehistoric, Punic and Roman items. Also Pinacoteca.

CANOSA DI PUGLIA, Apulia
37 **Cathedral**   Much restored 11th c Romanesque showing Byzantine influence. Interior: 11th c pulpit and episcopal throne; tomb of Bohemond, son of Robert Guiscard, (d. 1111); door by Roger of Malfi.

CAPRAROLA, Latium
38 **Palazzo Farnese**   Masterpiece by Vignola, massive flight of steps in front of façade. Interior: winding staircase, frescos.

CAREGGI, Tuscany
39 **Villa Medici**   First of the famous country houses of the Medici enlarged by Michelozzo for Cosimo and again by Lorenzo the Magnificent. Restored by Pontormo and Bronzino.

CASERTA, Campania
40 **Palazzo Reale**   Baroque, built 1692–1772 to the plans of Luigi Vanvitelli for the kings of Naples. Inspired by Versailles; large rectangular plan. Rich decoration in royal apartments; Empire-style furniture.

CASTEL DEL MONTE, Apulia
41 **Castle**   Built c. 1240 by Frederick II, in Gothic style looking forward to Renaissance.

CASTELFRANCO, Veneto
42 **Cathedral**   Contains important work by Giorgione.

CASTELSEPRIO, Lombardy
43 **Santa Maria in Castelseprio**   Graceful frescos, probably of 7th c.

CEFALU, Sicily
44 **Cathedral**   Magnificent Romanesque, begun by Roger II in 1131; façade designed by Giovanni Panettera started in 1240. Interior: magnificent mosaics, best-preserved in Sicily.
45 **Museo Mandralisca**   Antonello da Messina, *Portrait,* Byzantine painting, Greek vases.

CHIANCIANO TERME, Tuscany
46 **Casino**   Spectacular ceiling of the casino designed by modern architect-engineer, Nervi.

CHIUSI, Tuscany
47 **Etruscan Tombs**   Near town, Tomb of the Grand-Duke, Tomb of the Monkey etc.

CIVIDALE DEL FRIULI, Friuli-Venezia Giulia
48 **Tempietto**   Part of 8th c church, contemporary stucco reliefs of female saints.
49 **Archaeological Museum**   Roman and medieval exhibits. Psalters of Bishop Egbert of Trèves and St Elisabeth of Hungary.

CIVITA CASTELLANA, Latium
50 **Cathedral**   11th c Romanesque building with portal, façade and thrones by the Cosmati.
51 **Rocca**   Pentagonal fortress built by Sangallo the Elder 1494–1500. Keep 1512.

COMO, Lombardy
52 **Cathedral**   Important example of the fusion of Gothic and Renaissance styles. Principal architects Rodari and Solari with s door attributed to Bramante 1491, dome 1770 by Juvarra. Interior: good paintings by Ferrari and Luini.
53 **Sant' Abbondio**   11th c building with two graceful campanili.

CORTONA, Tuscany
54 **Museo Diocesano**   Wooden ceiling 1536. Paintings of Sienese school; works by Signorelli and Fra Angelico.
55 **Palazzo Pretorio**   Contains the Etruscan museum.

CREMONA, Lombardy
56 **Cathedral**   Started 1107 in Romanesque style but contains much Gothic and Renaissance work. Octagonal baptistery planned by Teodosio Orlandino 1167 with Renaissance additions.

ESTE, Veneto
57 **Museo Nazionale Atestino**   In the Palazzo Mocenigo (late 16th c). Pre-Roman and Roman exhibits including 1st c bronze Medusa's head.

FAENZA, Emilia-Romagna
58 **Cathedral**   Late 15th c, built by Giuliano da Maiano.
59 **Museo Internazionale delle Ceramiche**   Collection of ceramics of all periods, including Picasso and Matisse.

FANO, Marches
60 **Santa Maria Nuova**   16th–18th c, with 2 altarpieces by Perugino.
61 **Arch of Augustus**   Triumphal arch of 1st c.

FENIS, Lombardy
62 **Castle**   Well-preserved Gothic.

FERMO, Marches
63 **Cathedral**   Gothic façade by Giorgio da Como 1227. Interior reconstructed end of 18th c; mosaic floor 5th c.

FERRARA, Emilia-Romagna
64 **Cathedral**   Mid-12th c Romanesque. Impressive w front, campanile by Alberti.
65 **Museo della Cattedrale**   Cosimo Tura, *St George* and *The Annunciation.*
66 **Castello Estense**   Former palace of the Este dukes, built 1385 and enlarged in the 16th c. Early ceiling paintings.
67 **Palazzo di Lodovico il Moro**   Built by Rossetti, late 15th c. Large courtyard, 3 rooms with painted ceilings, probably by Garofalo. Museum with exhibits from Spina 6th–3rd c BC.
68 **Palazzo di Schifanoia**   Begun 1391, completed by Benvenuti and Rossetti of 1467–69. Frescos by Cossa and Tura of life of Borso d' Este.
69 **Pinacoteca**   Paintings of the Ferrarese school including Cosimo Tura, Cossa and Ercole Roberti.

FIESOLE, Tuscany
70 **Cathedral**   Plain building of 1028 with 13th–14th c additions.
71 **Badia Fiesolana**   Until 1028 the cathedral of Fiesole, 11th c façade. Imposing interior.
72 **San Domenico di Fiesole**   1405–35, beautiful Renaissance arches to nave chapels. Works by Fra Angelico.
73 **Roman Theatre**   Roman Theatre 80 BC. Museum contains Roman exhibits.

FLORENCE, Tuscany
74 **Cathedral**   (Santa Maria del Fiore) Started 1296 by Arnolfo di Cambio, continued in 14th c after designs by Talenti. Dome by Brunelleschi constructed from 1420–61. Façade destroyed at end of 16th c and replaced in 19th c. Exterior: s door, Portale dei Canonici, end of 14th c;

sculpture by D'Ambrogio and Tedesco. Interior: in dome fresco of the Last Judgment, an outstanding work by Vasari and Federico Zuccari; there are a number of important works by Luca della Robbia; a bronze urn by Ghiberti; Michelangelo, *Descent from the Cross*; two equestrian frescos by Uccello and Castagno. **Baptistery of San Giovanni** Octagonal building of 4th–5th c. rebuilt 11th–12th c; outstanding bronze doors with gilded bas-reliefs; s door by Pisano (1336); N and E doors (Porta del Paradiso) by Ghiberti early 15th c. Interior: dome lined with 13th c mosaics; tomb of John XXIII and *Mary Magdalen* by Donatello. **Campanile** Begun 1334 by Giotto, continued by Andrea Pisano (1343) and completed by Talenti 1348–59. On lower storey are bas-reliefs by A. Pisano and Della Robbia.

75 **The Carmine** Brancacci Chapel: very important series of frescos by Masolino and Masaccio, completed by Filippino Lippi.

76 **Ognissanti** Interior: works by Ghirlandaio and Botticelli, *St Augustine*.

77 **Or San Michele** Good example of the transition from Gothic to Renaissance. Exterior: pilasters with canopied niches containing statues by masters including Ghiberti, Verrocchio and Donatello. Interior: Gothic tabernacle by Orcagna (1349–59).

78 **Santissima Annunziata** Rebuilt by Michelozzo. Interior: Perugino, *Annunciation*, and late Renaissance works.

79 **Sant' Apollonia** Fresco of the *Last Supper* by Castagno.

80 **Santa Croce** Franciscan church rebuilt about 1294 with 19th c façade. Interior: many monuments to notable citizens. Frescos by Giotto and Agnolo Gaddi, also works by Orcagna, Veneziano, Donatello and Della Robbia. **Pazzi Chapel** Very beautiful early Renaissance chapel by Brunelleschi. **Museum** Housed in old refectory; works by Gaddi, Donatello, Giotto and Vasari.

81 **San Lorenzo** Begun by Brunelleschi (1442–46). Interior completed by Manetti (1447–60). Interior façade, library and new sacristy added by Michelangelo. **Old Sacristy** By Brunelleschi containing works by Donatello. **New Sacristy** Contains funerary chapel for the Medici and statues by Michelangelo.

82 **Santa Maria Novella** Large Dominican church built between 1278–1350. Façade designed by Alberti. Important frescos: Masaccio, *Trinity*; also Ghirlandaio, Orcagna and Filippo Lippi. In the Gondi Chapel a crucifix by Brunelleschi. Cloisters contain further important frescos attributed to Buonaiuto (late 14th c). Cappella degli Spagnuoli by Talenti; frescos by Andrea da Firenze and assistants.

83 **San Miniato al Monte** One of the most beautiful Romanesque churches in Italy. Façade from 1062 to late 13th c, plain interior in practically original state.

84 **Santa Trinità** 11th c, rebuilt 13th c and 14th c with Baroque front. Fine Gothic interior with works by Lorenzo Monaco and Ghirlandaio and interesting tombs.

85 **Convent of San Marco** Dominican monastery now a museum, reconstructed by Michelozzo from 1437 and decorated with outstanding frescos by Fra Angelico. Pilgrim's Hospice: fine works by Fra Angelico.

86 **Convent of Santa Maria Maddalena dei Pazzi** Frescos by Perugino.

87 **Biblioteca Laurenziana** Begun by Michelangelo, completed by Vasari. Museum displays part of the very valuable collection of MSS and books.

88 **Casa Buonarroti** Museum containing works by and relating to Michelangelo.

89 **Galleria d'Arte Moderna** 19th and 20th c paintings and sculpture mostly Italian.

90 **Galleria dell'Accademia di Belle Arti** Contains famous sculptures by Michelangelo, *David* and the Slave series; also Botticelli, Orcagna, Monaco, Lippi, Fra Bartolomeo, Lorenzo di Credi and works of the Tuscan school.

91 **Loggia dei Lanzi** A spacious open hall containing important sculptures: Giambologna, *Rape of the Sabines, Hercules and Nessus*; Cellini, *Perseus*.

92 **Museo Archeologico** Collection of Graeco-Roman and Egyptian works of art, especially rich in Etruscan antiquities: François Vase, Arezzo Chimera, Arringatore.

93 **Museo Bardini** Antiquities, sculpture and decorative arts including Pollaiuolo, *Hercules and the Hydra*.

94 **Museo dell'Opera del Duomo** Contains designs, models and works of art connected with the cathedral and campanile. Sculpture including: Donatello, *Jeremiah* and *Habakkuk*; 2 choir galleries (cantorie) by Luca della Robbia and Donatello; silver altar of St John the Baptist, 14th–15th c.

95 **Museo Horne** Paintings, drawings and decorative arts in Herbert Percy Horne's home, includes works by Martini, Giotto, Tiepolo.

96 **Museo Nazionale (Bargello)** Ancient medieval palace begun 1254, now museum of sculpture, arms and armour and decorative arts. Splendid collection of medieval and Renaissance sculpture includes: Michelangelo, *Bacchus*; Donatello, *David* and *St George*; Cellini, *Cosimo I de' Medici*; Verrocchio, *David*; Pollaiuolo, *Hercules and Antaeus*; Giambologna, *Mercury*.

97 **Palazzo della Signoria (Palazzo Vecchio)** Rectangular fortress-palace built by Arnolfo di Cambio with tower. Just outside: Donatello, *Judith and Holofernes*. Interior: Verrocchio, *Winged Genie* and frescos by Vasari and others.

98 **Palazzo Medici-Riccardi** Typical Florentine Renaissance palace, begun 1444 by Michelozzo and home of the Medici family for nearly a century. Now houses the **Museo Mediceo** which contains works of art which belonged to the Medici family. **Medici Chapel** Decorated with frescos by Benozzo Gozzoli including *Journey of the Magi to Bethlehem*.

99 **Palazzo Pitti** Renaissance palace, begun *c.* 1440 to design by Brunelleschi, enlarged with additional wings 17th–19th c, now an art gallery. Paintings include magnificent collection of works by Raphael, Andrea del Sarto, Titian, Tintoretto, Rubens. **Museo degli Argenti** Housed in the Palazzo Pitti; decorative arts including gold and silversmith's work, and gems.

100 **Palazzo Strozzi** Prototype of 15th c town mansion, half fortress, half palace.

101 **Spedali degli Innocenti** Colonnaded façade by Brunelleschi with terra-cotta medallions of babies by Andrea della Robbia.

102 **Uffizi Gallery** Collection of works of art started by the Medici housed in the palace built for them by Vasari in 1574. Paintings, sculpture, prints and drawings, tapestries. Famous sculpture: *Medici Venus*; *Arrotino*. Famous paintings: Giotto, *Madonna Enthroned with Angels and Saints*; Simone Martini, *Annunciation*; Filippo Lippi, *Madonna and Child*; Botticelli, *Primavera*; Leonardo da Vinci, sketch of Adoration of the Magi; Raphael, *Madonna of the Goldfinch*; Michelangelo, *Holy Family*; Titian, *Venus of Urbino*; Dürer, *Adoration of the Magi*.

FOSSANOVA, Latium
103 **Abbey** Cistercian, late 12th c abbey and monastic buildings.

FRASCATI, Latium
104 **Villa Aldobrandini (Belvedere)** Built 1598–1603 by Giacomo della Porta for prince Aldobrandini. Decorated with 17th c paintings.

GALLIANO, Lombardy
105 **San Vincenzo** In apse one of most impressive wall paintings of 11th c.

GEMONA, Friuli-Venezia Giulia.
106 **Cathedral** 13th c, transition from Romanesque to Gothic. Façade has much sculpture.

GENOA, Liguria
107 **Cathedral** Started in 12th c, Romanesque, Gothic and Renaissance in style. Interior: good Renaissance chapel of St John the Baptist.
108 **Palazzo Bianco** 17th c, built by Orsolino and Ponzello. Contains important art collection; good examples of Dutch and Flemish schools: Rubens, *Mars and Venus*; Van Dyck, *Christ and the Money Changers*; also 13th c frescos.
109 **Palazzo Reale** Built 1650 by P. F. Cantoni and others, altered 1705 by Fontana. Richly decorated rooms with paintings.
110 **Palazzo Rosso** Magnificent 17th c build-

ing by P. A. Corradi. Richly decorated with contemporary frescos. Contains picture gallery: strong collection of Van Dyck portraits.

GRADO, Friuli-Venezia Giulia
111 **Cathedral** Basilica of 6th c, Byzantine capitals, mosaic pavement. Pulpit includes 6th–9th c work. 14th c Venetian silver altarpiece.

GUBBIO, Umbria
112 **Palazzo dei Consoli** Gothic building of 1332–46 attributed to Matteo di Giovannello which houses the museum and art gallery.

HERCULANEUM, Campania
113 Remains of a Roman town destroyed in AD 79 by an eruption of Vesuvius, rediscovered 1709, excavations still proceeding. Many important buildings have been excavated including: the finely-preserved House of the Mosaic Atrium, House of the Wooden Partition, House of the Neptune Mosaic, House of the Deer.

IESI, Marches
114 **Palazzo della Signoria** Built 1486–90 by Francesco di Giorgio Martini. The Pinacoteca contains 5 important works by Lorenzo Lotto.

LECCE, Apulia
115 **Basilica di Santa Croce** Built 1549–1695 in Baroque style. Rich façade reminiscent of Spanish plateresque.
116 **Museo Castromediano** Greek and Roman exhibits.
117 **Piazza del Duomo** A fine group of Baroque buildings: the **Cathedral** 1670, the **Bishop's Palace** 1709; the **Seminary** 1709.

LORETO, Marches
118 **Santuario della Santa Casa** Sanctuary begun in 1468 and continued by a number of Renaissance masters: cupola by Sangallo; side chapels and screen by Bramante. Interior richly decorated.

LUCCA, Tuscany
119 **Cathedral** Rebuilt 11th c, Romanesque exterior; façade: arches with tiers of arcading by Guido and Guidetto da Como. Interior, Gothic, rebuilt 14th–15th c. Octagonal marble chapel, by Civitali. Tomb of Ilaria del Carretto earliest-known work of Jacopo della Quercia. Fra Bartolomeo, *Virgin and Child Enthroned*.
120 **San Michele** Perfect example of Pisan-Romanesque style of early 13th c. Interior: 12th c crucifixion.
121 **Museo Civico** In the Villa Quarquonia, Roman, Romanesque and medieval sculpture, Matteo Civitali, *Head of Christ*.

LUCERA, Apulia
122 **Castello** Built by Frederick II in 1233 and enlarged by Charles I (1269–83).
123 **Museo Fiorelli** Greek and Roman exhibits and medieval ceramics.

MANFREDONIA, Apulia
124 **Santa Maria di Siponto** Important Romanesque cathedral built by the Normans in 12th c.

MANTUA, Lombardy
125 **Sant' Andrea** Important and influential early Renaissance building built to the designs of Alberti by Luca Fancelli. Dome added by Juvarra; frescos and other works by Giulio Romano.
126 **San Sebastiano** Designed by Alberti and constructed by Fancelli. Superb entrance.
127 **Reggia dei Gonzaga** Fortress-palace of the Gonzaga family founded in 13th c and extensively redecorated 16th–18th c. Cortile della Cavallerizza by Giulio Romano, important developed Mannerist design. Interior: Graeco-Roman sculpture (caryatid 5th c BC); Renaissance sculpture; works by Van Dyck, Tintoretto, Rubens; frescos by Romano. Appartamento degli Arazzi: tapestries (perhaps the oldest in existence) designed after Raphael's Acts of the Apostles series. Camera degli Sposi: magnificent frescos by Mantegna.
128 **Palazzo Colleredo** Designed by Giulio Romano. Impressive Mannerist façade.
129 **Palazzo del Tè** Built by Giulio Romano as summer palace of the Gonzagas. Very influential Mannerist building. Frescos by Romano, e.g. *Fall of the Giants*.

MASER, Venetia
130 **Villa Barbaro (Villa Giacomelli)** Built

by Andrea Palladio c. 1555–59 as combination of farm and gentleman's residence. All rooms on upper floor have frescos by Paolo Veronese.

MERANO, Trentino-Alto Adige
131 **Castel Tirolo** 12th c fortress built for the counts of Tyrol 11 km from Merano.

MESSINA, Sicily
132 **Museo Nazionale** Medieval paintings and mosaics including Antonello da Messina, *Virgin and Child with Saint* and work by 17th c local artists.

MILAN, Lombardy
133 **Cathedral** Started 1386, w front completed 1813. Largest Gothic building in Italy, strongly influenced by transalpine example. Interior: tomb of G. G. Medici by Leoni 1562.

134 **Basilica of Sant' Ambrogio** Romanesque prototype of Lombard basilica and rare example of church which retains its atrium. 9th c bronze doors. Interior: pulpit c. 1000 with Romanesque decoration; richly decorated 9th c altar front; 5th c chapel of San Vittore in Ciel d'Oro with contemporary mosaics.

135 **Sant' Eustorgio** Romanesque basilica dating from 9th c. Cappella Portinari: beautiful Renaissance chapel by Michelozzo and Foppa.

136 **Santa Maria delle Grazie** Renaissance building (1465) of brick and terra-cotta, added to by Bramante. In refectory Leonardo's *Last Supper* of outstanding beauty and importance. Chiostrino and Sacristry by Bramante.

137 **San Satiro** Rebuilt by Bramante, façade 19th c. Interesting interior.

138 **Biblioteca Ambrosiana** Built 1609 for Cardinal Federigo Borromeo, now library with an important collection of printed books and manuscripts (Petrarch's Virgil illuminated by Simone Martini) and an art gallery. The collection of Italian paintings includes: drawings by Leonardo, including the Codice Atlantico with 1,750 drawings and notes on artistic and scientific subjects; also Raphael, *The School of Athens*.

139 **Castello Sforzesco** Square castle built for Francesco Sforza 1450, decorated by Bramante and Leonardo. **Museo Archeologico** (beautifully arranged) Pre-Roman, Greek, Roman and Etruscan exhibits. Medieval and Renaissance sculpture: Michelangelo, unfinished *Pietà*. Important collection of Italian paintings.

140 **Museo Poldi-Pezzoli** Important collection of paintings and other works of art. Paintings are mostly Italian including: Antonio Pollaiuolo, *Portrait of a Woman*; Mantegna, *Virgin and Child*; Giovanni Bellini, *Ecce Homo* also Della Francesca, Botticelli, Perugino.

141 **Palazzo Clerici** Bought in 17th c from the Visconti by the Clerici family. Main salon has magnificent frescoed ceiling by Tiepolo.

142 **Pinacoteca di Brera** Art gallery in 17th c Palazzo di Brera. Rich collection of Italian and other paintings, especially north Italian and Lombard works. Works by: Mantegna, including *The Dead Christ*; Giovanni Bellini; Carlo Crivelli; Raphael, *Betrothal of the Virgin*; Titian; Tintoretto; Veronese.

MODENA, Emilia-Romagna
143 **Cathedral** Important Romanesque building begun by Lanfranco in 1099. Notable sculpture on the main w portal and the s side by Wiligelmo. Beautiful 14th c Torre Ghirlandina.

144 **Palazzo dei Musei** Biblioteca Estense: library containing 350,000 volumes and 12,000 MSS, 15th c illustrated bible *Bibbia di Borso d'Este* illuminated by Taddeo Crivelli and Franco Russi. **Galleria Estense** Paintings mostly Italian. Strong in works by Emilian artists also Cima, Tura, Correggio, Tintoretto, Guardi, Bernini.

MONREALE, Sicily
145 **Cathedral** Outstanding Norman church, built by William II 1172–76. Façade flanked by square towers and decorated with interlaced arches, bronze door by Bonanno da Pisa 1186. Interior: richly decorated with mosaics. Lovely cloisters with decorated columns and capitals.

MONTEFALCO, Umbria
146 **San Francesco** Gothic with Renaissance portal. Now a museum containing paintings and frescos by Benozzo Gozzoli.

MONTE OLIVETO MAGGIORE, Tuscany
147 **Abbey** Founded in 1313 by Tolomei. Large cloister contains series of 36 frescos by Signorelli and Sodoma.

MONTEPULCIANO, Tuscany
148 **Madonna di San Biaglo** A main work of Sangallo the Elder (1518–37). Central plan with a dome.

149 **Museo Civico** In the 14th c. Palazzo Comunale. Terra-cottas by Della Robbia and painting.

MONTE SANT'ANGELO, Apulia
150 **Santuario di San Michele** Built in Romanesque-Gothic by Charles I of Anjou. Byzantine bronze door; 11th c episcopal throne.

MONZA, Lombardy
151 **Cathedral** Façade of white, green and black marble by Matteo di Campione 1390–96. Interior: reconstructed in 17th c. Chapel of Queen Theodolinda decorated with frescos by Zavattari.

MURANO, Veneto
152 **Museo d'Arte Vetraria** Comprehensive collection of glass from antiquity to the present.

NAPLES, Campania
153 **Cathedral** Begun 1272 (Gothic, French influence). Interior: chapel of St Januarius with beautiful Baroque bronze grill. Cappella Carafa, below high altar, good Renaissance work.

154 **Certosa di San Martino** Most complete example of 17th c Neapolitan Baroque.

155 **Gesù Nuovo** Interior of church 1584–1601 rich in coloured marbles and 17th c decoration. Above principal door fresco by Solimena.

156 **Monte Oliveto** Renaissance church with much Florentine sculpture of contemporary date.

157 **Santa Chiara** 14th c church contains several Angevin monuments. 14th c cloister transformed in 1742 into a rustic garden with majolica tiles and terra-cottas.

158 **Castel Nuovo** Built for Charles I of Anjou by Pierre de Chaulnes, but reconstructed several times. Main façade reached through a triumphal arch erected 1454–67, an outstanding Renaissance monument.

159 **Museo Nazionale** The 16th c palace contains one of the richest collections of antique sculpture: antiquities from Pompeii and Herculaneum, Graeco-Roman sculpture, murals, mosaics, bronzes, Greek vases and coins. Includes: *Doryphorus* (from Pompeii); *Aphrodite* attributed to Praxiteles; *Farnese Bull*; *Tazza Farnese*.

160 **Palazzo Reale** Built early 17th c, restored 19th c; chapel by Cosimo Fanzago, 1668. It contains furniture, tapestries, ceramics, and paintings. Houses the Biblioteca Nazionale founded by Charles of Bourbon in 1734.

161 **Palazzo Reale di Capodimonte** The 18th c palace houses the Museo e Galleria Nazionale: an art gallery and royal apartments contain paintings, porcelain, ivories, armour and tapestries. Titian, *St Paul*; Farnese casket; portraits by David, Goya, Kauffmann; works by Bruegel, Cranach, Martini, Masaccio, Botticelli, Lippi, Antonello da Messina, Mantegna, Correggio.

162 **Villa Floridiana** Magnificent Neo-classical villa contains the Museo Nazionale della Ceramica.

NORA, Sardinia
163 Remains of Roman and Phoenican town including forum, theatre and villa.

ORVIETO, Umbria
164 **Cathedral** Fine building started 1290. 14th c façade is especially beautiful, designed and started by Lorenzo Maitani of Siena, continued by Pisano and Orcagna. Frescos by Fra Angelico and Luca Signorelli.

165 **Palazzo dei Papi** Houses the collections of the cathedral museum including Martini, Nino Pisano and Etruscan vases.

166 **Palazzo Faina** Greek and Etruscan vases.

OSTIA, Latium
167 **Ostia Antica** Remains of the ancient port of Rome: many houses and public buildings including the Mithraeum, Temple of Rome and Augustus (1st c) and Baths of Neptune.

PADUA, Venetia
168 **Sant'Antonio** Begun 1231 as temple for tomb of St Anthony of Padua, finished in 14th c. Byzantine exterior with 6 domes raised on drums. Interior: Gothic in form, Byzantine in spirit containing many works of art. Late 14th c chapel of St Felix also chapel of St Anthony; altar designed by Donatello 1445–50.

169 **Cappella degli Scrovegni (Arena Chapel)** Interior decorated with outstanding frescos by Giotto.

170 **Museo Civico** Paintings, mostly Italian, including works by Bellini, Tintoretto, Veronese, Tiepolo, also Roman and Byzantine exhibits.

171 **Palazzo della Ragione** Rebuilt in present form 1306 by Fra Giovanni degli Eremitani. Interior: single vast hall with frescos by Nicola Mireto (1420) replacing originals by Giotto.

172 **Statue of Gattamelata** Donatello's masterly bronze of the Venetian condottiere.

PAESTUM, Campania
173 Many important Greek remains including: basilica, Temple of Neptune, Temple of Ceres also museum.

PALERMO, Sicily
174 **Cathedral** Founded end of 12th c; Norman style with Saracenic influence.

175 **The Martorana** Founded 1143, fine façade and mosaics.

176 **Museo Nazionale Archeologico** One of the most interesting museums in Italy for its collection Greek sculpture and vases. Metopes of Selinus 6th–5th c BC, Etruscan items from Chiusi. Topographical collection of Greek and Roman Sicilian terra-cottas and bronzes.

177 **National Gallery of Sicily** Major collection of Sicilian art from 13th to 18th c. Antonello da Messina, *Annunciation*, 15th–16th c Flemish works.

178 **Palazzo dei Normanni** Built by the Saracens, enlarged by Roger II and successors and much altered. Palatine Chapel: outstanding Norman-Saracen building by Roger II, 1132–40, with mosaics. Royal apartments: Sala di Re Ruggero has mosaic hunting scenes, 1140.

PALESTRINA, Latium
179 **Tempio della Fortuna** Remains of a vast temple built by Sulla 82 BC in the Latin town of Praeneste. The upper and lower sanctuaries contain the remains of a number of Roman buildings. Museum: Roman exhibits including mosaic of the Nile in Flood.

PARMA, Emilia-Romagna
180 **Cathedral** 11th c Romanesque with 13th c porch showing the months. Interior: nave decorated with frescos; dome has frescos of the Assumption by Correggio. Baptistery: outstanding octagonal building in Romanesque style.

181 **Camera di San Paolo** Early frescos of mythological scenes by Correggio.

182 **Madonna della Steccata** Built 1521–34; decoration of chapels excellent examples 10th c style.

183 **San Giovanni Evangelista** Frescos by Correggio in dome and in lunette in transept.

184 **Palazzo della Pilotta** Built 1583–1602 for the Farnese family containing the important collections of the city. **Museo Nazionale d'Antichità** Prehistoric and Roman exhibits. **Galleria Nazionale** Paintings, especially works by Emilian, Tuscan and Venetian artists; several works by Correggio.

PASSANIANO, Venetia.
185 **Villa Marion** Largest of Venetian villas built in 18th c. Enormous façade and loggias.

PAVIA, Lombardy
186 **Castello Visconteo** Square fortress built by Galeazzo II Visconti 1360–65. Two of original corner towers remain. It now contains the archaeological museum which has a good collection of Roman exhibits and Renaissance sculpture.

187 **Certosa di Pavia** Begun 1396, completed early 16th c. Illustrates the development of early Renaissance design in Lombardy. Important façade begun 1491. Interior: Gothic features; tomb of Lodovico il Moro and Beatrice d'Este executed by Solari in 1499. Small cloister has fine terra-cotta decoration.

188 **San Pietro in Ciel d'Oro** 12th c church containing bas-reliefs illustrating the life of St

Augustine (the Arca di San Agostino) *c.* 1362, the work of Pisan masters, one of the great sculptural shrines of Italy.

189 **Museo Civico** Paintings, engravings, prints including work by Correggio, Antonello da Messina and Crivelli.

PEGLI, Liguria

190 **Villa Durazzo Pallavicino** Museum of Ligurian archaeology, sculpture, vases, bronzes terra-cottas.

PERUGIA, Umbria

191 **Collegio del Cambio** Built 1452–57 for money changers, contains frescos by Perugino and his school.

192 **Etruscan arch** The principal gate in the Etruscan city wall.

193 **Palazzo dei Priori** Large building by Giacomo di Servado and Giovanello di Benvenuto 1293, completed 1443, impressive exterior staircase. **Galleria Nazionale dell'Umbria** The most important collection of Umbrian paintings 13th–16th C; in the Sala Maggiore works of 17th and 18th C including many works by Perugino, Pinturicchio.

194 **San Domenico** Gothic (1305) rebuilt on the design of Maderno 1632. Interior: rich altar with bas-reliefs and statues by Agostino di Duccio. Choir contains 15th C glass. **Prehistoric Museum of Central Italy** Important palaeontological collection. **Museum of Etruscan and Roman Antiquities** Etruscan and Roman exhibits and medals.

195 **San Pietro** Entered by the Porta San Pietro (Agostino di Duccio 1475). 10th C, reconstructed in Renaissance style. Octagonal campanile 1468.

PESARO, Marches

196 **Musei Civici** Very important collection of ceramics and in the Pinacoteca a good collection of Italian primitives as well as several works by Giovanni Bellini.

197 **Villa Imperiale** 15th C and Renaissance villa of the town built by the Gonzaga. Frescos of battle scenes and allegories.

PIAZZA ARMERINA, Sicily

198 **Villa Imperiale** Remains of large Roman villa with mosaics of hunting scenes.

PIENZA, Tuscany

199 **Museo** Paintings of the Sienese school. Flemish tapestries 15th–16th C. Cope of Pius II (14th C English).

200 **Palazzo Piccolomini** Typical early Renaissance palace built by Rossellino.

PISA, Tuscany

201 **Cathedral** Romanesque building of great importance, begun by Buscheto 1063 and continued by Rainaldo; restored 1602–16. Interior: pulpit by Giovanni Pisano; tomb of Henry VII by Tino di Camaino. Apse vault mosaic by Cimabue.

202 **Baptistery** Remodelled by Nicola and Giovanni Pisano 1260–90. Interior: famous pulpit by Nicola Pisano 1260; font by Guido da Como 1246.

203 **Campanile** Known as the Leaning Tower of Pisa.

204 **Camposanto** Cemetery with interesting frescos including *The Triumph of Death* attributed to the Pisan Francesco Traini and others; also scenes from the Old Testament by Benozzo Gozzoli.

205 **Museo dell'Opera del Duomo** Works of art mostly from the Camposanto; several works by Giovanni Pisano, including an ivory Madonna *c.* 1299.

206 **Museo Nazionale** Works of the Pisan, Lucchese and Sienese schools.

207 **San Paolo a Ripa d'Arno** Church consecrated in 1148 with magnificent 13th C Pisan style façade.

208 **Santa Caterina** Built 1251–1300, remarkable façade 1330. Works by Nino Pisano.

209 **Santa Maria della Spina** Gothic, fine decoration on façade by the school of Pisano. Interior: Andrea Pisano, *Madonna and Child*.

PISTOIA, Tuscany

210 **Cathedral** Romanesque, 12th C façade. Porch 1311 with terra-cottas by Andrea della Robbia. Interior: silver altar of San Jacopo; *Madonna and Saints* by Verrocchio and Da Credi.

Baptistery: charming Gothic design by Andrea Pisano.

211 **San Andrea** Romanesque façade, 1166; bas-relief on central portal. Interior: magnificent pulpit by Giovanni Pisano.

POMPEII, Campania

212 Ruins of town destroyed AD 79 by eruption of Vesuvius. Many very important Roman remains.

POMPOSA, Emilia-Romagna

213 **Abbey** 11th C Romanesque church with Hellenic influence; fine campanile 1069.

POZZUOLI, Campania

214 The remains of a Roman port including an amphitheatre built in the time of Vespasian.

PRATO, Tuscany

215 **Cathedral** Romanesque. Interior: Donatello and Michelozzo, Pulpit of the Sacred Girdle; Giovanni Pisano, *Madonna and Child*; Filippo Lippi, frescos.

216 **Galleria Comunale** The Palazzo Pretorio (13th–14th C) contains sculpture and paintings including works by Filippo and Filippino Lippi.

RAVELLO, Campania

217 **Cathedral** Built 1086, remodelled 1786; bronze doors by Barisano da Trani 1179. Interior: Byzantine pulpit decorated with mosaics; richly decorated pulpit by Nicola da Foggia 1272.

RAVENNA, Emilia-Romagna

218 **Baptistery of the Orthodox** Plain exterior. Dome decorated with mosaics.

219 **Mausoleum of Galla Placidia** Small cruciform building erected by Galla Placidia, mid-5th C. Interior decorated with outstanding mosaics.

220 **Mausoleum of Theodoric** Built 526 for Theodoric. Monolithic cupola of Istrian limestone presents an unsolved problem of construction.

221 **Sant' Apollinare in Classe** Built 535–538 with very beautiful 9th C campanile. Interior: 24 Greek marble columns with Byzantine capitals and bases. Triumphal arch and choir are decorated with 6th–7th C mosaics.

222 **Sant' Apollinare Nuovo** Built by Theodoric early 6th C. Interior: fine 6th C mosaics on nave wall.

223 **San Vitale** Supreme example of Byzantine art in w Europe; consecrated 547. Interior: decorated with marble and mosaics, triumphal arch to choir. In the apse beautiful mosaics of Justinian and Theodora with their court.

224 **Museo Arcivescovile** Includes the 6th C ivory throne of Maximian. Mosaics in Oratory of St Andrew.

225 **Museo Nazionale** Collection of Roman exhibits, Byzantine ivories, ceramics and glass.

REGGIO DI CALABRIA, Calabria

226 **Museo Nazionale** Items from Greek settlements in Italy, Christian art of 11th–12th C and paintings of the school of Antonello da Messina.

RIMINI, Emilia-Romagna

227 **Tempio Malatestiano** Late 13th C Franciscan church, transformed in mid-14th C on the direction of Sigismondo Malatesta, now used as the cathedral. Exterior: famous early Renaissance façade by Alberti. Interior: sculpture of fine quality by Agostino di Duccio; tombs of the Malatesta, also fine fresco of Sigismondo Malatesta by Piero della Francesca.

228 **Arch of Augustus** One of the finest triumphal arches in Italy built 27 BC.

ROME, Latium

229 **St Peter's** Built on site of tomb of St Peter. First basilica started 319, mostly demolished early 16th C by Bramante, continued by many architects including Raphael, Michelangelo, Vignola, Della Porta and Maderno. Exterior: large Baroque façade and portico by Maderno 1612. Bronze doors from old basilica decorated by Antonio Filarete 1439–45. In tympanum, *La Navicella*, mosaic by Giotto from old basilica. Left of portico, Scala Regia designed by Bernini with statue of Constantine. Interior: Roman cross, nave, aisles (decorated by Bernini), side chapels, transepts. Marble walls and pavements by Della Porta and Bernini. Ceiling, with gilded coffering, designed by Bramante. Vast dome over crossing

supported on 4 pentagonal piers with balconies and niches by Bernini. Niches with Rococo statues; pendentives with mosaics of Evangelists. Bronze altar canopy by Bernini 1633. Bronze statue of St Peter 5th or 6th C. Right aisle: Michelangelo, *Pietà*, 1499; Borromini, Cappella del Santissimo Sacrimento. Monuments by Canova, Bernini, Della Porta, Pollaiuolo.

230 **Chiesa Nuova** Built 1575–1605. Vault, apse, dome, sacristy ceiling decorated by Cortona. In sanctuary, 3 paintings by Rubens.

231 **The Gesù** Designed by Vignola in 1568 and executed by Della Porta. Mannerist façade much imitated throughout Europe. Interior: very richly decorated.

232 **Sant'Agnese fuori le Mura** Built 324 and restored several times. In apse vaulting 7th C Byzantine mosaic. Catacombs of St Agnes (before 305) well preserved and characteristic.

233 **Sant' Agnese in Agone** Rebuilt 1642 by Rainaldi, Baroque façade added by Borromini 1635.

234 **Sant' Agostino** Early Renaissance, built by Giacomo da Pietrasanta 1479–83 with material taken from the Colosseum. Interior: Sansovino, *Madonna del Parto*; frescos by Raphael, *Isaiah*; altarpiece by Caravaggio, *Our Lady of Loreto*.

235 **Sant' Andrea al Quirinale** Built by Bernini, one of the most harmonious Roman Baroque buildings, richly decorated by his pupils.

236 **Sant' Andrea della Valle** Domed church completed by Maderno and façade by Rainaldi. Interior: frescos by Domenichino, chapel by Fontana.

237 **Santa Cecilia in Trastevere** Founded 3rd C; rebuilt 9th and much altered 16th–19th C. Interior: Arnolfo di Cambio, tabernacle 1293; Stefano Maderna, *St Cecilia*; Pietro Cavallini, *Last Judgment*, *c.* 1292.

238 **San Clemente** Best-preserved medieval basilica in Rome. 2 churches superimposed. Upper church: begun 1108, basilican interior, 12th C mosaics. Lower church: built above a Roman Mithraeum; decorated with 10th and 11th C frescos.

239 **San Francesco a Ripa** Built 1229, modernised 17th C. Chapel to Lodovica Albertoni by Bernini.

240 **San Giovanni in Laterano** The cathedral of Rome. First church built early 4th C. 1650 Borromini was commissioned to undertake a further rebuilding, E façade added 1734. Apse reconstructed and mosaics reset 1875–85. Interior: 426 ft long. Marble pavement of Cosmatesque design. On nave piers, frescos attributed to Giotto. Richly decorated cloister by Jacopo and Pietro Vassalletto 1223–30.

241 **Sant' Ignazio** Designed by the Jesuit Orazio Grassi 1626–85. Interior: rich Baroque.

242 **Sant' Ivo della Sapienza** Spiral tower by Borromini 1642–60 in the form of a bee in honour of the Barberini pope, Urban VIII.

243 **San Lorenzo fuori le Mura** Large basilica formed of 2 churches end to end. Original church built by Constantine 330, rebuilt 579 and church of Madonna *c.* 435; united in 1215. Interior: decorated with mosaics; 6th C mosaic on triumphal arch; 12th C fine mosaic pavement by the Cosmati.

244 **San Luigi dei Francesi** Built 1518–89. Façade by Della Porta. Interior: altarpiece and paintings, life of St Matthew by Caravaggio, his first public work (1597).

245 **San Marcello** Re-erected by Sansovino 1519, late Baroque façade by Fontana 1708.

246 **Santa Maria Antiqua** 6th C basilica within a monumental antique building. 7th–8th C frescos.

247 **Santa Maria della Pace** Built by Sixtus IV 1471–84. Semi-circular porch with Tuscan columns by Cortona. Interior: Raphael, *Sibyls*, 1514. Cloisters, fine work by Bramante 1504.

248 **Santa Maria del Popolo** Rebuilt 1472–77 under Sixtus IV in Renaissance style. Façade attributed to Andrea Bregno. Interior: renovated by Bernini. Contains many works of art: paintings by Pinturicchio; tomb of Cardinal della Rovere 1477; tabernacle by Bregno in the sacristy; apse by Bramante contains frescos by

Pinturicchio and 2 tombs by Sansovino; Chigi Chapel built from design by Raphael (also designed the mosaics in dome); *Jonah*, designed by Raphael, executed by Lorenzetto.

249 Santa Maria della Vittoria Built by Maderno 1605; façade by G. B. Soria. Interior: Bernini, *Ecstasy of St Theresa*.

250 Santa Maria in Aracoeli Dates from before 6th C; exterior rebuilt in Romanesque style, staircase 1348. Interior: Andrea Bregno, tomb of Cardinal Lebretto 1465; Donatello, tomb of the archdeacon Giovanni Crivelli 1432; pulpits by Lorenzo and Giacomo Cosmas *c.* 1200; frescos of the life of St Bernardino by Pinturicchio *c.* 1485.

251 Santa Maria in Cosmedin Good example of a medieval Roman church. Interior: antique nave piers; decoration by the Cosmati.

252 Santa Maria Maggiore Built 352–1292. Apse rebuilt 1670–76 and main façade added 1740–58. Campanile completed 1377. Interior: vast, preserves basilican form. 5th C mosaics, apse mosaic, Jacopo Torriti, *Christ Crowning the Virgin*. Renaissance Sixtine Chapel by Domenico Fontana; tomb of Cardinal Consalvo Rodriguez (d. 1299) by Giovanni Cosmati. Baroque Borghese Chapel, built to plans of Flamino Ponzio 1611.

253 Santa Maria sopra Minerva Built on site of Temple of Minerva, rebuilt 1280. Only Gothic church in Rome; Renaissance façade *c.* 1453. Interior: important works of art and Baroque monuments. Cappella Carafa, balustrade and cupids by Verrocchio; frescos by Filippino Lippi; in choir Michelangelo, *Christ Bearing the Cross*, 1514–21.

254 Santa Martina e San Luca 7th C lower church rebuilt *c.* 1640 by Cortona who added upper church with dome.

255 San Paolo fuori le Mura Commemorates the martyrdom of St Paul. Present building 19th C replaces basilica destroyed by fire in 1823. Triumphal arch with 5th C mosaics. Over high altar, tabernacle by Arnolfo and Pietro da Cambio 1295.

256 Santa Prassede Rebuilt 9th C. Interior: important Byzantine chapel of St Zeno.

257 San Pietro in Montorio Rebuilt late 15th C at expense of Ferdinand and Isabella of Spain. Interior: Del Piombo, *Scourging of Christ*, 1518. Tempietto by Bramante 1499–1502. Built on the supposed exact site of St Peter's martyrdom.

258 San Pietro in Vincoli Traditionally founded in 442 as shrine for the chains of St Peter. Restored 1475 by Meo del Caprina who built façade with colonnaded portico. Interior: tomb of Julius II, unfinished figures of Moses, Leah and Rachel by Michelangelo.

259 Santa Sabina Built by Cardinal Peter of Illyria 425–432. Restored 824, 1216 and later. Vestibule contains wooden door of 5th C. Interior: only 5th C basilica in Rome of the Ravenna type.

260 Santa Susanna Baroque façade by Maderno 1603.

261 Baths of Caracalla Magnificent Roman baths.

262 Baths of Diocletian Started 306. Very large baths with frigidarium, calidarium, tepidarium. Part converted by Michelangelo into the church of Santa Maria degli Angeli. Houdon, statue of St Bruno; see Museo Nazionale Romano.

263 Castel Sant' Angelo Originally Hadrian's mausoleum, finished AD 139 by Antonius Pius. Now contains the Museo Nazionale di Castel Sant' Angelo: paintings and decorative arts.

264 Catacombs Extend around Rome in a wide circle, over forty have been found. The more interesting are the catacombs of St Calixtus, St Sebastian, Domitilla, St Praetextatus, St Priscilla, St Agnes.

265 Colosseum Vast amphitheatre for 50,000 spectators started by Vespasian, dedicated AD 80.

266 Domus Aurea Extensive remains of a palace built by Nero after AD 64.

267 Fontana del Tritone Fountain by Bernini 1640.

268 Fontana di Trevi Magnificent fountain begun by Nicola Salvi 1732.

269 Forum Imperialum Remains of Roman monumental squares. Among the remains are: Forum of Trajan 111–114; Trajan's Column 113; Market of Trajan; Forum of Augustus; Basilica of Constantine.

270 Forum Romanum Commercial and legal centre of imperial city. Remains include: Temple of Vespasian AD 81; Arch of Septimus Severus AD 203; Temple of Castor and Pollux 484 BC; House of the Vestal Virgins; Temple of Antoninus and Faustina; Arch of Titus.

271 Galleria Borghese Housed in the Casino Borghese, a small palace built 1613–16 by Jan van Santen. Collection of paintings and sculpture founded by Cardinal Scipione Borghese. Sculptures include: Canova, *Pauline Borghese*; Houdon, *St John the Baptist*; early works by Bernini including *Rape of Proserpine*, *David*, *Apollo and Daphne*. Paintings: Raphael, *Deposition*; Titian, *Sacred and Profane Love*.

272 Galleria Nazionale d'Arte Moderna Major collection of 19th and 20th C Italian art.

273 Galleria Pallavicini In the Palazzo Rospigliosi built by Cardinal Scipio Borghese in 1603. Paintings: Botticelli, *La Derelitta*; Lorenzo Lotto, *Triumph of Chastity*; Guido Reni, fresco of *Aurora*.

274 Galleria Spada In the Palazzo Spada built by Giulio Mazzoni 1540, statues and stucco decoration added by Borromini. Small but important collection of 17th and 18th C art.

275 Museo Artistico Industriale Collection of works of applied art: Greek, Etruscan and Renaissance ceramics; Coptic, Byzantine and Renaissance fabrics; Islamic and medieval bronzes and ivories.

276 Museo Barracco Ancient Babylonian, Assyrian, Greek and Egyptian sculpture housed in the Piccola Farnesina built 1523, probably by Antonio Sangallo the Younger.

277 Museo Nazionale Romano Roman antiquities and Greek and Hellenistic sculpture: *Daughter of Niobe*, Greek 5th C BC; *Maiden of Anzio*, Greek 4th–3rd C BC; *Venus of Cyrene*, Greek, 4th C BC. Ludovisi Collection: Ludovisi Throne depicting birth of Aphrodite, Greek 5th C BC.

278 Museo Preistorico Etnografico Luigi Pigorini Important ethnographic and archaeological museum. Most of the archaeological exhibits are Italian. Objects from Bernardini Tomb from Palestrina, Venus of Savignano and Sardinian figures.

279 Palatine The one of the seven hills which has preserved most relics of ancient Rome. Remains include: House of Livia, rich house with mural paintings; Palace of the Flavians; Palace of Septimus Severus. Palatine Museum contains all items found on the Palatine since 1870.

280 Pantheon The only ancient Roman building which has been preserved. Begun by Agrippa AD 27, reconstructed by Hadrian 110–125. Used as a temple; subsequently converted into a church by Boniface IV 609.

281 Palazzo Barberini One of grandest Baroque palaces in Rome. Begun by Carlo Maderno for Urban VIII in 1624, continued by Borromini, finished by Bernini. Frescos by Pietro da Cortona. Contains Italian Baroque paintings, works by Cortona, Bronzino, Reni, Del Piombo, Giulio Romano.

282 Palazzo della Cancelleria 15th C, probably built by Andrea Bregno. Court attributed to Bramante, doorway by Vignola.

283 Palazzo Colonna Rich patrician house with important paintings and works of art.

284 Palazzo dei Conservatori Begun *c.* 1450 and remodelled 1564–68 from designs by Michelangelo. **Sale dei Conservatori** Works of art: marble statue by Bernini of Urban VIII; *Spinaro* 5th C BC; *She-Wolf*, Etruscan bronze 5th C BC. **Museo del Palazzo dei Conservatori** Esquiline Venus; Greek and Roman sculpture; Greek vases. **Museo Nuovo** Sculpture. **Pinacoteca Capitolina** Notable collection of paintings: Velasquez, *Self-portrait*; Rubens, *Romulus and Remus*; Dosso Dossi, *Holy Family*, also ceramics.

285 Palazzo Doria Begun 1435. Fine Rococo façade by Gabriele Valvassori *c.* 1690; s façade by Paolo Ameli 1743; N façade by Antonio del Grande *c.* 1660. **Galleria Doria-Pamphili** Important Roman patrician art collection. Paintings mainly 16th–17th C; Velasquez, *Innocent X*, Lorenzo Lotto, Rubens, Titian, Raphael, Claude, Carracci.

286 Palazzo Farnese Begun *c.* 1515 by Sangallo the Younger; continued by Michelangelo who built entablature; rear portion by Giacomo della Porta. On 1st floor frescos by painters of the Bolognese school.

287 Palazzo del Laterano Palace of the popes before 1309, reconstructed 1586. Contains Lateran Museums: **Museo Profano** Important collection of ancient Roman items. **Museo Christiano** Antiquities mainly from the catacombs and Christian sarcophagi.

288 Palazzo dello Sport Built of prefabricated concrete by Nervi with great technical daring. The smaller **Palazzetto dello Sport,** charming concrete construction also by Nervi.

289 Palazzo Madama 16th C with 17th C Baroque façade by L. Cigoli and Paolo Marucelli. Seat of the Italian Senate.

290 Palazzo del Museo Capitolino Built 1644–55. Contains museum of antique sculpture: *Dying Gaul, Capitoline Venus*.

291 Palazzo di Venezia Example of transitional Gothic/Renaissance style *c.* 1455. Now contains the Museo del Palazzo di Venezia: paintings, Romanesque wood sculpture and ivories, Renaissance bronzes, Hispano-Moresque maiolica, silver, tapestries and cassoni.

292 Piazza Navona Fine piazza with the Fountain of the Rivers by Bernini.

293 Spanish Steps Magnificent Baroque staircase by Francesco de Sanctis, 1723–26.

294 Temple of Fortuna Virilis Dates from end of 3rd C BC. Largely unchanged and consecrated as church of Santa Maria Egiziaca 872.

295 Termini Station Magnificent railway station incorporating 4th C BC wall.

296 Theatre of Marcellus Begun by Julius Caesar and completed by Augustus 13 BC.

297 Vatican Museums Include **Museo Chiaramonti, Braccio Nuovo, Museo Egizio. Museo Etrusco Gregoriano** Very important collection of items from south Etruria. Outstanding examples of Greek and Roman art, Greek, Italic and Etruscan vases. **Museo Pio-Clementino** Sculpture, mosaics, sarcophagi. Mosaics from Hadrian's Villa; *Apollo Sauroctonus*; the Barberini candelabra, sepulchral stele. *Venus of Cnidos*, copy of statue by Praxiteles; *Laocoön*; *Apollo Belvedere*; *Hermes*; *Belvedere Torso*; statues by Canova.

298 Vatican Palace Houses **Pinacoteca Vaticana** strong in schools of Siena, Umbria and the Marches. Melozzo da Forlì, *The Foundation of the Vatican Library*; Raphael, *Madonna of Foligno* and other works; Leonardo da Vinci, Titian, Caravaggio, Domenichino. **Appartamento Borgia** Richly decorated personal suite of Alexander VI 1492–1503. Frescos by Pinturicchio and his school 1492–95. **Museo Sacro** Founded by Benedict XIV 1765; enlarged in 19th C. Items illustrating Early Christian art, mainly from the catacombs; papyri; jewels; Ramboyna Diptych *c.* 900; vestments; small articles of church furniture. Room of the Aldobrandini Marriage: prints; early Roman frescos. **Sistine Chapel** Built for Sixtus IV by Giovanni de Dolci in 1473–81, now serves as the private chapel of the popes. Choir gallery and marble screen by Mino da Fiesole, Giovanni Dalmata and Andrea Bregno, 15th C mosaic pavement. Long walls decorated with important frescos by leading Tuscan and Umbrian fifteenth-century artists: Botticelli, *The Burning Bush* and *Punishment of Korali*; Perugino, *Christ giving the Keys to St Peter*. Barrel-vault covered with outstanding frescos by Michelangelo 1508–12. Altar wall: fresco by Michelangelo, *Last Judgment*, 1534–41. **Sistine Hall** Founded by Sixtus V, built 1587–89 by Domenico Fontana. Decorations have the themes of the glorification of literature and the pontificate of Sixtus V. Collection of manuscripts. **Stanze of Raphael** Stanza dell'Incendio: Perugino, *Glorification of the Holy Trinity*; walls painted by Giulio Romano, Francesco Penni and perhaps Perin del

Vaga. Stanza della Segnatura: painted by Raphael 1509–11; *Disputation of the Holy Sacrament*; *Parnassus* and small octagon in the ceiling by Bramante. Stanza d'Eliodoro: painted by Raphael 1512–14; *Expulsion of Theodorus from the Temple*; *Mass of Bolsena*; *Leo I Repulsing Attila*; *Deliverance of St Peter*. **Loggia of Raphael** Long gallery of 13 bays begun by Bramante, continued by Raphael and pupils. **Sala di Constantino** Painted by Giulio Romano with the help of Francesco Penni and Raffaele del Colle. Represents scenes from the life of Constantine.

299 **Villa Farnesina** Built by Peruzzi 1508–11 as the suburban residence of Agostino Chigi. Long gallery: frescos by Raphael, *Triumph of Galatea*; Giulio Romano, Francesco Penni and Giovanni da Udine. Bedroom: Sodoma, *Wedding of Alexander and Roxana*.

300 **Villa Giulia** Built 1550–55 for Pope Julius III by Vignola and Ammanati. Houses superb museum of pre-Roman antiquities: Cista Ficoroni; Chigi Vase; Apollo of Veii and sarcophagi.

301 **Villa Torlonia** Built 1760 by Carlo Marchionni for Cardinal Alessandro Albani. Important collection of sculpture.

SABBIONETA, Lombardy

302 **Teatro Olimpico** Built by Scamozzi based on Palladio, with frescos. Good example of 16th c town planning.

SALERNO, Campania

303 **Cathedral** Romanesque, rebuilt 1076–85 by Robert Guiscard. Atrium has 28 Roman columns brought from Paestum. Central doorway has 11th c decoration and bronze doors made in Constantinople. Museum has fine altar front of 54 ivory panels late 12th c.

304 **Museo Provinciale** Archaeological exhibits from excavations in the province, including a 1st c head of Apollo.

SAN CLEMENTE CASAURIA, Abruzzi and Molise

305 **Abbey** Cistercian, rebuilt in 12th c, but with a crypt of 871; portico and bronze door of late 12th c. Interior: pulpit, candelabrum and fine altar canopy of late 12th c.

SAN GIMIGNANO, Tuscany

306 **Cathedral** In medieval town with towers; 12th c Romanesque with façade of 1818. Interior: important frescos of 14th–15th c; marquetry chancel stalls by Giuliano da Maiano, 1475.

307 **Sant' Agostino** Late 13th c, Gothic. In chancel *Life of St Augustine*; frescos by Benozzo Gozzoli.

308 **Museo Civico** Paintings of the Sienese school 12th–15th c.

SAN SEPOLCRO, Tuscany

309 **Santa Chiara** Fresco by Piero della Francesca.

310 **Pinacoteca** Della Francesca, *Resurrection* and *The Virgin*.

SASSARI, Sardinia

311 **Cathedral** c. 1480 in Spanish style, 18th c façade.

SEGESTA, Sicily

312 Ruins of Greek temple and theatre in splendid setting.

SELINUS, Sicily

313 Impressive Greek city with several temples.

SIENA, Tuscany

314 **Cathedral** The most sophisticated Gothic design in Italy. Begun c. 1226 completed in 14th c. Façade: lower part by Giovanni Pisano has 3 portals; upper part, large rose window and modern mosaics. Interior: nave and 2 aisles. Unique pavement is formed by a series of 56 designs dating from 1369. Pillars: banded columns of black and white limestone; Pulpit by Nicola Pisano, assisted by Giovanni Pisano and Arnolfo di Cambio 1265–68; Cappella di San Giovanni by Sassetta 1482; Donatello, *John the Baptist*, 1457; **Baptistery** In the cathedral crypt; font and several statues by Jacopo della Quercia; Donatello, *Herod's Feast*.

315 **San Domenico** Gothic, 1226–1465, with crenellated tower of 1340. Cappella di Santa Caterina contains frescos by Sodoma.

316 **Museo dell' Opera del Duomo** Fragments from the façade and pavement and other items from the cathedral. *The Three Graces*, Roman copy of the original by Praxiteles. Impressive altarpiece by Duccio, *The Maestà*, completed 1311.

317 **Libreria Piccolomini** Founded 1495 by Cardinal Piccolomini, charming Renaissance work. Fine frescos by Pinturicchio and pupils 1502–09.

318 **Palazzo Pubblico** Gothic 1297–1310. Arcade at street level. Central section has 4 storeys topped by battlements. Torre del Mangia by Muccio and Francesco di Rinaldo 1338–48. It contains many works of art mostly of Sienese school: Simone Martini, *Maestà* and *Guidoriccio da Fogliano*, frescos by Ambrogio Lorenzetti, *Good and Bad Government*.

319 **Pinacoteca** In the 14th c Palazzo Buonsignori, restored in 1848. Paintings 13th–17th c, especially of the Sienese school. Several works by Duccio, also Sodoma, Beccafumi and Ambrogio and Pietro Lorenzetti.

320 **Spedale della Scala** Hospital decorated with frescos.

SPELLO, Umbria

321 **Santa Maria Maggiore** 12th c with a Baroque interior, and a 17th c façade. Frescos and *Madonna* by Pinturicchio; another Pinturicchio in the museum.

SPOLETO, Umbria

322 **Cathedral** 12th c, but much altered; Renaissance portico with 2 pulpits. Interior: frescos by Filippo Lippi and his tomb.

STRA, Veneto

323 **Villa Foscari** (Malcontenta) Important villa built by Andrea Palladio before 1560. Two major storeys, porch with one storey on a high base.

324 **Villa Nazionale (Pisani)** 18th c villa with fine frescos by Tiepolo.

STUPINIGI, Piedmont

325 **Villa Reale** Built at end of 18th c by Juvarra as a hunting lodge for Charles Emmanuel III of Savoy. Interior: furniture and objets d'art; ceiling paintings by Van Loo and others.

SULMONA, Abruzzi and Molise

326 **Palazzo of the Annunciata** Founded 1320, Gothic and Renaissance elements are blended harmoniously. Museum has interesting goldsmiths' work.

SYRACUSE, Sicily

327 **Cathedral** Reconstructed by Bishop Zosimus in 7th c from ruins of Doric temple of Athena. Rebuilt 1693; Baroque façade 1728–54 by Andrea Palma.

328 **Museo Nazionale** Major archaeological collection, very strong on items from E Sicily.

329 **Neapolis** Among the ruins are: Roman 2nd c ampitheatre; Greek theatre c. 335 BC, largest Greek theatre known; castle of Euryalus 402–397 BC, most important extant Greek military work.

TARANTO, Apulia

330 **Museo Nazionale** Exhibits from local excavations, particularly interesting is work of Greek settlements in Italy.

TARQUINIA, Latium

331 **Etruscan necropolis** Four main groups of tombs with remarkable frescos of 6th–2nd c BC.

332 **Museo Nazionale Tarquinese** 15th c palace houses an important collection of Etruscan and Roman exhibits.

TIVOLI, Latium

333 **Temple of Vesta** Also known as the Temple of the Sibyl. Small circular temple with ten of its original Corinthian columns standing.

334 **Villa d'Este** In 1550 Cardinal Ippolito d'Este commissioned Piero Ligorio to transform the original Benedictine convent into a villa. It was subsequently further embellished. Gardens with statues, grottos and many fountains.

TODI, Umbria

335 **Santa Maria della Consolazione** Fine High Renaissance church, started 1508, completed 1609, centralised plan.

TORRALBA, Sardinia

336 Most famous nuraghe of which there are hundreds throughout the island.

TORCELLO, Veneto

337 **Cathedral** Mostly 9th and 11th c, typical Venetian Byzantine. Interior: fine capitals, mosaic, pulpit and ambo and iconostasis.

TRANI, Apulia

338 **Cathedral** Good 12th c Romanesque building with marked Norman influence. Façade with sculptured portal and bronze doors by Barisano 1175–79.

TREMEZZO, Lombardy

339 **Villa Carlotta** Completed in 1747. Interior: sculptures including works by Canova and Thorwaldsen.

TRENTO, Trentino-Alto Adige

340 **Cathedral** 13th c Romanesque surrounded by an external gallery.

341 **Castello del Buon Consiglio** Fortress dating from 13th c to Renaissance.

TREVISO, Venetia

342 **Museo Civico** Includes a picture gallery, library and museum. Works by Pisanello and Bellini.

TRIESTE, Friuli-Venezia Giulia

343 **Cathedral of San Giusto** Created in 14th c by combining 2 11th c buildings. Interior: basilica with 5 asymmetric aisles; in apse 3rd c mosaics.

344 **Castle** Built 1471 by Frederick III of Austria, enlarged 1508, completed 1630. Collection armour.

345 **Orto Lapidario e Museo di Storia** Roman remains, Egyptian exhibits, Greek and Roman sculpture, goldsmiths' work.

TURIN, Piedmont

346 **Cathedral** Renaissance, built at end of 15th c by Cardinal della Rovere. Façade: three doors with fine sculpture by Meo del Caprino. Campanile completed 1720 by Juvarra. Interior: 17th c Cappella della Santa Sidone by Guarini.

347 **San Lorenzo** Built by Guarini (1687) with elaborately decorated Baroque interior and bold dome.

348 **Basilica of Superga** Considered to be Juvarra's masterpiece. Impressive columned portico, dome, and campanili.

349 **Italia 61 Pavilion** Built by P. L. and A. Nervi, a gigantic hall with mushroom pillars.

350 **Palazzo dell' Accademia delle Scienze** Three museums in a building constructed by Guarini 1678. **Museum of Antiquities** Archaeological items, Greek and Etruscan vases, ceramics. **Egyptian Museum** One of the richest Egyptian collections in Europe; statue of Rameses II, seated figure of Thothmes III. **Galleria Sabauda** Largest collection of paintings by non-Italians in Italy. Many Flemish and Dutch works: Memling, *Passion of Christ*; Paul Potter, *Bulls*. Also Florentine furniture of 16th–17th c and Italian painting: Fra Angelico, Botticelli, Lorenzo di Credi, Pollaiuolo, Mantegna, Veronese.

351 **Palazzo Madama** Palace transformed by Castellamonte and Juvarra with façade and wonderful double symmetric stairway. Now contains a museum which includes works by Daddi, Antonello da Messina, Vivarini. Also a book of hours with work by Van Eyck and collections glass, porcelain and objets d'art.

352 **Palazzo Reale** Built by Amedeo di Castellamonte in 17th c. Apartments with 18th c decoration, paintings and statues of the Savoy princes. **Armeria Reale** A very fine collection of arms and armour. **Royal Library** Collection manuscripts including Leonardo da Vinci, *Self-portrait*.

UDINE, Friuli-Venezia Giulia

353 **Palazzo Arcivescovile** Frescos by Tiepolo.

URBINO, Marches

354 **Palazzo Ducale** One of the masterpieces of the Renaissance with a magnificent courtyard by Laurana continued by Bramante and others. Now houses the Galleria Nazionale delle Marche: sculpture and furniture. Important paintings in the ducal apartments including works by Raphael, Botticelli, Piero della Francesca, Justus of Ghent, Uccello, Titian, Signorelli. Marquetry work in Duke Federigo's room.

VENICE, Veneto

355 **Basilica of St Mark** Byzantine in inspiration, begun 829, rebuilt 976, reconstructed in 11th c in form of a Greek cross. Covered by 5 nearly

equal domes. Façade: in 2 tiers, each of 5 semi-circular arches, richly decorated with mosaics and sculpture and Greek horses of hand-beaten copper. Atrium: earliest pointed arches in Italy; covered by 6 small domes with mainly 13th c mosaics. Interior: marble decoration below, mosaics on a gold ground above; mosaic pavement of marble with representations of animals; very rich capitals; 4 large round-headed arches at the crossing. Fine rood screen by Jacopo Benato, 1394. Behind and above altar, Pala d'Oro with precious stones made in 1105 with many additions. Renaissance sacristy by Giorgio Spavento 1486–1490. Baptistery: font by Sansovino 1546. Cappella Zen: tomb of Cardinal G. B. Zeno by Antonio Lombardo. Treasury: many items taken from Constantinople.

356 **Frari** Franciscan Santa Maria Gloriosa dei Frari begun c. 1250 and finished 15th c. Interior: many tombs and works of art: Titian, *Assumption* and *Madonna di Casa Pesano*.

357 **Gesuati** Santa Maria del Rosario by Massari with a fine ceiling and other work by Tiepolo.

358 **Madonna dell' Orto** Romanesque with Gothic detail c. 1350. Portal with Renaissance elements 1460. Contains: Cima, *St John the Baptist*; Bellini, *Presentation of the Virgin* and works by Tintoretto.

359 **Redentore** Built by Andrea Palladio 1577–92 for the Venetian senate to mark deliverance from a plague. Most complete and typical of Palladio's churches incorporating many Roman ideas in the design.

360 **San Francesco della Vigna** Designed by Sansovino, 1535, with façade added by Palladio, 1568–72.

361 **San Giorgio degli Schiavoni** Façade by Sansovino. Contains series of paintings by Carpaccio particularly *St Jerome in his Study*, *St George Slaying the Dragon*.

362 **San Giorgio Maggiore** Started by Palladio 1566 and completed by Scamozzi 1610. Experimental in plan; an attempt to combine humanist principles with current liturgical practice.

363 **Santi Giovanni e Paolo** Gothic brick church begun 1246 containing tombs of the doges. Notable is the tomb of Doge Antonio Vendramin by Tullio Lombardo and work by Pietro Lombardo.

364 **Santa Maria dei Miracoli** Outstanding early Renaissance church of white marble built by Pietro Lombardo 1481–89.

365 **Santa Maria della Salute** Built by Longhena 1632–56 as a thanksgiving for deliverance from the plague. Octagonal in plan with a large dome.

366 **San Salvatore** Built by Spavento, Tullio Lombardo, Sansovino and Baroque façade by G. Sardi. Contains statues by Sansovino, fine *Annunciation* and *Transfiguration* by Titian.

367 **San Sebastiano** Built 1544–47 by Scarpagnino and others and decorated by Veronese. Contains work by Veronese, Titian, Sansovino.

368 **San Zaccaria** Built by Antonio Gambello and Mauro Coducci 1444–64. Transition from Gothic to Renaissance. Contains Giovanni Bellini, *Virgin Enthroned*, 1505.

369 **Scuola di San Rocco** Built for the community of St Roch by Bartolomeo Bon 1517, continued by Sante Lombardo 1524–27, completed by Scarpagnino 1549 with a splendid façade. Contains 56 paintings of New Testament subjects by Tintoretto and Titian, *Annunciation*.

370 **Accademia di Belle Arti** Most important collection of Venetian paintings from 14th to 18th c. Many first-class works by Giovanni Bellini, Titian, Tintoretto and Veronese, also Carpaccio legend of St Ursula series.

371 **Ca' d'Oro** Gothic palace built for Marino Contarini 1421–40 by Giovanni and Bartolomeo Bon and others. Contains the Galleria Franchetti: Italian paintings, sculpture, bronzes, including work by Carpaccio, Mantegna, Veneziano and Tintoretto.

372 **Campanile of St Mark and Loggetta** Both rebuilt 1912. Campanile: 15th c design. Loggetta: masterpiece by Sansovino with statues by him.

373 **Doges' Palace** Former official residence of the doges and chief magistrates, founded 814; rebuilt and remodelled until 17th c. Façade: Gothic with arcade of 36 columns surmounted by a loggia of 71 columns; above, marble façade pierced by large windows. Relief decorations including *Judgment of Solomon* by Pietro Lamberti and Giovanni di Martino. Porta della Carta 1439–43 is a graceful gateway. The Cortile has decoration of different periods. Statues including bronze well heads, sculpture by Rizzo and the Scale dei Giganti with colossal statues by Sansovino. Interior: richly decorated rooms, ceilings painted by Tintoretto, decorations by Palladio. Tiepolo, *Neptune offering his Gifts*; Veronese, *Rape of Europa*, *Vulcan's Forge*. Sala del Collegio has ceiling by Francesco Bello with paintings by Veronese. Sala del Senato (seat of doge and senators): Tintoretto, *Descent from the Cross*. Other rooms have paintings by Veronese. Collection of arms and armour in the Sale d'Armi del Consiglio dei Dieci. Doge's private apartment: Titian, *St Christopher*, Sala del Maggior Consiglio: Tintoretto gigantic painting *Paradise*.

374 **Libreria Vecchia** Constructed by Sansovino, completed by Scamozzi 1536–82. Contains the Biblioteca Nazionale Marciana and the Old Library containing: Titian, fresco of Wisdom; the Grimani Breviary illuminated by Flemish artists. **Archaeological Museum** Remarkable collection Greek and Roman sculpture.

375 **Museo Correr** Museum of art and history founded by a wealthy citizen. Contains: Carpaccio, *Two Venetian Courtesans*; work by Da Messina, Tura, Van der Goes, Tintoretto.

376 **Palazzo Corner della Ca' Grande** Dignified Renaissance building by Sansovino.

377 **Palazzo Grassi** Built by Massari, stairs have trescoed carnival scenes by Longhi.

378 **Palazzo Grimani** Masterpiece by Sanmicheli.

379 **Palazzo Labia** Central saloon has magnificent decorations by Tiepolo, showing the story of Anthony and Cleopatra.

380 **Palazzo Pesaro** Fine Baroque building by Longhena now contains the Museo Internazionale d'Arte Moderna: paintings of all schools mostly bought from the Biennale exhibitions. Also the Museum of Oriental Art with fine collection of Japanese and Chinese works.

381 **Palazzo Querini-Stampalia** 17th building. Now contains notable collection 18th c works of art, including paintings by Longhi also work by Lorenzo di Credi, Giovanni Bellini and Tiepolo.

382 **Palazzo Rezzonico** By Longhena c. 1660 and Massari 1745, contains the city's collection of 18th c art. Sumptuously decorated 18th c rooms, particularly the chapel with a wedding by Tiepolo; also frescos brought from Tiepolo's country house; Longhi, scenes of Venetian life and fine costumes, tapestries and furniture.

383 **Palazzo Vendramin Calergi** Completed by the Lombardo, the finest Lombardesque palace in Venice.

384 **Peggy Guggenheim Collection** Outstanding collection 20th c painting and sculpture particularly surrealist. Includes works by Ernst, Tanguy, Giacometti, Mirò, Magritte also Picasso, Kandinsky, Klee, Arp.

385 **Statue of Bartolomeo Colleoni** Grand and simple work by Verrocchio of the famous condottiere.

VERONA, Veneto

386 **Cathedral** Reconstruction started 1139; building continued until 16th c. Choir: Romanesque; nave: Gothic. Entrance porch 12th c flanked by statues of Roland and Oliver. Interior: red marble pillars with curious capitals; Titian, *Assumption*; Cappella Mazzanti by Domenico da Lugo, 1508.

387 **Sant' Anastasia** Gothic, begun at end of 13th c, completed in 15th c. Façade has a double w door. Interior: 24 terra-cottas of the life of Jesus by Michele da Firenze, 1435; several good frescos; Pisanello, *St George and the Princess*, 1437–38.

388 **San Fermo Maggiore** Lower church started c. 1065. Upper church Romanesque but rebuilt early 14th c in Gothic style. Interior:

aisleless nave with 14th c frescos. Pisanello, *Annunciation*, 1423–24, his earliest surviving major work.

389 **San Giorgio Maggiore (in Braida)** Begun in 1477 on site of earlier church. Dome and campanile (unfinished) designed by Sanmicheli. Interior: in apse Veronese, *Martyrdom of St George*; Moretto, *Female Saints*.

390 **Santa Maria Antica** Romanesque; 12th c campanile. Interior: tombs of the Scaligers including those of Mastino II and Cansignorio by Bonino.

391 **San Zeno Maggiore** Fine Romanesque church built 1117–1225, apse rebuilt 1389–96; campanile 1045–1175. Porch by Nicolo and interesting bas-reliefs by Nicolo and Guglielmo; main doors with superb bronze reliefs 11th–12th c. Early circular window on w front c. 1150. Interior: Mantegna, *Madonna and Saints*.

392 **Arena** One of the biggest and best-preserved Roman amphitheatres.

393 **Castelvecchio** Castle, started 1354 by Cangrande II to designs of Bevilacqua. Contains the Museum of Art: paintings by Veronese artists 14th–18th c and equestrian statue of Cangrande.

394 **Palazzo Bevilacqua** Built by Sanmicheli; shows influence of Giulio Romano and Mannerist ideas.

395 **Palazzo Canossa** Built by Sanmicheli, fresco by Tiepolo.

396 **Palazzo del Consiglio** (Loggia) Elegant Renaissance building, 1493, by Fra Giocondo.

VICENZA, Veneto

397 **Cathedral** Founded 12th c, rebuilt 15th c, campanile 11th c.

398 **Basilica** Major work of Andrea Palladio, and his first public commission, started 1549. Consists of an open colonnaded screen round the Gothic Palazzo della Ragione.

399 **Loggia del Capitano** Built by Palladio, 1571.

400 **Palazzo Chiericati** Excellent palace started 1550 by Andrea Palladio, houses the Museo Civico: paintings including works of the Venetian school.

401 **Palazzo Valmarana** Designed by Palladio and started 1565–66, façade only completed.

402 **Teatro Olimpico** Wood and stucco building with fixed scenery of a piazza and streets, designed by Andrea Palladio on the model of a Roman theatre; completed by Scamozzi 1583.

403 **Villa Rotonda (Capra)** A belvedere by Palladio 1550–51, built on a hilltop with porches on each side and a dome over the centre.

404 **Villa Valmarana** By A. Muttoni, 1669, with grotesque figures on the walls and early frescos by Tiepolo.

VIGEVANO, Lombardy

405 **Castello della Sforzesca** Designed by Bramante for Lodovico il Moro in 1486.

406 **Castello Visconteo** Built c. 1340, enlarged 1492. Tower and loggia by Bramante.

VILLA ADRIANA, Latium

407 **Hadrian's Villa** Largest and most imposing of Roman imperial villas, built by Hadrian 125–135. Remains of many buildings including: Greek theatre in its original form, public baths and an extensive imperial palace built around four peristyles.

VITERBO, Latium

408 **Museo Civico** Etruscan exhibits and paintings.

409 **Palazzo Papale** Built c. 1266; important example of civic Gothic architecture.

VOLTERRA, Tuscany

410 **Cathedral** Restored Romanesque. Interior: 13th c ambo, tabernacle by Mino da Fiesole and fresco, *Adoration of the Wise Men* by Benozzo Gozzoli.

411 **Museo Etrusco Guarnacci** Contains over 600 Etruscan cinerary urns or chests. On the lids are recumbent effigies of the deceased and on sides reliefs showing Etruscan life or mythological scenes.

412 **Palazzo dei Priori** Gothic built 1208–57. Art gallery contains work by Ghirlandaio, Signorelli and the Sienese school.

413 **Porta dell' Arco** Etruscan arch with three heads.

Index

The numbers in Roman type refer to text and captions, the heavy type to illustrations, the italics to the Museums and Monuments index.

Acknowledgements

The photographs were supplied by Scala, Florence, except in the following cases:
Alinari, Florence title page, 8, 14, 36, 61, 88, 116, 120, 166, 177, 178, 189, 192, 194, 197, 198, 202, 200, 204, 215, 216, 218, 226, 236, 244, 245, 269; Anderson, Rome 41, 68, 115, 182, 193, 217; Arts Council of Great Britain 266; Robert Emmett Bright, Rome 191, 227, 262; Peter Cannon-Brookes, Birmingham 263, 264; Gabinetto Fotografico Nazionale, Rome contents page, 60, 126, 239, 238, 257, 265; Studio Giulio Gazzoni, Florence 120; Paul Hamlyn Archive 203; Hirmer Fotoarchiv, Munich 68; Irifoto, Verona 3; Mansell/Alinari, London 106, 117, 138, 161, 167; Leonard von Matt, photograph S.W.B., Buochs 221; Radio Times Hulton Picture Library, London introduction; Soprintendenza di Monumenti alle Gallerie della Venezia Giulia e del Friuli, Udine 69; Vasari, Rome 223; Villani, Bologna 25; Foto Wells, Bergamo 118; Vatican Photo Service, Rome 37, 268.

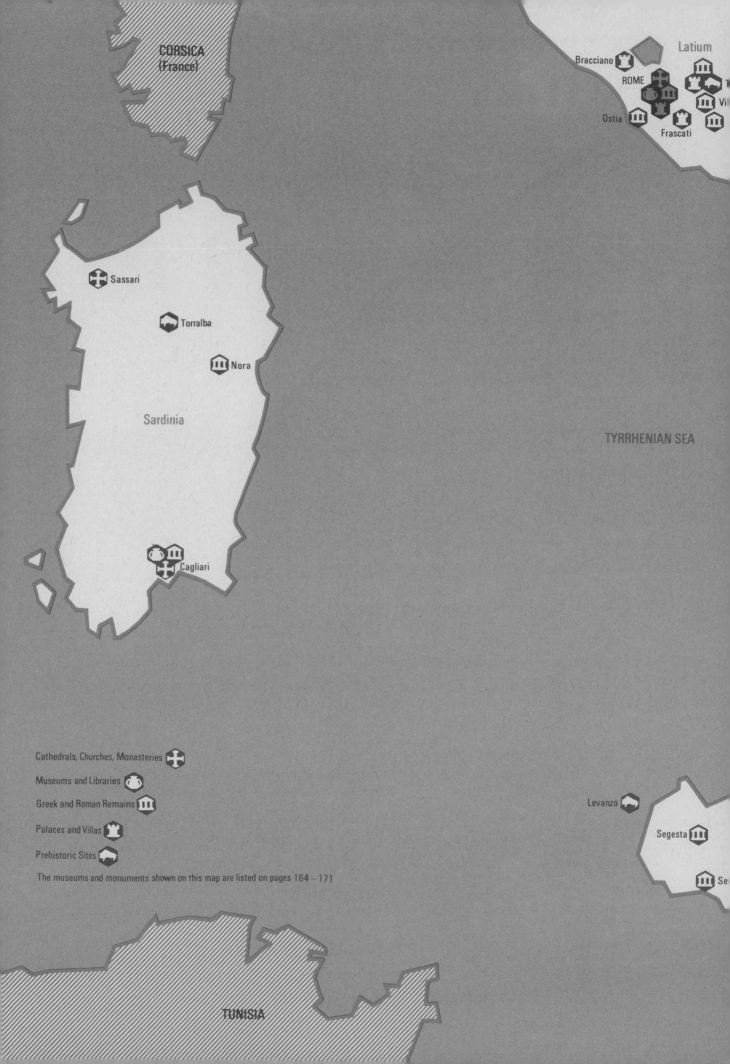

CORSICA
(France)

Latium

Bracciano

ROME

Vil

Ostia

Frascati

Sassari

Torralba

Nora

Sardinia

TYRRHENIAN SEA

Cagliari

Cathedrals, Churches, Monasteries

Museums and Libraries

Greek and Roman Remains

Palaces and Villas

Prehistoric Sites

The museums and monuments shown on this map are listed on pages 164 – 171

Levanzo

Segesta

Se

TUNISIA